ANDA A

C000084726

Produced by AA Publishing

European Regional Guide

Written by George Kean

Copy editor: Helen Douglas-Cooper

Edited, designed and produced by AA Publishing. Maps © The Automobile Association 1993.

Distributed in the United Kingdom by AA Publishing, Fanum House, Basingstoke, Hampshire, RG21 2EA.

The contents of this publication are believed correct at the time of printing. Nevertheless, the publishers cannot accept responsibility for errors or omissions, or for changes in details given. We have tried to ensure accuracy in this guide, but things do change and we would be grateful if readers would advise us of any inaccuracies they may encounter.

A CIP catalogue record for this book is available from the British Library.

ISBN 0 7495 0584 2

Published by The Automobile Association.

Colour separation: Daylight Colour Art Pte, Singapore

Printed by Printers Trento S.R.L., Italy

Cover picture: **Hilltop town, Málaga**
Opposite: **The Alhambra, Granada**
Pages 4–5: **Tile in the Plaza de España, Sevilla**

·CONTENTS·

FEATURES

MAPS

The main entries in this book are cross-referenced to the regional map on pages 108-9. All heights on maps are in metres.

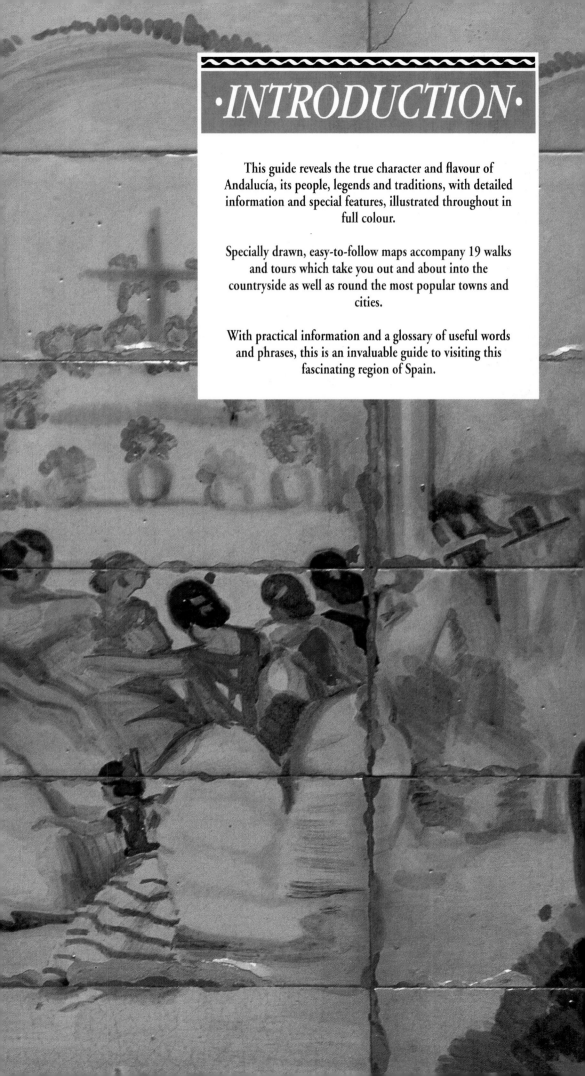

·INTRODUCTION·

This guide reveals the true character and flavour of
Andalucía, its people, legends and traditions, with detailed
information and special features, illustrated throughout in
full colour.

Specially drawn, easy-to-follow maps accompany 19 walks
and tours which take you out and about into the
countryside as well as round the most popular towns and
cities.

With practical information and a glossary of useful words
and phrases, this is an invaluable guide to visiting this
fascinating region of Spain.

·THE REGION·

Andalucía occupies a very large part of Spain – most of the south. It is a good deal bigger than the three Benelux countries and more than four times the size of Wales. Andalucía borders the Atlantic Ocean and the Mediterranean Sea. It has ski slopes, deserts, the area with Spain's highest rainfall and the largest percentage of land area designated as nature reserves within Europe. It has a mind-boggling historical and cultural heritage, magnificent mountains, fast-paced cities, and sleepy towns and villages. It has customs trapped in the Dark Ages and working methods caught in a timewarp, and is experiencing a rush of socio-economic progress and technological development outstripping that of most European regions. It is a complex confection, tempting to taste, satisfying to savour.

Spanish-looking Christ on a church in Jerez de la Frontera

IMAGES OF ANDALUCIA

Andalucía is a land of dramatic images: the tautness in the face of a flamenco singer and the agony in the song; the expressions among a bullring crowd; the come-on look of a swaggering Don Juan; the dismissive wave of a demure Carmen's painted fan; the pagan piety of onlookers at a religious procession; a sunset view of the Alhambra against a backdrop of the snow-covered Sierra Nevada. All good material for the countless words, photographs and publicity posters depicting Andalucía.

For three decades there was an unplanned rush to build a holiday playground and retirement park for North Europeans along the sunniest parts of Andalucía's coastline. Deep-blue conservatives from Britain and Germany became lotus-eaters in a country and region that has repeatedly elected socialist governments since 1982. The numbers of invaders in search of sun, sea, sand and *sangría* swelled annually in the days when Spain had one of the lowest price structures in Europe. Now the number of foreign visitors to Andalucía's shores has declined. Shabbiness, rowdiness, pollution and indifferent service also tarnished the golden image. In an economy much dependent upon tourism, there had to be a rethink. It has gone in the direction of improving the quality and diversifying the range of amenities along the coast, and promoting the varied attractions of the region's interior, which was so much treasured by previous civilisations.

BEGINNINGS

Early man has left many traces of habitation in this region, and it was from here that some people moved as far afield as Britain and Denmark. Much later, around 1000BC, new settlers arrived from North Africa, and became known as the Iberians. The rich and fabled state of Tartessos was established in the area of present-day Huelva. Phoenicians, and later Greeks, came to trade and established colonies. Next came the Carthaginians, and southern Iberia was a major theatre of

fighting in the first two Punic Wars (264–201BC). For the next 600 years the victorious Romans imposed their sovereignty over their new province of *Baetica*. Remnants of their aqueducts, roads and cities remain throughout the region. Their language, legal and civil codes became the base for those now used in Spain. When Rome's empire was disintegrating in the 5th century, *Baetica* was overrun by the Vandals, a Germanic tribe. They were soon chased to North Africa by allies of Rome, the Visigoths, also Germanic but converts to Arianism, the Christianity of Byzantium. In 711, the Visigoths were defeated by a small army of Moslems (Moors) from North Africa.

AL-ANDALUS

Moslems had a ruling presence for the next 780 years in what they named *Al-Andalus*. For these desert-dwellers it was a land of milk and honey to which they began contributing their greater wisdom, advanced administration, knowledge about agriculture and finer architecture. They also implanted their racial stock, religious norms and culture. This is the legacy that today distinguishes Andalucíans from other Spaniards. It can be seen in people's features, their behaviour and the style of their villages.

In 1492, when the last Moorish king in *Al-Andalus*, Boabdil of Granada, was deposed by the Catholic monarchs Ferdinand and Isabel, Christopher Columbus (Cristóbal Colón) had their leave to sail from Andalucía to reach the Indies. He was stalled by the Americas. The quincentenary celebration of his voyage and Andalucía's hosting of EXPO '92 in Sevilla during 1992 have provoked transformation in all of the region's eight provinces. It is the objective of its government, the Junta de Andalucía, to make the region into the 'California of Europe'.

PLANS FOR THE FUTURE

A vast investment programme has been unleashed. Much of it has gone into the transport and communications infrastructure: a high-speed line of 482km cuts the rail journey time between Madrid and Sevilla to under three hours; more than 1,000km of dual carriageways have been constructed to facilitate road transport within the region and improve its link with the European road network; cities have been surrounded by ringroads; capacity

at Sevilla, Málaga and other airports has been increased; and the region's telecommunications system will advance 15 years with the installation of a digital network infrastructure based on fibre optics. The European Community has generously supported the region's development programme, which includes aid to boost productivity in traditional and new activities in the agricultural and fishery sectors.

Private initiatives have a legal framework, tax incentives and public subsidies to encourage them to set up in Andalucía. Private enterprise has been responsible for greatly extending and improving the quality of hotel accommodation. Public and private funds have been directed at restoring historic buildings and monuments, and improving the cultural environment by providing more and improved venues and better funding of the arts. Málaga's Technological Park is attracting some of the world's top companies, and so is CARTUJA '93 a project to spark off technical innovation for the region reusing Expo '92's legacy of infrastructure, buildings and equipment on La Cartuja Island.

Like any foreign land, Andalucía is for the traveller what he or she makes of it, whether they spend a few days in feverish sightseeing or years of thoughtful discovery and reach few absolute conclusions, save concurrence with the Arabic calligraphy on the walls of the prayer niche in Córdoba's mosque, 'All praise to Allah for leading us to this place.'

Aracena's airy hill and ruined castle make a fine playground

GEOGRAPHY AND CLIMATE

Andalucía is one of Spain's 17 autonomous communities. Its area of 87,268sq km represents 17 per cent of Spanish territory and is home to 17 per cent of Spain's 38 million people. Sevilla is the capital of the region and of its own province. Seven other provinces are named after their capital cities: Almería, Cádiz, Córdoba, Granada, Huelva, Jaén and Málaga.

In the north, the rugged mountains of the Sierra Morena separate Andalucía from the autonomous communities of Extremadura and Castila La Mancha. In the south and east are the mountains of the Sistema Bética, which fan out northeastwards into the Subbética system of the Sierras of Cazorla y Segura in Jaén province and run eastwards as the Penibética system, in which the Sierra Nevada of Granada province reach the highest point in the Iberian peninsula at Mulhacén, 3,482m above sea-level. The Río Guadalquivir, Spain's fifth-longest river, rises in the mountains of Jaén and runs for 657km through that province and also Córdoba and Sevilla provinces to enter the Atlantic Ocean in the marshlands of Huelva province. Its name derives from *al-wadi al-kabir*, the Arabic for 'great river'. When the golden city was the capital of *Al-Andalus*, boats could sail up to Córdoba, but now it is navigable only as far as the city of Sevilla. Before the Moors, the fertile plain of the *Betis*, the river's Roman name, had also been the breadbasket of the Roman Empire. Today, the Guadalquivir basin remains the heartland of Andalucía's large-scale agriculture. An intensive irrigation network seeks to use every available drop of the river's water while industry and populations along its course also make their demands. The ecological impact is felt in Coto de Doñana, one of Europe's most important resting spots for migratory birds, where water levels are dropping dangerously.

Atlantic rollers break with a strong surf on the white sand of the Costa de la Luz (Coast of Light), which starts at the border with Portugal and runs along Huelva and Cádiz provinces. Only the wide sweep of the Bay of Cádiz and a few rocky promontories break the long line of wide beaches. North of Cádiz and the mouth of the Guadalquivir, the marshlands of Coto de Doñana are lined by low coastal dunes, and sandbars protect the estuaries of other rivers. Near Tarifa, continental Europe's most southerly point and a boardsailing paradise, high dunes are blown up by the almost continuous winds, which can howl at more than 120km/h in the winter. East of Tarifa, a polluting industrial zone surrounds the bay of Algericas and Gibraltar.

The Costa del Sol (Coast of the Sun) belongs to Málaga province. Beaches vary from rock, shingle, coarse and fine sand to very fine, white imported sand at luxury beach clubs. For much of its length of 160km, the Costa del

A stretch of the Río Tinto. The river has long been associated with the mining of metals

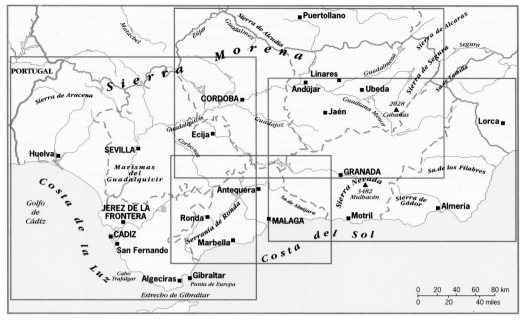

Sol is an almost continuous city abutting a coastal plain of varying width, with an attractive backdrop of the Penibética mountain system. Along the western part of this coastline are the big-name resorts of Estepona, Marbella, Fuengirola and Torremolinos. Beyond the lively port city of Málaga and its mountain ring, the coastal towns do not yet all run together, and smallholdings cover much of the coastal plain. Around the resort of Nerja the mountains come down almost to the sea.

A corniche road runs into Granada province, which has dubbed its coastline the Costa Tropical. Beaches are mostly pebbly or of coarse, grey sand. The town of Almuñécar was Spain's successful pioneer in commercially cultivating tropical fruits. Further east the coastal plain is covered in sugar plantations; then a shimmering sea of plastic, under which a wide variety of crops are grown, begins to stretch into Almería province.

The Costa de Almería has a concentration of tourist amenities west of the port city. Eastwards a piece of coastline with some of Andalucía's best beaches of fine sand is protected within the Parque Natural de Cabo de Gata-Nijar. Beyond the Sierra Cabrera, which abuts the sea, is the resort development of Mojácar, and beyond that a long stretch of sandy beaches, backed by a wide, dry plain, runs up to the border with the autonomous community of Murcia.

It is to its beaches that most of Andalucía's foreign visitors flock, but the interior is richer in natural beauty, with stunning vistas across agricultural lands, lakes, high mountains and some lunar landscapes. Here, too, the most monumental cities and towns, the most picturesque villages and gentler ways of life are found. And it is inland where tourist authorities are now enticing travellers: the new road system speeds journey times, although there are still hundreds of minor roads along which to meander gently; monuments have been renovated and other cultural attractions have been sparked; and new hotels and other amenities await the traveller.

Andalucía is a region to visit at any time of the year. Although in such a large and varied region where local topography and wind patterns make generalisations very difficult, some broad observations can be made.

The interior is at its best in spring and autumn. Winters, although chilly, are sunny, have fewer sightseers and a brilliant light for photography, and the ski resort of the Sierra Nevada, Solynieve, is open. Summers are searingly hot and temperatures can rise to 45˚C. The Costa del Sol, Costa Tropical and western part of the Costa de Almería have Europe's most equitable annual climatic pattern, and can be enjoyed throughout the year. From July to September the popular resorts are buzzing; in spring and autumn their pace is slower. In the mild winters, which the coastal mountain ranges assure by blocking cold, northerly winds, Andalucía's south coast is climatically the most pleasant place in Europe. Strong prevailing winds make both the Costa de la Luz and the eastern part of the Costa de Almería less pleasant.

Olive trees stud the slopes around Lucena in the north

PEOPLE AND WAY OF LIFE

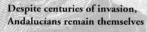

Despite centuries of invasion,
Andalucíans remain themselves

Although it is difficult to generalise about all 6½ million Andalucíans, especially in a rapidly changing society, many foreigners come up with rigid stereotypes of the national character. What is undeniable is that the indigenous people of southern Spain have, while changing them, absorbed some character traits and customs of others, including conquerors and settlers from Castile and northern parts of Spain. However, it is the legacy of almost 800 years of Arab rule in many parts that has left the deepest mark on individual and communal behaviour.

Foreign visitors – settlers in the sun and now, increasingly, business people, scientists and other workers – are the latest in a series of invasions that Andalucíans have been inclined not to resist. They have let the climate, the beauty of the land and their own inscrutability and charm do the work of moulding the invader into a gentler, more courteous inhabitant with a world view closer to their own. What Andalucíans think about them, foreigners will rarely hear expressed. What Andalucíans think about their own region and people will depend on where they come from, what province or town, what village or part of town.

A perspective of life and the world is formed within the family, still very much a matriarchal unit in which the mother is both the most revered and the most hard-worked member. The second most powerful influence is the perception of the community, based on its collective experience, which can be very different in isolated villages, large city areas or tourist resorts. Then there is the close and closed circle of friends in which an *Andaluz* (Andalucían) also finds solidarity and comfort.

These three mingled influences protect a person, but their strength can also strangle fresh thought and progress. Foreigners in search of acceptance by an *Andaluz* must somehow gain acceptance within one sphere of influence and then wiggle their way into the others by acceptable behaviour and using introductions, the Andalucían means for social and career progress. Traditional values have attributed less worth to a person's wealth than to their presence of personality. Judgements of others by the younger generation, however, have more to do with materialistic values.

Travellers should be prepared to be perplexed and forget all preconceptions about Andalucíans, especially the one that they are lazy. Andalucíans are, however, dismissive of time constraints and may be happier to leave until *mañana* (tomorrow) what North Europeans may insist should be done today. However, they have a lower incidence of stress-related diseases and live longer. They love noise and are demonstrative in their emotions. They live life to the full and for the moment, spending savings and caring little about tomorrow. They admire *un listo*, a 'clever one' who can easily wax into verse, burst into song or make music well. And anyone who outsmarts bureaucracy is an instant hero. The collective sanction or praise of the local community is usually more meaningful than the sanction of authorities and any outside recognition.

The Andalucían's humour is black and fatalistic and many old jokes are about death. Among themselves they disparage their politicians, other areas, towns and provinces, even their own place of birth at times, but they do not welcome outsiders doing so. They admire a man's virility and a woman's fertility. They are highly tolerant of anyone's children and hugely indulgent of their own. The old are seldom cast out into retirement homes, nor are handicapped and retarded people often rejected by the family and community.

Among the great majority, home is a place for the family and strangers are rarely invited. Daily social intercourse takes place in the street outside, in shops and bars, along promenades and on the beach in summer months. Even the smallest village has what passes for a disco, where the young set gather. Sunday is the favourite day for families and their circles to get together for extended lunches in a village *meson*, countryside *venta* or beachside *merendero*, and one of the party will usually know the owner. Christenings, confirmations and weddings are celebrations on which no money is spared, however humble the family's means.

In villages and small towns many of the inhabitants are related and, even if they are not, everybody seems not only to know everybody else, but also each other's detailed affairs. Anonymity is not easily found. There are definite ways and intricate rules for getting things done. They are often incomprehensible to barnstorming foreigners, who get little more than high blood pressure. A middle man who knows somebody who knows somebody is usually indispensable.

Annual *fiestas* (festivals), *ferias* (agricultural fairs), and *romerías* (pilgrimages) – the distinctions are subtle – are times for dressing up and showing off; for music, dance, deafening noise and fireworks. No matter if the main purpose of the event is religious, it is usually also a time for merrymaking. Many hours are spent in its preparation,

many words spoken in its anticipation and in its post mortem. Andalucía also puts on Spain's most solemn and awesome *Semana Santa* (Holy Week) processions, which some foreign onlookers find spine-chilling.

There is obviously a great difference between lifestyles and attitudes in the countryside and those in big urban centres like Sevilla, where the daily routines and concerns of people are much the same as they are in Liverpool or Hamburg. However, common to the country and city is the impact of television, with glamorous advertising and the endless running of dubbed movies extolling the American way.

Andalucían society is rapidly changing, and it is also a society of distinct classes. The large mass is on a big-stepped ladder of upward mobility, and for many their memory of poverty is fresh. Below them a large number have not yet touched the first rung, and for some their hopelessness generates a life of drug abuse and crime to support their habit. At the pinnacle are aristocrats and large landowners whose ancestors gained their titles and wealth long ago by means fair or foul. Among the new rich are one-time peasants who made it lucky with sales of land for tourist projects, property developers, owners of service and manufacturing industries and the like.

To answer the colonial explorer's question, 'Are the natives friendly and trustworthy?', in regard to Andalucíans the answer is an unequivocal affirmative.

Fisherman mending his nets – some old ways continue

SEVILLA, HUELVA AND CADIZ

These three province have a common boundary point near the mouth of the Río Guadalquivir. Huelva and Sevilla provinces have northern mountainous areas, which are part of the Sierra Morena chain; the eastern end of the Sistema Bética protrudes into Cádiz province. All three capitals are port cities. Although Sevilla province is landlocked, the Río Guadalquivir is navigable up to the capital city. Huelva and Cádiz provinces share the Costa de la Luz (Coast of Light) along the Atlantic seaboard and Cádiz also has a Mediterranean coastline east of Gibraltar, where Algeciras is an important port.

Various minerals are mined and refined in parts of Huelva and Sevilla provinces. Rice and cotton are principal products of Sevilla's agriculture; the cultivation of cereals, vines and olives heads the list in Cádiz and Huelva provinces. Cattle (for meat and dairy products) and pig farming are important in all three and in northern parts of Sevilla sheep are reared for their wool. Textiles, foodstuffs, agricultural machinery, chemicals and cement are main

Huelva's Columbus monument by US sculptor Gertrude Whitney

elements of Sevilla's industry; chemicals, forestry and artificial fibres are crucial in Huelva, which, like Cádiz, also has a large fishing industry and is a producer of wines. The city of Sevilla is a significant earner from tourism; summer tourism is a big contributor to the economy of Cádiz province and its importance is growing in Huelva province.

Evidence of prehistoric settlement is found throughout the area. For the ancients of the eastern Mediterranean, this territory lay beyond the limits of their world. The Phoenicians were the first to venture beyond the Pillars of Hercules to trade with Tartessians settled in the area of present-day Huelva, who were extracting the area's minerals and whose wealth is mentioned in the Bible. The Phoenician settlements of *Hispalis* and *Gadir* became Sevilla and Cádiz respectively, and the latter was the last stronghold on the Carthaginian Peninsula. When those great builders, the Romans, took over, their 'national highway', the Via Augusta, ran from Tartessos to Rome. At Itálica and other sites their sophisticated urban arrangements have been

revealed. The imprint of some 500 years of Moorish domination is most strongly felt in villages whose layout has changed very little since those times, and where Christians used Moorish sites and materials to raise their fortifications, churches and palaces. They also used Moorish craftsmen and there are many fine examples of Mudéjar architecture, nowhere more so than in Sevilla's Reales Alcázares (Royal Fortress).

Few people will not know something about Sevilla after all the media exposure the city has had because of EXPO '92. Even before that, Sevilla was one of those 'essential' cities, like London, Paris and Florence, on the list of well-travelled people. Few others can match its boast: founded, according to legend, by Hercules, settled by Phoenicians and Carthaginians, fortified by Julius Caesar, capital of Visigothic and Moorish kingdoms, once among the world's four biggest cities, gloriously endowed architecturally by the wealth of Spain hauled back from the Americas, rich in collections of art up to contemporary times and the inspiration for great operas in the international repertoire. Now, all spruced up and with new attractions awaiting visitors on La Cartuja island, Sevilla is even more enticing. And the authorities are hoping that with the CARTUJA '93 project, many of the world's technological research and manufacturing companies will also be attracted to the city. Within the province, the very historic and monumental town of Carmona, the handsome towns of La Campiña, the plain like Osuna and Ecija and the hills, valleys and villages of the Sierra Norte await to delight visitors.

In Cádiz province a string of coastal towns and summer resorts add to the area's attractions. Different ambiences prevail in the two 'sherry ports' of El Puerto de Santa María and Sanlúcar de Barrameda. Luxury residential and marina developments at Sotogrande and Puerto Sherry, where grand yachts are berthed, contrast with sleepy Conil de la Frontera, where small fishing boats lie, and laid-back Tarifa, where windsurfers rule beautiful beaches. Impressively situated, Cádiz city retains its seaward defences and maritime atmosphere.

Jerez de la Frontera, capital of the sherry barons, offers visits to *bodegas* and performances by dancing horses. Fighting bulls and fine horses roam in many pastures.

Arcos de la Frontera proudly crowns a hill, and more white villages are scattered through the province. Nature-lovers can enjoy rest or relaxation in the wooded heights of the Sierra de Grazelma natural park.

There is not much in Huelva's capital to attract visitors, but the province does have three varied natural attractions. Coto de Doñana, which covers marshlands around the mouth of the Río Guadalquivir, is regarded as the most important wildlife sanctuary in Europe. The beaches of the Costa de la Luz are rated as among the best on the continent. In the Sierra de Aracena pretty villages lie among silvan slopes and criss-crossing valleys, through which run bubbling rivers. Sadly, human exploitation is wounding these natural bequests: upstream use of water is threatening Coto de Doñana; beaches are dirtied by industrial pollution; mining and forestry activities have changed natural aspects of the *sierras*.

These three provinces were in the vanguard of Spain's American 'experience'. The vessels which first reached the Americas sailed from Huelva province; those which for some three centuries

returned laden with treasure unloaded at ports in all three provinces. Sevilla held the *Casa de Contratacíon* monopoly of trade with the New World from 1503, and later it was held by Cádiz. Contacts with Christopher Columbus (Cristóbal Colón) are many: in Huelva province he schemed and planned at the monastery of La Rábida, and on his first voyage departed from and returned to Palos de la Frontera,

Sevilla's extravagant Plaza de España was built for the 1929 Ibero-América Exhibition

near to which a large monument was raised. In Cádiz province he set off from both the capital and Sanlúcar de Barrameda. In Sevilla he maintained a long relationship with the monks of La Cartuja, where his coffin later rested for some time, and his 'tomb' is in the city's cathedral.

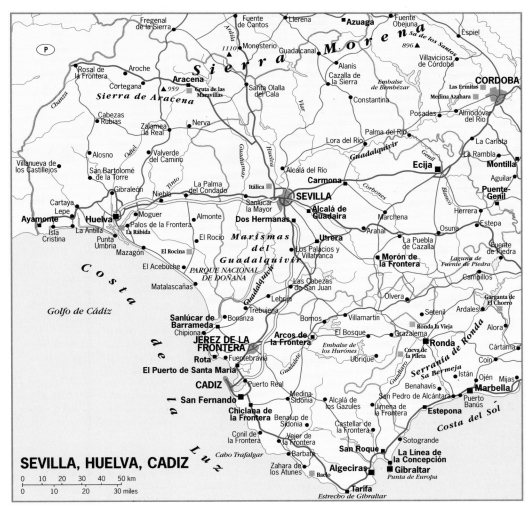

ARACENA

MAP REF: 108 A2

The Gruta de las Maravillas is the main draw for visitors to this town on the northern slopes of the Sierra de Aracena. Guided tours are taken deep into the Cave of Marvels, which has galleries some 1,500m in length, 12 large chambers, six lakes and many brightly coloured rock forms. Times of tours should be checked with the tourist office, Plaza San Pedro (tel: (955) 11 03 55).

Others sights are the Iglesia de Nuestra Señora de la Asuncíon (Church of Our Lady of the Assumption), with an impressive Renaissance façade, and, above the town, a church built by the Knights Templar in the 13th century, which has a Mudéjar tower. Casas, Pozo Nieve 41, is one of the places at which to sample the good pork and hams for which the area is known. The mushrooms collected in autumn are another culinary favourite of the area. A newly built *Villa Turística* (Tourist Village) provides simple, modern accommodation and an excellent base from which to explore.
Nearby Three attractive mountain villages are worth visiting. Alájar is a discreet resort for people in the know. Philip II visited Arias Montano, theologian and philosopher, who had retreated

to the Ermita de Nuestra Señora de los Angeles here.

Fuenteheridos is a tightly packed and irregular collection of whitewashed houses with wooden balconies in a lush setting. Galaroza lies in a protected valley where a variety of fruits grow well, and is among the most carefully maintained villages in the province.

Quiet Aracena is noted for its healthy climate

MOTOR TOUR

There is splendid and varied scenery along the route through an area with thick woods of chestnut, walnut, cork oak, holm oak, cherry and pomegranate trees. Recent reforestation and the building of irrigation dams have changed aspects of the area, but not much changes in its villages.

Arcos de la Frontera, on its rock high above the Río Guadalete

From Aracena take the H501 signposted Campofrio. After about 35km several mines come into view.

Minas de Ríotinto
Slag heaps from Roman times still exist in an area that has important deposits of iron, copper, pyrites and sulphur. Exploitation rights were sold to the English Rio Tinto company in 1866 and 1873, and there is a collection of typically English houses.

Some 10km to the west is another mining town.

Zalamea la Real
La Ponderosa mines are especially rich in copper, and manganese is also mined near the town, which the archbishopric of Sevilla was once pleased to own. The town's most notable building is the Iglesia de la Asunción, an elegant neoclassical monument from the 17th century.

Going north the N435 winds back into the Sierra de Aracena along a scenic route. After 35km, go west.

Almonaster la Real
Natural beauty spots in the vicinity include the Balneario de Manzano spa and the mountain of San

Cristóbal. Additions were made to its Moorish castle and the mosque was converted into a hermitage. The Iglesia de San Martín (Church of St Martin) has a portal in the 15th-century Portuguese style, a reminder of that country's proximity. Some of the town's houses retain Mudéjar and Gothic features.

Continue west past Cortegana, another pretty place, and for 14km on the N433.

Aroche
In an area of many holm and cork oaks, the town, first fortified by the Romans, retains parts of early Moorish walls and a castle of the Almoravides, in which there is now a bullring. Its Renaissance church also shows Gothic elements. Some six noble families built houses which still grace the town. Stone Age implements are on show in the small museum.

It is 43km back to Aracena along the N433 with the opportunity to visit Jabugo, Galaroza and Fuenteheridos on the way.

Elegant baroque carving to be seen in Arcos de la Frontera

JABUGO AND ITS JAMON
A huge number of mountain hams are produced in this area, and Jabugo probably has the highest reputation throughout Spain for its *pata negra,* so called because the brown breed of pigs from which it comes have black *patas* (feet). They roam the surrounding cork-oak forests and live on a diet of acorns, which gives a special flavour to their meat. Long curing takes place on the premises of local producers, who can be visited. The microclimate, fresh in summer and dry and cold in winter, is part of the secret of success. The church is 18th-century and there is an attractive cluster of houses from the same period. Near by is pretty Castaño del Robledo, the highest hamlet in Huelva province.

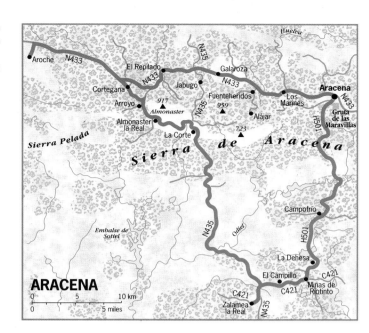

ARCOS DE LA FRONTERA
MAP REF: 108 B1

Arcos presents a stunning sight perched high on a cliffside above the Río Guadalete and its lake. Its *conjunto histórico* (historic quarter) is a maze of narrow streets with many fine buildings in a mix of architecture from Moorish to baroque. From the Plaza de España there are wide views over the curving Guadalete and its plain. Facing the plaza is the Iglesia de Santa María, originally Visigothic but mainly 16th- to 18th-century. It has a baroque choir by Diego Roldán and painting by Alonso Cano. Also on the plaza is the Parador Nacional Casa del Corregidor, another successful conversion of an old building to make a very comfortable hotel. The Ayuntamiento (town hall) completes the plaza.

Not far away is the Gothic Iglesia de San Pedro (Church of St Peter) with a fine portico and altar paintings to which Zurbarán, Pacheco and Ribera contributed.

BARBATE
MAP REF: 108 B1

This is an unpretentious town living off its fishing and canning industry, and is popular for its simple places serving the freshest of fish. A river of the same name ends in an area of marshlands. **Nearby** Zahara de los Atunes is another fishing village seeing fast growth as a summer and residential resort because of its fine beaches.

Walks of different durations can be taken through a pleasant area of pinewoods backing the coast between Barbate and the low headland off which Nelson's fleet routed a French and Spanish force in 1805. It is some 13km from the town to Cabo de Trafalgar.

At the tiny village of Los Caños de Meca sweet spring water pours from the cliffs. Good sandy beaches stretch on either side of the point.

Fishing boats on the beach at Barbate. Tuna is the most important catch for canners

CADIZ

MAP REF: 108 A1

As with Sevilla, myth claims Hercules as the city's founder. What is true is that this narrow promontory has been continuously inhabited for some 3,000 years since it was the Phoenician settlement of *Gadir*. Much later it played an important maritime role in Spain's New World enterprise, and held the monopoly of trade with the New World during part of the 18th century. In 1587 the English navigator and pirate, Sir Francis Drake, sacked the city to 'singe the King of Spain's beard'; in 1797 Admiral Nelson was back to bombard and destroy much of the rebuilt city. During Spain's War of Independence against Napoleon, Cádiz was for a short time the nation's capital, and in 1812 Spain's first constitution was signed in the Oratorio de San Felipe Neri, a fact of which most of the city's 160,000 or so independently minded inhabitants are very proud.

The Puerta de Tierra is an impressive remnant of 18th-century fortifications, and most of the promontory is encased in solid walls and bastions. Castillo Santa Catalina (St Catalina's Castle) looks out across the Atlantic breakers. The Barrio del Populo dates from the 13th century and is at the core of the city's most atmospheric part. Neoclassical and baroque styles, the latter sometimes showing colonial features, predominate in the principal buildings.

Dominating the skyline is the 18th- and 19th-century cathedral. The Iglesia del Rosario (Church of the Rosary) is a typical expression of Gaditan late baroque; next door, the Oratoria de la Santa Cueva (Oratory of the Holy Cave) boasts paintings by Goya. Casa de Fragela and Casa de las Cadenas are two typical buildings from the 17th century. The Museo de Cádiz (Cádiz Museum) displays local archaeological finds and has works by Murillo, Ribera and Zurbarán as well as exhibits of folkloric interest. Local history is celebrated in the municipal museum.

Manuel de Falla (1876–1946), the composer, was born in Cádiz and is entombed in the cathedral. The theatre named after him is the hub of the city's cultural life. Fun-loving inhabitants of Cádiz give the city a sparkling nightlife and they put on the most elaborate celebration of *Carnaval* in the peninsula. As is to be expected, *fino* is the favourite aperitif, fish the favoured food, *pescaíto frito* the snack served everywhere.

At Playa de la Victoria high-rise blocks back a good beach and the Paseo Marítimo is lively in the summer months. On the opposite side of the promontory are busy commercial and fishing ports and important shipbuilding yards. Industrial outskirts spread around a wide bay, as do the fish farms of one of its fastest-growing industries. A popular excursion is the 45-minute trip to Puerto de Santa María (St Mary's Gate) on *El Vapor*, a ferry that departs from the port entrance.

Cádiz is one of those cities which it is a pleasure to visit not so much for seeing great sights or becoming enmeshed in history, but for enjoying its present-day atmosphere among people known for their wit and vivacity. Close to the ocean with which the city's fortunes have for so long been linked, the Hotel Atlántico offers the usual high standards and comfort of a Parador de Turismo.

Cádiz cathedral, begun in 1722 but not completed for 100 years

Church of San Felipe Neri in Cádiz, birthplace of Spanish democracy

CARMONA

MAP REF: 108 B2

This whole town has been declared a National Monument. It was a strategic site for Palaeolithic man, Iberians and Carthaginians, for Romans, who built its walls, and Moors, who fortified them. In the extensive Necropolis Romana, which a British archaeologist, George Bonsor, excavated between 1881 and 1914, there are over 800 family tombs, some dated to the 1st century BC. Most impressive are the Servilia, almost the size of a villa, and the Elefante, guarded by a statue of an elephant.

After the caliphate in Córdoba collapsed, Carmona was for a time the capital of a *taifa* (small kingdom) and its rulers raised fine buildings. Following its capture by Fernando *el Santo,* in 1247, it was favoured by successive monarchs and further endowed with fine architecture. Elements from both periods feature in the buildings along streets and squares that follow the Roman town plan. The Puerta de Sevilla, main entry to the old town, is part of the Alcázar Bajo (Lower Fortress), built by the Romans and altered by the Moors. Close by, the tower of the 15th-century Iglesia de San Pedro (Church of St Peter) was erected in 1704 and is a copy of Sevilla's Giralda.

The patio of the Ayuntamiento (town hall) is covered by a Roman mosaic depicting Medusa. Plaza de

San Fernando is lined with buildings in which Mudéjar elements are prominent. Iglesia de Santa María la Mayor is a Gothic structure on the site of a mosque, from which it retains the ablution patio and other elements. It has notable Plateresque altarpieces, ironwork and paintings. Two octagonal Roman towers flank the Puerta de Córdoba (Córdoba Gate). The Alcázar Arriba (Upper Fortress) of the Arabs was converted into a palace by Pedro the Cruel, but abandoned after an earthquake in the 16th century. It has been tastefully rebuilt to provide 122 comfortable rooms of the Parador Alcázar de Turismo del Rey Don Pedro. The chance to stay in a 17th-century palace, renovated and furnished with superb taste, is offered by the Casa de Carmona.

Plaza de la Constitución, Cádiz. The city was once capital of Spain

MOTOR TOUR

A mountain zone of much natural beauty lies not far northwest of Sevilla. When the city is sweltering in the summer heat, Sevilla's Sierra Norte offer cool and shady glens with bubbling brooks. The Sierra Norte are the foothills of the Sierra Morena, which form Andalucía's northern boundary. Extensive farmlands, pastures, forests, game reserves and valley collieries present a varied scenery.

From Carmona take the C432 north for 27km.

Lora del Río
On the banks of the Guadalquivir the town sits like a very large, white estate among an expanse of farmland whose richness was appreciated by Romans and Moors. Most of the 20,000 or so inhabitants are in some way involved in agriculture: cotton, cereals, potatoes and sugarbeet have been the traditional crops. The Zahariche ranch of the Miura family is famous for its fine bulls. Close to remains of its Moorish

castle, the Ermita de Señora Setefilla, dedicated to the town's patroness, has a notable altar. The Casa de Leones is one of a number of fine 18th-century houses.

Take the C432 north for 30km.

Constantina
It is difficult to imagine that the son of Emperor Constantine would have bothered about this slumbering place enough to donate his name to it; that the Moors would have seen fit to build its castle; that it was here in 1283 that King Alfonso X did battle with his son for the throne of Castile. Most picturesque is the Barrio de la Morería.

Continue north on the SE163/2 for a scenic drive of 25km.

Alanis
The walls of its Moorish castle remain, and notable among its buildings is the Iglesia de Nuestra Señora de las Nieves (Church of Our Lady of the Snows), which

displays beautiful tilework. Hunting and river fishing are popular pursuits in the area surrounding.

The C421 winds south for 17km.

Cazalla de la Sierra
Cocolubis wine from here reached the tables of Rome; now the town's production of *anís* liqueurs and fiery *aguardientes* are widely appreciated. At one time its iron foundries attracted visitors; now people visit it to enjoy its summertime leisure amenities. Notable among its buildings are the 14th-century Mudéjar Iglesia de Nuestra Señora de Consolacíon (Church of Our Lady of Consolation); 15th-century Convento de Madre de Dios (Convent of the Mother of God); and La Cartuja, a monastery affiliated with the famous one of Sevilla.

Along the C433 south, it is 80km to Sevilla and a further 40km to Carmona.

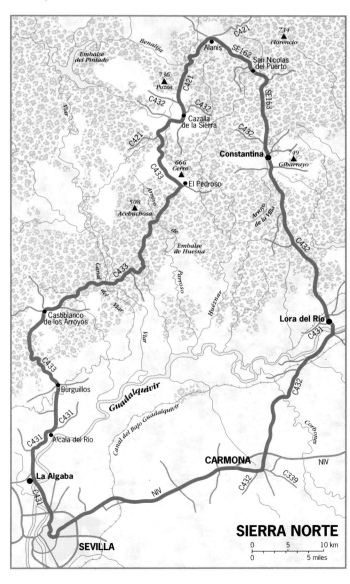

SIERRA NORTE

INVADERS AND SETTLERS

The settlement of Andalucía began a long time ago. Cro-Magnon man occupied caves at Nerja in Málaga province 25,000 years ago; Carmona was a large settlement of a Neolithic tribe some 20,000 years later; during the Bronze Age an advanced knowledge of mining and refining ores gained from the East was being used by the Argaric people in the northeast of what today is Almería province.

After 1000BC a fresh wave of settlers, now known as Iberians, arrived from North Africa and spread throughout Andalucía. By 1000BC, the rich and fabled state of Tartessos was established in the area of present-day Huelva. The Bible records its existence at the time of King Solomon. The nearby Río Tinto district was rich in ores, which the Tartessians mined and traded with the Phoenicians, the people of Tyre.

The Phoenicians had founded their colony of *Gadir* on the site of Cádiz, which justifiably claims to be the oldest continuously inhabited city in the Western world. They brought writing, improved methods for metal working and the use of money. Four centuries later Phocaeans (Greeks) were also trading with Tartessos from colonies west of their main settlement at Mainake (near Málaga). They contributed their culture, the olive and the vine to the region.

Phoenician influence in the region was adopted by their descendants from the North African city of Carthage, who in turn displaced all Greek influence, destroyed Tartessos, increased their foothold in the region and began challenging Rome for control of the Mediterranean. After the First Punic War (264-241BC),

when they were also under attack by the Iberians, the Carthaginians were left with little more than Cádiz. Hamilcar was successful in regaining much territory and, soon after taking command in 221BC, Hannibal provoked the Second Punic War (219-201BC), in which the region was a major theatre of fighting. The Roman, Scipio Africanus, had a decisive victory over Hasdrubal's forces at Carmona in 206BC and the subsequent fall of Cádiz ended Carthaginian power in the Iberian peninsula.

Rome consolidated its rule in its new province of Hispania Ulterior and in 151BC Córdoba was established as the administrative capital. Roman architecture, urban planning, country estates, agricultural arrangements and road networks became dominant features in the landscape. From Cádiz the Via Augusta was built along the coast to end in the imperial city. Order was imposed with Roman civil and legal codes and Latin as the language for all.

Córdoba was the birthplace of the philosopher Seneca (about 4BC-AD65); Itálica, near Sevilla, that of the emperors Trajan (52-117) and Hadrian (76-138); other places throughout the region produced men who made their mark in the wider empire.

The Christian Reconquest of Málaga as depicted in tiles on Sevilla's Plaza de España

Christianity, which had filtered in during the first century, was suppressed until early in the 4th century. By the time of the death of Theodosius in 395, Christianity was the official religion and the empire, already in serious decline, was divided between his two sons. Arcadio, born in Spain, became emperor of the Eastern Empire. Honorio, emperor of the Western Empire, had lost Spain, Britain and Gaul by the end of his reign in 423. Of the Germanic tribes that overran Roman Spain, it was the Vandals who first spread across *Baetica*. They were soon chased to North Africa by the Visigoths.

In 456, the Visigoths broke with Rome and in 475 Rome conceded that the Visigoths were rulers of what had been its Iberian provinces. The Visigoths were few in number and ruled through a military aristocracy and elected monarchy. They adopted Latin and much else that was Roman. By 590, Catholicism was the state religion. Racial integration continued, but effective government was continuously undermined by rivalry for the monarchy, religious strife and dissidence among the subjects. Oppa, Archbishop of Sevilla, conspired with Musa, Moslem emir in North Africa, to invade the peninsula in a bid to secure the crown for his nephew. On the banks of the Río Guadalete (Cádiz province) in 711, Berber forces led by Tarik, nominee of Musa, routed the army of King Roderick.

The Islamic conquest of the whole peninsula was rapid. Feuding Visigoths were no match; most of the population was indifferent to the invasion; persecuted minorities like the Jews welcomed it. But there was also rivalry among the different Moslem tribes and factions.

The sole survivor of the Omayyad dynasty in Damascus landed at Almuñécar (Granada province) and gathered support on his way to Córdoba where, as Abderraman I, he established himself as an independent emir in 756 and ruled until 788. Abderraman II, who reigned for 30 years from 822, strengthened the administration, but it was under the 49-year reign of Abderraman III from 912 that Moslem power was consolidated in the peninsula. In 929 he broke with the Eastern Caliphate by declaring himself Caliph and, when London was but a rudimentary settlement, Córdoba was set to become the West's most civilised city. Abderraman III strengthened the defence lines against Christian kingdoms in the

Incident in the Battle of Trafalgar
illustrated by W L Wyllie

north of the peninsula, and developed relations with Byzantium and the German empire. *Al-Andalus* was a bright beacon of learning and culture on a continent that had entered the Dark Ages.

Hakam II, who ruled from 961 to 976, maintained the pattern set by his father and further enhanced the cultural development of *Al-Andalus*. His successor, Hisham III, was ineffective and, for most of his rule, real power was held by Almansur, a military strongman who conducted successful campaigns against Christian kingdoms. Almansur was also strong on civic pride and he initiated many public works projects. When he died in 1002 the caliphate began its decline and Hisham III, the last caliph, abdicated in 1031. Moslem Spain split into 26 *taifas* (small kingdoms). Some warred with each other; some made pacts with Christian rulers in the north; some consolidated. The kingdoms of Sevilla and Granada predominated.

After the loss to the Christians of Toledo in 1085, some *taifas* asked the Almoravid emir in North Africa for help. From 1090, the Almoravides began uniting the *taifas* and imposing a strict religious order, which included the persecution of Christians and Jews. Their rivals in North Africa, the Almohades, arrived in *Al-Andalus* in 1147 and by 1170 had replaced the Almoravides. They improved the economy and were keen builders. Initially, they offered religious freedom. After their defeat in 1212 by the Christian forces of Castile at the battle of Las Navas de Tolosa near Jaén, the Moslems again split into factions.

COTO DE DOÑANA

MAP REF: 108 A2

Spain's largest National Park and its adjoining protected areas cover 75,000 hectares of marshlands, scrublands, oak forests and dunes at the estuary of the Río Guadalquivir, and provide different microclimates favoured by different fauna and flora.

Doñana is Europe's most important resting and feeding area for the continent's many migratory birds. Huge flocks of geese, flamingos, storks, herons, egrets, spoonbills and other birds winter here. In the scrublands there are deer, wild boar, polecats, badgers and unique species of lynx and mongoose. Among birds of prey, threatened imperial eagles still rule the skies.

Las marismas (the marshes), which dry out in summer, are threatened by an ecological disaster as increasing use of water upriver is dangerously lowering the water level of the marshes throughout the year, permanently drying out some. Pollution of the water upstream is also a threat to the park's delicate ecosystem. Property development on its borders is another.

Doñana is a very controversial issue in national and Andalucían politics and the European Commissioner for the Environment has warned Spain that

Cork oak trees growing near rainy Grazalema

Europe will not 'close its eyes to the catastrophe'.

Excursions lasting four hours and covering 70km through the park are made in four-wheel-drive vehicles from the park's reception centre at El Acebuche. Reservations are essential. La Rocina information centre, near the village of El Rocío, gives information about areas adjoining the park that can be visited without guides. It is hoped that visitors will become committed converts to the cause of protecting one of Europe's most important natural areas.

ECIJA

MAP REF: 108 B2

One of the earliest archbishops' sees in Spain under St Crispin was established here and local legend claims that St Paul was a visitor. Vestiges of the town's importance in the Roman period are scattered near by. Ecija is called 'the town of sun and towers', but it is also known as 'the frying pan of Andalucía' because summer temperatures often go above 45°C in the shade and have reached 52°C. Of towers there are certainly many: 11 of them and 15 belfries. A rich inheritance of Renaissance and baroque architecture adorns the compact town. The Plaza de España is surrounded by good-looking buildings and is popularly known as *el salón* (sitting room), perhaps because so many retired or unemployed agricultural workers are usually sitting around in the plaza. Parts of the Palacio de los Marqués de Peñaflor (Peñaflor Palace) can be visited, and two other notable Renaissance palaces are those of Condes de Valdehermoso and Valverde. The Palacio de Benamejí, a National Monument and now occupied by the military, was built in the 18th century and has a large marble

Sizzling Ecija, a town where temperatures soar in summer

front. Inside are an attractive patio and stables with a collection of carriages. Among Ecija's many notable churches are: Santa María, Santa Inés, Santa Bárbara and San Juan Bautista (St John the Baptist), which boasts the most impressive tower; Las Descalzas is a full expression of Sevilla's baroque style.

GRAZALEMA

MAP REF: 108 B1

The highest annual rainfall in Spain is regularly recorded in this neatly sited village, surrounded by El Torrejón and other peaks that force rain-bearing clouds drifting in from the Atlantic to unleash their load. The Parque Natural de Sierra de Grazalema covers 52,000 hectares of the western end of the Sistema Bética mountain chain, and most of it is lushly covered with trees, including the indigenous *pinsapo* fir.

Grazalema had a wide reputation for the quality of its blankets woven from the wool of sheep which once roamed the hills in great numbers. Recently there has been a revived interest in the craft and the Fabrica de Mantas is a museum-piece factory in operation. Goats' milk cheese is another product for which Grazalema has some fame, and it can be bought directly from the factory.

Wiggling lanes are lined with white houses adorned with solid ironwork and a profusion of flowerpots. From above, the village is a patchwork of pantiled roofs. A rustic 'mini parador' operated by the provincial authorities has comfortable rooms and serves local dishes. A project which will further enhance the area's attraction as an inland centre for leisure and recreation includes the building of a 'tourist village' to provide simple, comfortable accommodation at moderate prices.

Nearby El Bosque, some 18km west along a scenic road, is at the edge of the mountain region and overlooks agricultural plains. Trout are farmed in fresh mountain waters, as they are in the nearby hamlet of Benamahoma, and are on the menu of the village's 'mini parador', the Hostal Las Truchas.

Ubrique is 25km from Grazalema and 16km from El Bosque along scenic roads and is much larger than both. The town, in which many fountains bubble, lies in a valley below the Sierra de Ubrique

Iglesia de Santiago in Ecija, one of several fine churches here

An endangered refuge: Coto de Doñana National Park

and close to the large expanse of the Embalse de los Hurónes. Many of its 18,000 people are involved in the leather industry and the *Piel de Ubrique* label denotes good quality. Factories also turn out designer items for big-name international fashion houses. Craftsmen can be seen at work.

CYCLE TOUR

A 59km round route from Grazalema to El Bosque, Ubrique and back goes through delightful scenery on tarred roads that do not have much traffic. Gradients are all easily manageable for the fairly fit.

WALKS

On the road from Grazalema to El Bosque and just before the hamlet of Benamahoma, is a picnic and camping area that is a favourite setting-off place for hikers on routes of varying durations through forests of pines, cork oaks, poplars, eucalyptus and *pinsapos*. A three-day staged walk can follow the route suggested above as a cycle tour. There are campsites in Grazalema and El Bosque and low-cost hostels in Ubrique. All three places have public swimming-pools.

CHRISTIAN RECONQUEST

Unification of the kingdoms of Castile and León in the person of Ferdinand III, and disarray among Moslem factions following the battle of Las Navas de Tolosa in 1212, helped Christian forces rapidly to pick up major prizes: Ferdinand took Córdoba in 1236, Jaén in 1246, Sevilla in 1248; Alfonso X added Huelva and Cádiz in 1262. Remains of Fernando *el Santo* (The Saint), and Fernando *el Sabio* (The Wise), are revered in Sevilla's great cathedral. Conquests of territory were followed by the immigration of people from the north, adding to Andalucía's racial mix and the imposition of a less advanced culture and administration. Eagerness to consolidate the Faith led to an outburst of religious building in which the architectural style of northern regions was combined with Arab styles. Land was divided among the nobility, church and military orders. *Latifundios*, large estates harking back to Roman times, and ruling families were created. Their existence has caused much socio-economic damage in the region up to the present time.

Inflammatory engraving showing Moslems torturing Christians

Moslems remaining in Christian territories were known as *mudéjares*. Mudéjar is the term for Moslem craftsmanship and architecture carried out under Christian rule. Moslem converts to Christianity were called *moriscos*. Jews were forced to live in *juderías* (enclosed city districts) under the protection of kings whom their scholars, traders and administrators served. A delicate co-existence was maintained among the races and religions. The Nasrid kingdom of Granada still retained a large area of *Al-Andalus*, including Málaga and much of the south coast. By a strategy of strong defences and treaties, it survived and its city blossomed into the most cultured in the peninsula.

Ferdinand and Isabel, the Catholic Monarchs (los Reyes Católicos), who married in 1469, had their campaign against the Moslems blessed by the Pope as a Holy Crusade, and they instituted the ruthless Inquisition to root out heretics. From the fortress of Sevilla, Córdoba and other strategic places, they nibbled away at the boundaries of Granada and planned their final assault on the city. On 2 January 1492, King Boabdil gave them the keys of his city. They had promised him that his people could live peacefully, practising their beliefs and customs. It was not a promise they kept. They banished all Jews from Spain and their treatment of gypsies was also harsh. In the same year, the Genovese seafarer, Christopher Columbus (Cristóbal Colón), sailed to the New World, which he claimed in the name of the Catholic Monarchs.

UNITED SPAIN
Spain began hauling back the treasure trove it found in the

Americas. Grand Renaissance buildings were commissioned in cities and towns in an extravagant display of wealth; at its most elaborate the style is known as Plateresque as it resembles the fine works of silversmiths. From his maternal grandparents, the Catholic Monarchs, Charles V (1516–56) inherited a united Spain and its colonies in the Mediterranean and New World; from his paternal Habsburg grandfather he gained Austria, the Low Countries, most of Germany and parts of France.

Charles and his son, Philip II (1556–98), one of the most powerful rulers the world had known, used Spain's immense wealth in waging wars aimed at gaining territory and fighting the Protestants. The defeat of Philip's Armada by the English in 1588 signalled the waning of Spain's unmatched power in the world. With the expulsion of Jews and Moslems, and the subjugation and final expulsion of *moriscos* (1609), Andalucía's productivity had progressively declined. Many Andalucían people had left to settle in the New World.

THE GOLDEN AGE

During the 17th century Spain became weaker politically, but culture flourished in the nation's *Siglo de Oro* (Golden Age). Baroque was the dominant architectural style, and there was a wealth of talent in Andalucía to give it exuberant expression and leave the treasured legacy of architecture, painting and sculpture at which visitors can marvel today. Velázquez and Murillo of Sevilla and Alonso Cano of Granada were painting their masterpieces. Sevilla's Museo de Bellas Artes (Fine Arts Museum) has the most representative collection of the region's great art from the period. In literature, Luis de Góngora from Córdoba was the brightest light.

The 18th century started off with the War of the Spanish Succession in which the Bourbon claimant, Philip V, was successful and Britain gained Gibraltar. Sporadic wars with Britain and the loss of American colonies followed, until Britain's victory at the Battle of Trafalgar in 1805. Three years later and until 1814, Britain was Spain's ally in the Peninsular War against Napoleon's forces, who looted or destroyed many architectural and artistic treasures, causing great losses throughout Andalucía. The 19th century was marked by continuous political upheaval, including a two-year period of the First Republic enthusiastically supported in Andalucía. By 1898 Spain had lost most of its colonial empire after its war with the United States.

THE 20TH CENTURY

Andalucía, largely owned by absentee landlords, was sadly neglected by Madrid's central government and movements in favour of agrarian reform were usually ruthlessly suppressed. Political confusion and economic stagnation continued and with the support of King Alfonso XIII, General Primo de Rivera ran the country from 1923 to 1930. He fled and the king left the next year. The majority in Andalucía strongly supported the socialists who won Spain's general elections of 1931.

Again, the country could not pull itself out of political chaos within its Second Republic. In July 1936, army factions – Nationalists – led by General Francisco Franco, rose against the Popular Front government. Control of Sevilla was taken by General Queipo de Llano in July 1936 and Franco had his headquarters in the city for a time. The ensuing civil war lasted until early 1939 and each village, town and city has its sad and separate story of the horrors. Franco, *el Caudillo* (the Leader), ran the country until his death in 1975. Andalucía received little benevolence from a man who saw himself as a kind father of the people. From the late 1950s the phenomenon of mass tourism began to be exploited along Málaga's coastline. It was greatly encouraged by Franco, hungry for foreign exchange, and unplanned, rampant over-development was allowed in some places.

Under Spain's democratic constitution, Andalucía became an autonomous region in 1982. Its parliament sits in the newly converted Renaissance building of the Hospital de las Cinco Llagas (Hospital of the Five Wounds) in Sevilla. The 18th-century Palacio de San Telmo is the seat of the regional government, the Junta de Andalucía. Felipe González, President of Spain's government (Prime Minister) since 1982, comes from Sevilla, where he began his clandestine support and work for the PSOE (Socialist Party) during the dark Franco years. Alfonso Guerra, also from Sevilla, was then his closest collaborator and is vice-general secretary of the PSOE. Manuel Chaves, another member of the 'Sevilla Clan', is President of the Junta de Andalucía.

Philip II, whose reign saw the beginning of Spain's decline

Philippus de II, Coninck van Hispanien, ende Indien Aertshertoch van Oostenryck Hertoch van Bourgondien etc.

HUELVA

MAP REF: 108 A2

Not many tourists spend time in this industrial and port city because, in comparison with all the sightseeing Andalucía has to offer, Huelva has little. However, like any city, it has a life and style of its own which, given time, visitors come to enjoy. It may have been an important place in the time of the Tartessian kingdom. The Phoenicians had a settlement named *Onuba* from which today's 150,000 *onubenses* get their nickname. The Moors called it *Ghelbah,* from which Huelva is derived.

After the Christian conquest it lived in the shadow of Sevilla. In 1755 an earthquake caused massive destruction, and in the 19th century it became capital of its own province. The British boosted its trade by exporting copper, silver and gold from their Riotinto mines through its port, and the English-style Barrio Reina Victoria, which the company built for its workers in 1917, is one of the city's most notable 'sights'.

What attracts visitors is the proximity of places related to Christopher Columbus (see pages 30 and 31). The monument to Columbus (Colón), a grandiose sculpture by Gertrude Whitney, at Punta del Sebo, where the estuaries of the Odiel and Tinto rivers meet, was a gift from the United States in 1929. In the Museo Provincial (Provincial Museum) are objects relating to Dolmen and Tartessian civilisations and a fine arts section with contemporary works by Vázquez Díaz (1882-1969), who

Jerez de la Frontera: statue of San Juan de la Salle

was born in the province. Oldest of the city's buildings are the Iglesia de San Pedro (Church of St Peter), built on the site of a mosque, and the cathedral, much of which was previously a convent.

Nearby Niebla, on the road to Sevilla, is the most attractive town on the province's coastal plain. Its walls have stood intact for over 1,000 years and its main church is almost as old. Punta Umbria, La Antilla and Isla Cristina have developed as summer resorts west of the city, where there are fine beaches up to the border with Portugal at Ayamonte. Pollution of the sea frequently makes it inadvisable to swim at beaches along this stretch.

JEREZ DE LA FRONTERA

MAP REF: 108 B1

Jerez - Pura Andalucía is the town's promotional slogan and it is true that in Jerez many of the idealised images of this region come alive: rich land barons, grand palaces and large estates, finely bred horses and fighting bulls, lively and passionate flamenco, beautiful women and handsome men, and much flowing wine.

Built on the bedrock of sherry and brandy production, Jerez has for long been among Spain's most commercially successful towns. The old Anglo-Andaluz sherry dynasties still wield much social influence and economic power, in spite of the arrival of multinational corporations and opposing politicians. The outskirts of town have a modern aspect and many of the 180,000 inhabitants occupy new apartment blocks. A very attractive old quarter remains at the heart of the town.

Few visitors to Jerez do not go on a tour of one of the sherry *bodegas* to see the production process and to sample the product. Another essential visit is to the Real Escuela Andaluza del Arte Ecuestre, the school of equestrian art, where on most days it is possible to see the stables, a collection of carriages and training sessions; on Thursday a fascinating and perfected performance is given of an equestrian ballet, with Spanish music and costumes from the 17th century.

Everybody is concerned with time and in the Museo de Relojes is one of Europe's most varied and interesting collections of time-keeping instruments. A wander

Defensive remains in old Jerez

through the old town does not take long and there is much to note. In Plaza de la Asunción is the 16th-century Casa del Cabildo Viejo (old town hall), which houses a small archaeological museum and library. Here, too, is the 15th-century Gothic-Mudéjar Iglesia de San Dionisio (Church of St Dionisio), patron saint of Jerez. The Alcázar-Mezquita was built in the 12th century as a residence for the Emir of Sevilla and its mosque was later converted into a church. Among the most notable churches are: Santiago (St James), with its florid Gothic front; San Miguel, (St Michael) a Gothic building that features an altarpiece by Martínez Montañés; and Iglesia-Convento de Santo Domingo (Convent Church of St Dominic), started shortly after the Reconquest, where exhibitions are often held in the cloisters. Near by is one of the finest mansions of a sherry dynasty, Casa Domecq.

Just out of town on the road to Medina Sidonia is the monumental ensemble of La Cartuja de Santa María de la Defension, a monastery founded in 1477, which is inhabited by a silent order.

With a good selection of accommodation, restaurants and nightspots, an enlarged international airport, a motorway connection to Sevilla, new sports and leisure facilities and the proximity of fine beaches, scenic countryside and picturesque villages, Jerez is an ideal base from which to explore and enjoy this part of Andalucía. Local businesses and authorities are active in promoting the town and enhancing its attractions.

BULLS AND HORSES

These two animals are very important in the local popular consciousness, and the ranches on which they are reared occupy large tracts of Cádiz province. One such ranch is Los Alburejos near Medina Sidonia where Alvaro Domecq, once a *rejoneador* (mounted bullfighter) raises Torrestrella fighting bulls and where the testing of the bulls can be seen in spring. Bull-breeders follow individual criteria for preparing bulls for the ring, but all tend to claim that there is no financial reward from their work and that it is passion that motivates them. For *aficionados* of the *corrida* (bull-fight), the bull's breeder is almost as important in the ritual as the *torero* who kills it. According to legend, Hercules, who forced Europe and Africa apart, came to these parts to perform one of his 12 labours – to kill a bull.

The Cartujano breed is regarded as the aristocrat of horses in Andalucía, and it was the monks of La Cartuja who concentrated on its perfection. Born a chestnut colour, the horses turn to grey or piebald and have long, silky manes. At the equestrian school these beautiful animals have shown an ability to move to music and proudly perform intricate steps, which includes the *cabriolé*, a sharp kick backwards when all four feet are in the air. During the *Feria del Caballo* (horse show) in late April and early May, horses are the centre of attraction and inhabitants of Jerez parade their best animals and show themselves off in their finest costumes. It is one of Spain's oldest fairs and in the Middle Ages traders came from all over Europe. Traditionally at this fair, the sale of a horse is confirmed when the purchaser takes it by the reins.

Far from the passion of the *corrida*, fighting bulls graze peacefully

FOOD AND DRINK

When Arabs ruled this region, it had the West's most sophisticated cuisine. During centuries of economic stagnation, the peasants' diet became the culinary tradition. In our times, mass tourism caused an eruption of eating places serving poorly prepared and presented local or foreign-style dishes. Farmers, fishermen and foreigners with no training in catering pretended to be restaurateurs. Some fine restaurants did, however, arise. Gourmets have had little praise for Andalucían cooking, except for that of a few outstanding restaurants, but in recent years they have welcomed wider trends.

Local tipple includes good table wines as well as sherry

A revived interest in traditional regional cooking has been part of the general increased awareness and promotion of all that is typically *Andaluz*. There is some harking back to Arab times and the wider adaptation of traditional recipes, or the creation of new ones, to make light dishes that satisfy modern tastes and dietary concerns. Innovative chefs come up with imaginative combinations of ingredients from the best of local produce during different seasons.

El Centro Andaluz de Investigaciónes Gastronomicas, in the village of Dúrcal near Granada, is a centre for the investigation of culinary arts, a living museum of *Andaluz* cooking and a training school supported by the Andalucían government. Its El Molina restaurant is a favourite with purists. Now, at many restaurants throughout the region, memorable and sophisticated meals can be enjoyed at prices which are very favourable by international comparison. There are also many unpretentious places where traditional dishes, well prepared from good quality ingredients, can be enjoyed.

Olive oil *(aceite de oliva)* and garlic *(ajo)* are staple ingredients. Tomato *(tomate)*, onion *(cebolla)* and green or red pepper *(pimiento)* also feature strongly. Chicken *(pollo)* and pork *(cerdo)* were the most used poultry *(aves)* and meat *(carnes)*, but veal *(ternera)* and beef *(vaca)* are now widely available. Cured ham from mountain areas *(jamón serrano)*, by itself or in combination, such as with melon *(melón)*, are among the most popular snacks and starters. Red paprika sausage *(chorizo)* and blood sausage *(morcilla)* are the most used prepared meat products. The wide choice of fish *(pescados)* and shellfish *(mariscos)* comes from both Mediterranean and Atlantic catches, and from the mountain streams. Eggs *(huevos)* are used hard-boiled *(duros)* in salads, scrambled *(revueltos)* or in many types of omelettes *(tortillas)*. However, apart from potatoes *(patatas)* and carrots *(zanahorias)*, most vegetables *(verduras/legumbres)* have traditionally been above-ground varieties with an emphasis on green beans *(judías verdes)*, broad beans *(habas)*, peas *(guisantes)* and chick peas *(garbanzos)*.

The choice has widened. Sevilla province is an important producer of rice *(arroz),* main ingredient for *paella,* which is of Valencian origin. In addition to tomato and onion, cucumber *(pepino)* and lettuce *(lechuga)* are the staples for salads *(ensaladas).* Avocados *(aguacates),* of which Andalucía is now a major producer, are the base for many starters and salads.

Desserts *(postres)* and pastries *(pasteles)* show their Arab origins. Andalucía produces many different fruits *(frutas),* including exotic subtropical varieties. Cheeses *(quesos)* both local or from other countries, are becoming more widely available. Sauces *(salsas)* are few and food has traditionally been cooked on a griddle *(a la plancha),* fried *(frito),* grilled *(a la parrilla),* baked/roasted *(al horno/asado),* or plain-boiled *(cocido).*

There are provincial, and more localised, differences in cooking styles and dishes as well as rivalry in respect of some staples. Córdobans claim they make the best *gazpacho Andaluz,* a cold soup of tomato, onion, green pepper, garlic, bread, oil and vinegar. Sevillans say only they use the authentic recipe for *huevos a la flamenca,* a baked mix of eggs, ham, spicy sausage, beans, peas, onion, garlic and olive oil. For the people of Jaén province, others do not know how to cook *choto,* kid goat. *Malagueños* say their *pescado frito,* deep-fried fish, is the best. Huelva's claim that its *jamón serrano* is the best is countered by Granada's that hams from the village of Trevélez take the prize. In Almería they claim that their *sopas de mariscos,* a soup of shellfish with mayonnaise, beats similarly named soups elsewhere.

The Andalucían idea of *tapas* has spread throughout Spain and beyond. The word is derived from *tapar* (to cover) as glasses were covered with a small plate on which it became a custom to put a snack. Olives *(aceitunas),* nuts *(nuezes)* and potato crisps *(patatas fritas)* are the simplest snacks, but *tapas* can be small portions of almost any type of food in a variety of preparations.

WINE

Red *(tinto),* rosé *(rosado)* and white *(blanco)* wines *(vinos)* from Rioja and Penedés, the best-known wine regions of Spain, as well as those of other controlled wine-producing areas, *Denominaciones de Origen* or DOs, are widely available. Many villages have a *bodega* producing wine for local consumption. It can often be strong and heady, but is always cheap and flows freely during many *fiestas.* Málaga's sweet and luscious wine has long been a British favourite. Cádiz province produces the renowned sherries, and the Montilla-Moriles area of Córdoba province is another producer of wine for drinking before or after a meal. Good white table wines now also come from here as well as from Cádiz province and the Condado del Niebla area of Huelva province. Most restaurants have a house wine *(vino de la casa)* and other regional restaurants usually offer their region's wines. Excellent quality and value can be enjoyed among the *cavas,* sparkling wines produced by the champagne method.

SHERRY

Very chalky soil in an area of Cádiz province favours the grape types (Palomino, Pedro Ximénez, Moscatel) mainly used in the production of sherry, or *vino Jerez* as it is locally called. Production is centred on Jerez de la Frontera, El Puerto de Santa María and Sanlúcar de Barrameda.

Huevos a la flamenco: **baked eggs with ham and vegetables**

Expert blending by the cellar-man *(capataz)* ensures bottled sherries of uniform taste and quality for the different types: *fino,* very pale and dry; *amontillado,* a fuller, nuttier and older *fino; oloroso,* similar but darker and more fragrant; *palos cortados,* halfway between an *amontillado* and *oloroso* and rarely available. Cream sherries are sweet, either pale and light tasting or dark and velvety; *manzanilla,* made only in Sanlúcar, is like *fino.*

The Panteón Ducal in Osuna, where tombs of the powerful Dukes of Osuna may be seen

OSUNA
MAP REF: 108 B2

Julius Caesar conquered the Iberian town of *Urso,* which had allied itself with Pompey. After the Moorish town was taken in 1240, it passed under the control of the religious order of Calatrava and then into the Girón family. From 1562, when one of the family was given the title of Duke of Osuna by Philip II, the town was the fiefdom of one of Spain's most influential aristocratic families. When their power was at its height through the 17th and 18th centuries, the dukes and their acolytes endowed the town with many beautiful buildings, which have been well preserved. Buildings made with crafted stone stand out among whitewashed ones on which black *rejas* and *cancelas* (ironwork windows and door grilles) are contrasted. Calle San Pedro is one of many streets lined by fine houses of this period.

The Iglesia Colegial de Santa María de la Asunción (Collegiate Church of St Mary of the Assumption) has been declared a National Monument for the importance of its architecture, wealth of interior decoration and the art collection shown in the sacristy. Christs by Luis de Morales and Juan de Mesa, and the baroque altarpiece, are especially impressive and the Calvary painting by José de Ribera (1620) is regarded as one of the province's great treasures. Members of the ducal family are still interred in the Plateresque Panteón Ducal (Ducal Sepulchre) attached to the convent.

Nuns remain in residence in the

LEBRIJA
MAP REF: 108 B2

This white town lies close to the Río Guadalquivir among fields and vineyards. During the Roman epoch, Bacchus and Venus were venerated here and the area has yielded rich archaeological finds. Steven Spielberg filmed parts of *Empire of the Sun* here because of the quality of the light, the stunning sunsets and the similarity of the landscape to the part of China where J G Ballard's story (on which the film was based) was set. A famous son of the town is Antonio de Nebrija, chronicler of the Catholic Monarchs and author of the first Castilian grammar, which was published in 1492. Notable among buildings in Mudéjar, Renaissance and baroque styles are the Casa del Cabildo and the Iglesia de Santa María de la Oliva (Church of St Mary of the Olives), once a mosque, which has a tower resembling Sevilla's Giralda and an altarpiece by Alonso Cano.

MATALASCAÑAS
MAP REF: 108 A2

Matalascañas and Mazagón are the principal urban centres of Huelva's Costa de la Luz (Coast of Light), whose beaches rate among the very best in Europe. They are long and wide and have fine, golden sand washed by the Atlantic, backed by dunes in some places and by pinewoods in others. A road runs for 29km through pinewoods between the two towns.

Recent and rapid development has provided the full infrastructure for summer resorts, which are very busy in the season. Mazagón has more charm and is more family-oriented. Both places are good bases from which to visit the Coto de Doñana National Park (see page 20). Off-season the area is tranquil and the beaches are deserted. On a cliff-top near Mazagón the fairly modern Parador de Turismo de Cristóbal Colón offers the usual comfort and good value of this chain.

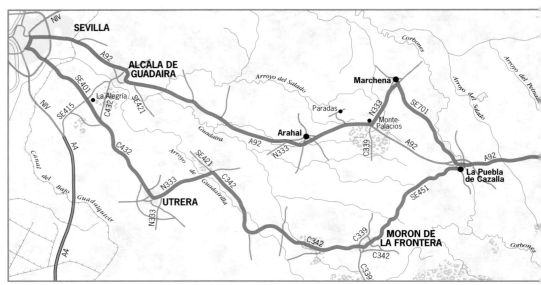

16th-century Monasterio de la Encarnación (Monastery of the Incarnation) which has a museum with valuable religious art and artefacts. Sevillian ceramic tiles of the 18th century decorate the cloister. The Antiqua Universidad, much praised by Cervantes, served as a university from 1549 to 1820. The imposing building is now a school. Once part of the town wall and now a National Monument, the Torre del Agua houses a small archaeological museum displaying Iberian and Roman items.

MOTOR TOUR

Peace and solitude – rare images for pulsating Matalascañas Beach

This route is through rich farmland, coveted through the centuries, where towns were endowed with fine architecture by feudal families.

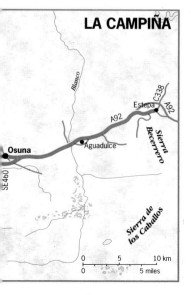

From Sevilla go southeast along the SE401/C432 for 35km.

Utrera

After its first conquest by Alfonso *el Sabio* (The Cruel), the Moors retook their town of Medina Utrirab three times until finally being ousted in 1340. In 1368, Mohamed V of Granada returned to make a fierce attack. Remnants of the castle and walls still stand.

The town is known as the cradle of fighting bulls; fine horses and fighting cocks are also raised. Some people claim the best green olives in Spain come from here and olives are very important to the town's economy. Another favoured product are its cinnamon-flavoured *mostachones*.

Notable baroque stonework adorns the Gothic Iglesia de la Asunción (Church of the Assumption); a florid Gothic style was adopted for the Iglesia de Santiago (Church of St James). The Convento de Nuestra Señora de la Consolación (Our Lady of the Consolation), patroness of the Andalucían countryside, is venerated in the Mudéjar sanctuary on the outskirts of the town, and a large *feria* (agricultural fair) and *fiesta* in her honour is held each September.

Potage Gitano, a gypsy festival of *cante jondo* (the oldest and most authentic form of flamenco) is held at the end of June.

After 9km on the N333 go southwest for 27km.

Morón de la Frontera

A hint of the town's former importance is given by Pliny's (AD23–79) description of it being 'the third city of Betica'. Parts remain of a castle whose origins are Phoenician, and which was slighted by the French in 1812. Many convents were founded in the town, and of its palaces that of the Marqués de Pilares is a very fine example. The Gothic temple of San Miguel Arcángel (St Michael the Archangel) is the most outstanding building.

Go northeast for 20km on the SE451, then east for 43km, visiting Osuna, pearl of La Campiña, on the way or on the return.

Estepa

Uphill through narrow and pristine streets is the Convento de Santa Clara (Convent of St Clare), built in 1598, which has a notable altarpiece showing the transition from Plateresque to baroque. It has an attractive patio and the nuns sell sweets. Adjoining is the 15th-century fortress church of Santa María de la Asunción (St Mary of the Assumption). From the Balcón de Andalucía is a view across the rooftops of Estepa and the plain of La Campiña. Built in the 18th century and now a National Monument, the Torre de la Victoria rises to 48m and is among the most beautiful towers in Andalucía. Estepa's sweet, shortcake-type biscuits – *polvorones*, *mantecados* and *roscos* – are popular throughout Andalucía, especially around Christmas.

Return westward on Autovia '92, going northwest on to the SE701 at La Puebla de Cazalla.

Marchena

Parts of ancient walls and towers are incorporated in other buildings. The Ponce de León family, Dukes of Arcos, held sway here after the Reconquest. Their palaces, and those of the gentility in Barrio de San Juan, give the town its noble air. Grand arches give access to the dignified Plaza Ducal. The Iglesia de Santa María includes Moorish elements; the tower of 15th-century San Juan (St John) is decorated with ceramic work and its altarpiece exhibits the Gothic-flamenco style of Sevilla. A small museum shows works of Zurbarán, Luis de Morales and José Ribera.

By rejoining the Autovia '92 it is some 60km back to Sevilla.

PALOS DE LA FRONTERA

MAP REF: 108 A2

In 1492 the Catholic Monarchs issued an edict charging the village to provide Christopher Columbus (Cristóbal Colón) with ships, sailors and provisions. In Calle Colón is the home of the Pinzón brothers, Martín and Vicente, who undertook the task and served as captains on the voyage. It was in the Iglesia de San Jorge (Church of St George) that Columbus and his crew prayed before their departure and at La Fontanilla, a well in its garden, that the small fleet's water was drawn. The wharf from which the *Santa María*, *Pinta* and *Niña* departed on 3 August 1492 no longer exists as the Río Tinto has long been silted up here.

The Monasterio de La Rábida has been home to Franciscan monks since the beginning of the 15th century. Its Gothic church has Mudéjar decoration, which is also the style of its peaceful cloister. Columbus and his son, Diego, first arrived here from Portugal in 1484 and humbly sought refuge and sustenance. Columbus discussed his theories with the friars Antonio de Marchena and Juan Pérez, who were later to help him in his petitions to the Catholic Monarchs. Murals done by Daniel Vázquez Díaz in 1930 depict the 'discovery' of America. Monks lead conducted tours of their monastery.

Nearby Moguer is now a strawberry-growing centre and retains a harmony between old and new. In the Gothic-Mudéjar Convento de Santa Clara (Convent of St Clare), Columbus and his men once gave thanks for surviving a storm. The convent's museum shows some Columbine material. Resembling Sevilla's Giralda is the tower of the parish church. A 'universal *Andaluz*', Nobel-prizewinning poet, Juan Ramón Jiménez (1881–1958), was born in Moguer, and the Casa-Museo displays an interesting collection of memorabilia of him and his wife.

Palm-shaded promenade in El Puerto de Santa María

PUERTO DE SANTA MARIA, EL

MAP REF: 108 A1

Located at the mouth of the Río Gaudalete only 14km from Jerez, El Puerto is another town with sherry and brandy production as its economic base. A number of *bodegas* offer conducted tours and sampling sessions. Along the riverside, the Ribera del Río is lined with bars and restaurants where the best of local seafoods are washed down with chilled dry sherry. More animated than Jerez, and with the advantage of its own beaches and the proximity of well-endowed resorts, El Puerto is a favourite of the 'in' people from Sevilla and Cádiz, as well as Americans from the nearby naval base of Rota.

The Castillo de San Marcos (St Mark's Castle), was erected on the site of a mosque, from which it retains the *mihrab* and some parts of the walls, as was the fortified church of Santa María del Puerto. The Iglesia de Prioral Mayor, which boasts a central choir, is mainly Gothic but includes later styles. Many fine houses, some displaying coats of arms, line the streets and are a reminder of the town's heyday during Spain's colonial exploits. The bullring, a favourite with some famous matadors, is regarded as one of the most beautiful in Spain. A ferry, *El Vapor*, connects the town with Cádiz.

Nearby Puerto Sherry is a luxurious marina and residential complex within a stretch of summer-resort development stretching west of the town and including Valdelagrana, El Ancla and Fuentebravia. There is good provision for many sports and off-beach diversions.

The 18th-century town hall of Moguer, near Palos de la Frontera

La Rábida monastery: stone detail

SANLUCAR DE BARRAMEDA

MAP REF: 108 A1

The third point in the sherry triangle lies at the mouth of the Río Guadalquivir and its speciality is *manzanilla*, a delicate, pale, dry sherry. *Bodegas* receive visitors.

Each weekday afternoon seafood is auctioned at Bonanza upriver, and various places in Sanlúcar offer simple, fresh food.

Notable buildings include the 15th-century ducal palace whose monumental Gothic façade is known as *Las Covachas*. Next to it, the Iglesia de Santa María de la O dates from the 14th century and has fine Gothic and Mudéjar portals. The mass of the medieval castle of Santiago dominates the town and parts of the original encircling walls still stand. Columbus set sail from here on his third voyage.

CRISTOBAL COLON

Christopher Columbus was probably born in Genoa in 1450. Between 1476 and 1484 he lived in Portugal, where he worked as a map-maker and tried to get support for his venture to reach the Far East by sailing west. His first son, Diego, was born in 1476. Penniless, father and son arrived at La Rábida monastery and Columbus began petitioning Ferdinand and Isabel for support, but the monarchs were engrossed in their reconquest of the Moorish kingdom of Granada, and the Church was sceptical of Columbus's theories. Columbus tried again with the crown of Portugal and also with those of England, France, Genoa and Venice. He married Beatrice Enriquez of Córdoba and their son, Hernando, was born in 1488.

Juan Pérez, friar of La Rábida, had been a confessor to Queen Isabel and his entreaties on behalf of Columbus had great influence in finally winning Columbus the approval of the Catholic Monarchs for his expedition. Under the agreement, Columbus was appointed an admiral and made viceroy and governor of all territories he discovered. There followed a long and complicated story of four voyages (1492–3, 1493–6, 1498–1500, 1502–4), his landfalls, and settlements, his triumphs, disappointments and disgrace until his death in Valladolid in 1506.

The resort and sherry port of El Puerto de Santa María

•SEVILLA•

Andalucía's capital is sensuous and seductive, and few other cities have the power to beguile visitors so rapidly. In Sevilla there is an abundance of energy, a vital spark in making the most of the moment, and *Sevillanos* are blessed with graciousness supported by good humour and an ever-present desire to have fun.

Much of Sevilla (map ref: 108 B2) is very beautiful, with a rich bequest of Gothic, Mudéjar, Renaissance and baroque architecture. When Spain was at its most powerful in the 16th and 17th centuries, Sevilla was the world's busiest port and was one of its four largest cities.

With the hosting of EXPO '92, Sevilla again claimed the international limelight. The full impact on the city and its 700,000 people of the six-month event cannot yet be measured, but it has left an important legacy, not least in vital infrastructural improvements and the enhancement of cultural amenities.

While some of Sevilla's *aficionados* fear that much of the city's charm will be rubbed off in the rush of modernisation, others are sure that its idiosyncrasies and bewitching ways will survive. There will still be the spookily solemn observance of *Semana Santa* (Holy Week) to contrast with frivolous abandonment during the *Feria de Abril* (April Fair) two weeks later, as in flamenco there will always be deep *cante jondo* to contrast with light *cante chico*.

On the Río Guadalquivir, some 115km from the Atlantic, Sevilla has a busy commercial port. Sports and leisure are enjoyed on the river and along its banks. Of most interest to visitors among the city's 24 *barrios* (municipal districts) are three on the east bank: Centro, El Arenal and Santa Cruz. The latter, pristine and picturesque, is an archetypal tourist zone. South of it, the Parque de María Luisa and its surroundings is another area of prime interest and, east of there, Nervion has a number of hotels as well as shopping areas.

Across the river is relatively modern Los Remedios, where the attractions are shopping and nightlife in its many modern music bars. North of here is Triana, whose residents consider themselves the only real Sevillans and where there is the flavour of a traditional residential quarter, now undergoing renovation, with many *tapas* bars, lower-priced restaurants and old-time shops.

North of Triana is the island of La Cartuja, site of EXPO '92 and consequently packed with gleaming modern buildings and new places of interest.

The Lonja, where archives include Columbus' diary and letters

ARCHIVO DE LAS INDIAS

Avenida de la Constitución
Juan de Herrera, Philip II's
favourite architect, completed the
sombre Lonja (Exchange) in 1598.
Two centuries later, the building
began serving its present purpose
as an archive where documents
relating to Spain's connections
with the New World are received
and preserved. One of the galleries
has an exhibition of sample
material, usually including pages
from the diaries or letters of
Columbus.

CATHEDRAL

Plaza del Triunfo
In 1401 the cathedral chapter
declared, 'Let us build a cathedral
so huge that on seeing it people
will think us madmen'. Work
continued until 1506, on the site
of what had been a Visigothic
church and Sevilla's principal
mosque. The main structure is
Gothic; some embellishments
and additions are late Gothic,
Plateresque and baroque. It is a
place of superlatives: the third
largest Christian church in the
world; the largest Gothic
cathedral; the largest interior
space of all with a width of some
83m, a length of 126m and a
height of 30m. In the Capilla
Mayor (Main Chapel) Christ's life
is depicted in 36 tableaux on the

**Gypsy flower-seller in Sevilla's
charming old Jewish quarter**

retable of gilded hardwood. This
altarpiece, measuring 18m wide
and 20m high, is the biggest in
Christendom and was completed
between 1482 and 1564. The
choir has notable wrought-iron
grilles and the carving of its ebony
stalls is in Mudéjar-Renaissance
style.

Predominantly Plateresque
decoration adorns the Capilla Real
(Royal Chapel), completed in
1575. A silver urn supposedly
contains the uncorrupted remains
of Ferdinand III, *el Santo*. Other
chapels display more work of
great artistic merit, and a wealth of
gold and silverware is shown in
the Sacristía Mayor (Main Sacristy).
Paintings in the Sacristía de los
Calices (Chalice Sacristy) include
work by Martínez Montañes,
Valdés Leal, Zurbarán and Goya.
Murillo painted the *Immaculate
Conception* in the dome of the
Sala Capitular (Chapterhouse), and
there is also a series of eight other
works by him. Columbus's body
spent a brief time in the cathedral
after it was finally brought from
Cuba and there is a monument to
him. The Patio de los Naranjos
(Court of the Orange-Trees) was
once the ablution courtyard of
the mosque.

BARRIO DE SANTA CRUZ

The buzz of the city does not
penetrate the enclosed quarter
of the old *judería* where
Fernando *el Santo* allowed
Jews from Toledo and
elsewhere to settle. No matter
how many tourists pass over
the cobbles of its narrow streets
and small squares, the *barrio*'s
charm does not wane.

Whitewashed buildings with
ochre-coloured decoration have
black, wrought-iron grilles and
balconies usually bright with
flowers. Behind heavy
doorways or solid grilles hide
private patios where more
flowers bloom and fountains
play. At times the air is heavy
with the scent of orange
blossom and jasmine. Progress
through the *barrio* is likely to
be delayed by sorties into art
and crafts shops or by lingering
awhile at an outdoor café.
During warm evenings, there is
an animated streetlife and the
many bars and eating places
become very lively.

In Calle Susona a ceramic tile
painted with a skull recalls one
of the *barrio*'s legends. In the
15th century, Jews led by one
named Susón conspired to kill
the most prominent Christians
and seize control of the city.
One of those on their list was
the secret lover of his daughter,
Susona, who, once aware of the
scheme, exposed it to her
caballero. Her father was
condemned to death and in
time she was deserted by her
lover. She died after a miserable
life and left a will stating that,
for her shame, her skull should
be displayed above her
doorway. Plaza Doña Elvira is
named after a luckier lady. She
inherited the buildings around
it from a father who had
benefited from Henry III's
confiscation of Jewish property
under the influence of the
Inquisition.

**Inside Sevilla's mighty 15th-
century cathedral**

CHURCHES

The following are the principal churches, which are generally open to the public. Sevilla has many more of note which are only accessible during times of services.

Jesús del Gran Poder

Plaza San Lorenzo

In the modern, baroque-style church of Jesús del Poder (Jesus the Powerful) is an image of Christ, done by Juan de Mesa in 1620, whose heel is kissed to speed the answering of prayers. This image is one the city's most revered and its *paso* (float) for carrying it in procession is among the most elaborate.

Magdalena

Plaza Magdalena

Magdalena was built in 1692 and is notable for its polychromed cupolas and belfries. The interior is very heavily decorated, and there are works by Valdés Leal, Lucas Valdés, Pedro Roldán, Juan Bautista Vázquez, Francisco Pacheco and Zurbarán.

San Lorenzo

Plaza San Lorenzo

The Mudéjar church of San Lorenzo (St Lawrence) has been much remodelled but retains worthy pieces of religious art from the 13th to 18th centuries, including a main altarpiece by Martínez Montañes and another, in the Capilla de la Concepción (Chapel of the Conception), by Francisco Pacheco.

San Salvador

Plaza Salvador

Popularly regarded as the city's second cathedral, San Salvador (St Saviour) was begun in 1674 on the site of a mosque whose patio still exists. It is most regarded for its baroque altar screen and for having the much venerated image of *Jesús de la Pasión* (Jesus of the Passion), carved by Martínez Montañes. It also has Juan de Mesa's carving of *Cristo del Amor* (Christ of Love).

Santa Ana

Calle Pelay

First built in the 13th century and much remodelled since, this church is, unusually in Sevilla, of brick construction and in a style transitional between Mudéjar and Gothic. It boasts a fine altarpiece and, like cathedrals, a central choir.

CONVENTS

After Fernando *el Santo* took Sevilla from the Almohades in 1248, there was a spate of building as religious orders established themselves in the city. Another followed when Sevilla became rich from holding the monopoly of trade with the New World. The city abounds with convents. Among the most interesting are the following:

San Leandro

Plaza San Leandro

Nuns do a good trade in the famous *yemas de San Leandro*, sweets made from egg yolks. And their church has an impressive altarpiece by Martínez Montañés.

Santa Clara

Calle de Santa Clara

The 13th-century Torre de Don Fabriqué, which shows the transition from Romanesque to Gothic in a defensive construction, rises above the convent, in which Gothic and Mudéjar elements are blended. The small collection of the Museo Arqueológico Municipal (Archaeological Museum) is on display in the tower.

Santa Inés

Calle de Doña María Coronel

María Coronel used hot oil to disfigure her face so as to shake off the besotted Pedro (Peter) the Cruel, and she then took refuge in this Gothic-Mudéjar convent, where her body lies. Nuns sell images of her as well as sweets.

Santa Paula

Calle de Santa Paula II

Here the nun's sell sweets made from Sevilla's bitter oranges, as well as jams and marmalades. Gothic, Mudéjar and Renaissance styles co-exist harmoniously.

The Archbishop's Palace, home of the Cardinal of Sevilla

TOWN WALK

Start in the Plaza del Triunfo.

1 This is the heart of the city's sightseeing attractions. In the centre of the plaza is *La Inmaculada*, a monument to the Immaculate Conception, so much venerated in the city. The Triunfo memorial recalls the big earthquake of 1755.

Leave on the right side of the cathedral into another attractive area, the Plaza de Virgen de los Reyes.

2 Café tables spill into the street and horse-drawn carriages continuously pass by the elaborate central lamp-post. On the left, behind orange trees, is the Convento de la Encarnación (Convent of the Incarnation), whose oldest parts date from the 14th century. Opposite is the coloured front of the Palacio Arzobispal (Archbishop's Palace), dating from the 18th century, which is occupied by the Cardinal of Sevilla. Abutting the cathedral, la Giralda rises proudly.

The finely detailed Plateresque façade of Sevilla's town hall

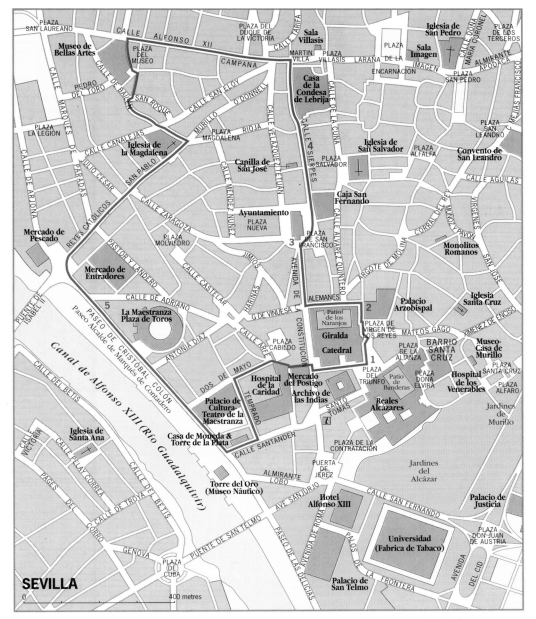

Walk along the side of the Giralda in Calle Alemanes, passing the steps of las Gadas, known since the time when Cervantes was in the city as a rascals' meeting place. Turn right up Avenida de la Constitución to Plaza de San Francisco.

3 Very impressive is the intricate Plateresque façade of the Ayuntamiento (town hall), which, after its restoration, is no longer used as a working city hall. A few interesting shops line the opposite side of the plaza.

Continue ahead to Calle Sierpes.

4 This and the network of pedestrianised streets, including Calle de la Cuna, form the heart of the city's prime shopping area.

At the end of Calle Sierpes, go left into Calle Campana. Bearing

right, you pass Plaza del Duque de la Victoria and the El Cortes Inglés department store to enter Calle Alfonso XII. Soon you reach the tree-filled Plaza del Museo in front of the Museo de Bellas Artes. Exit on the far left side of the plaza into Calle San Roque, cross right into Calle Bailén and right again into Calle San Pablo, with the Iglesia de la Magdalena on your right. Galerías Preciadas department store is opposite. Go over at the crossing and right into Calle de los Reyes Católicos. Ahead lies the Río Guadalquivir.

5 Paseo de Cristóbal Colón is a busy road, and Paseo Alcalde de Marqués del Contadero is a pleasant riverside promenade with views to the Puente de Isabel II, and to colourful old buildings along Triana's Calle del Betis on the west bank. Looking away from the river and moving south, there

is Plaza de Toros de la Maestranza , and next to it the new Teatro de la Maestranza, a fine cultural venue built behind the façade of old military barracks. Almost opposite is the Torre del Oro.

Cross the Paseo Colón and go into Calle Santander to reach the Torre de la Plata and adjoining Casa de Moneda; then turn left into Calle Temprado to the Hospital de la Caridad. Continue into Calle Dos de Mayo and look for old advertisements in ceramic tiles. Narrow streets on the left lead into the interesting quarter of El Arenal. Right along Calle Dos de Mayo and ahead is the Mercado del Postigo crafts market, and, near it through an archway on the left, is the enclosed Plaza Cabildo. Across Avenida de la Constitución is the front of the cathedral and the Plaza del Triunfo.

GIRALDA

Plaza del Triunfo

In 1184, the ruling emir of the Almohades, Abu Yacub Yusuf, ordered that the mosque then being built should be graced by a minaret of unsurpassed beauty. From a square base on foundations that include Roman tablets, four brick walls with typical *sebka* decoration were raised and in 1198 four superimposed bronze spheres were placed as the minaret's crowning ornament. They were destroyed by an earthquake in the 14th century. In 1558 work started on adding the present belfry and upper tower in the prevailing Renaissance style. Some 100m above ground, it was topped by a bronze *giraldilla* (weathervane) in the form of a figure of Faith. A ramp inside the tower, which horsemen could use, leads to the top.

HOSPITAL DE LA CARIDAD

Calle Temprado

Miguel de Mañara, who had been a high-living man about town, turned to a life of religious observance and good works after the unexpected death of his wife. He became the leader of the Very Humble Brotherhood and the Hospital of Charity was where they cared for their poverty-stricken charges. Its chapel, built between 1645 and 1721, has notable works by Valdés Leal: frescos in the presbytery's cupola and his two famous death paintings, which dramatically show life's transitory nature. Also notable are works in different styles by Murillo, and Pedro Roldán painted the *Holy Burial*, which is the main feature of the altarpiece. Mañara is buried in the crypt.

HOSPITAL DE LOS VENERABLES

Plaza Venerables

Another example of Sevilla's fine baroque buildings, this home for retired priests was completed in

1687. Valdés Leal did the ceiling frescos; his son Lucas Valdés did those on the walls. There are also works by Herrera the Elder, Pedro Roldán, Alonso Cano and Martínez Montañes.

LA CARTUJA

In 1400 the Bishop of Sevilla founded the Carthusian monastery of Santa María de las Cuevas (St Mary of the Caves) on the 'island', which is actually a peninsula of the Río Guadalquivir. It grew in a mix of Gothic, Mudéjar, Renaissance and baroque styles, and floods repeatedly damaged the buildings. After Spain's short-lived Liberal government expropriated church property, an Englishman, Charles Pickman, leased the buildings and in 1841 he began production in his ceramics factory. Centuries earlier, Almohades had dug *cuevas* (caves) to extract clay

The Giralda is named after its weathervane or *giraldilla*

from which to make their ceramics.

The Pickman factory ceased production on the site in 1982, when it became the property of the government of Andalucía. Part of the complex was restored to serve as the Royal Pavilion during EXPO '92. The headquarters of the Andalucían Institute for the Conservation of the Cultural Heritage is based here and has a museum. The public will be able to see and experience restoration work in progress.

La Cartuja Island, across which the extravaganza of EXPO '92 was spread, has given Sevilla a whole new zone of tourist interest with

Sevilla's archaeological museum houses treasures found near by

its museums, exhibition centres, the Omnimax Theatre and Planetarium, gardens, sports and leisure facilities and cultural venues like the Auditorio and Teatro Central. For the latest details, consult tourist offices.

MUSEUMS

The following are among the principal museums. Information about others can be obtained at tourist offices or from media listings. These are also a source for finding out what exhibitions or other special events are being staged at the many other cultural venues, including commercial art galleries.

Arqueológico
Plaza de América
Most of the pieces on display in the Archaeological Museum were found in the vicinity. The strongest part of the collection is of Roman material, much of it from nearby Itálica. For many, the museum's greatest prize is the Carambolo Treasure discovered in a hillside very close to the city in 1958. It comprises 21 pieces of finely worked, 24-carat gold jewellery, which was probably buried with a king or priest of Tartessos.

Arte Contemporaneo
Calle Santo Tomás
The Museum of Contemporary Art's collection is housed in the Cilla del Cabildo Catedral (Cathedral Tax House), which was

built in 1770 and in some ways resembles the nearby Lonja. Works of young and rising Andalucían artists are often on display and prominent local artists who are represented include Gordillo, Saénz, Pérez Aguilera, Francisco Molina and Blanca Mencos. It also has works by internationally known names like Chillida, Manrique, Miró, Tàpies and Saura.

Artés y Costumbres Populares
Plaza de América
Traditional work methods and crafts are celebrated in re-creations of rooms and workshops and exhibits of the tools used in the Costume and Folk Museum. There are displays of crafts for which the city and area are best known: lace, weaving, silver and gold work and pottery. Dress and accessories for court life, everyday and religious festivals are also displayed, as are furniture, domestic ornaments and musical instruments.

Bellas Artes
Plaza del Museo
After the Prado in Madrid, this is Spain's most important collection of fine art. The museum was opened in 1835 in the large, baroque Convento de la Merced and much of the collection came from other convents. Besides paintings there are fine exhibits of sculptures, gold work, embroidery, furniture and pottery. The three best-represented masters are: Francisco Zurbarán (1598–1664), the painter from

The Museo de Artés y Costumbres Populares gives an insight into local life

Extremadura who lived in Sevilla from 1629 to 1658 and whose *Apotheosis of Saint Thomas of Aquinas* is regarded as his finest canvas in the museum; Bartolomé Murillo (1617–92) whose *Virgen de Servilleta*, *San Tomás de Villanueva* and *Santas Justa and Rufina* are some of the museum's proudest possessions; and Valdés Leal (1622–90), a founder member of the Sevilla Arts Academy in 1660, whose grand canvases filled with vitality contrast with the macabre pessimism of some of his other works. Also represented are Pacheco, Varela, Roelas, Alonso Cano, Velázquez, Juan de Roelas, Juan de Castillo, José de Ribera, Alonso Vázquez, Herrera the Elder and others of the Sevillan School. The most prominent sculptors represented are Pedro de Mena and Martínez Montañes.

Casa de Murillo
Calle Santa Teresa
Bartolomé Esteban Murillo was born in Sevilla in 1617, spent most of his life in the city and died in 1682 in the Convento de Santa Teresa (Convent of St Theresa). Near by, the house where he is believed to have lived was restored and opened in 1982 as the Murillo Museum, and has displays of items from the artist's time as well as paintings by him and his pupils.

PALACES

Among grand homes retained by aristocratic families are three that can be visited.

Casa de la Condesa de Lebrija
Calle Cuna 18
There is restricted public access to the Countess of Lebrija's town house, which behind its somewhat forbidding façade is a typical Sevillan mansion. It is centred on a patio, adorned with Mudéjar work. What makes it exceptional is that there is a treasure of Roman mosaics and other pieces gleaned from sites around the city before they were protected for posterity. The most impressive mosaic, which covers the patio, was found in Itálica in 1914.

Casa de Pilatos
Plaza de Pilatos
Don Fabrique Enríquez de Ribera returned from the Holy Land in 1521 and, so one story goes, modelled the completion of his town mansion on what he had deduced from the ruins of Pilate's house in Jerusalem. Now owned by the Duke of Medinaceli, this is regarded as the grandest private residence in Sevilla. Mudéjar and Renaissance styles are pleasingly blended. A collection of classical statuary is on display in the patio and surrounding rooms. Fine frescos have been uncovered in the Salón de los Frescos and the chapel has more fine plasterwork. Francisco Pacheco, father-in-law of Velázquez, did the ceiling paintings in the room that bears his name.

Palacio de las Dueñas
Calle Dueñas
The Duke and Duchess of Alba permit limited public access to their Sevillan home (the Dueñas Palace), which features an arched and galleried patio-garden decorated with delicate Mudéjar plasterwork and filled with palms and fruit trees. Rooms are filled with the furniture, art and objects acquired by successive generations of one of Spain's most prominent aristocratic families.

PARQUE DE MARIA LUISA

In 1893, María Luisa Fernanda, sister of Queen Isabel II and a duchess of the Montpensier family, donated the park to the city. It has areas of formal gardens, trellises and ponds, others of bowers and grottos, and areas where a profusion of exotic trees flourish amid untamed under-growth. Pavilions and other buildings were constructed on the park's periphery and around the Plaza de América for the 1929 Ibero-América Exhibition.

PLAZA DE ESPAÑA

The principal construction of the Ibero-América Exhibition is an arcaded, brick-faced building, now housing government offices, in a semi-circle around a big square. A series of ceramic-tile pictures depict some identifying features of each of Spain's 50 provinces.

REALES ALCAZARES

Soon after their arrival in Sevilla in 712, Arab military chiefs built an *alcázar* on this site. In the 9th century the fortress was transformed into a palace for Abderraman II. When Sevilla was their capital, the Almohades added new areas like the Patio del Yeso (Plasterwork) and Patio del Crucero (Transept). Castilian kings brought their northern architectural style. Alfonso X added three large Gothic halls; Alfonso XI's contribution was the Sala de Justicia with its fine plasterwork and Mudéjar panelling, which is the oldest to be seen in the city.

It is, however, the core of this palace complex, ordered by Peter I, King of Castile from 1350 to 1369, that is the richest gem of Mudéjar secular architecture. Fragments from earlier Moorish buildings, particularly from Medina Azahara in Córdoba, were incorporated in the renovation and new construction.

The inspiration of Medina Azahara is very evident in the exceptionally handsome Salón de Embajadores (Ambassadors), where public and private sections of the palace join. The former is centred on the galleried Patio de las Doncellas (Maidens) with its very fine frieze and foliated arches. Domestic quarters surround the more hidden Patio de las Muñecas (Dolls), where delicate columns and capitals support the galleries.

Successive monarchs made additions to the palace of Pedro, *el Cruel*, most notably a Gothic church built by Fernando and Isabel and a set of apartments by Charles V, who was also responsible for extending the Jardines del Alcázar. It was here that the feared Pedro had done some of his misdeeds, and his mistress Doña María de Padilla took her bath to titillate watching courtiers. Today these rambling gardens offer a welcome escape from the city's summer heat and noise.

TORRE DEL ORO

Paseo de Cristóbal Colón
The Almohades completed the Gold Tower, and a long-gone one on the opposite bank, in 1220. A chain stretching across the river between the two was part of the defensive system, and so was the recently restored Torre de la Plata. Golden-coloured tiles on the original roof gave the tower its name. In 1760 the rounded top section was added to the tower, which now houses a small maritime museum (Museo Náutico).

Taking a peaceful ride among the trees of the splendid Parque de María Luisa

UNIVERSIDAD

Calle San Fernando
The science and law faculties of
Sevilla University now occupy the
second-largest building in Spain,
which was built as a tobacco
factory and completed in 1771. It
was here that the mythical Carmen
worked with more than 5,000
other women, rolling cigarettes.
Nearby Alcalá de Guadaira, some
10km to the southeast of Sevilla, is
now virtually a suburb of the city.
It has spread out below the
impressive castle, which was built
by the Almohades as an outer
defence when Sevilla was their
capital city in the late 12th
century, and which is the best
remaining example in Spain of
their military architecture.

**The Bécquer monument in the
Parque de María Luisa**

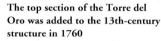

**The top section of the Torre del
Oro was added to the 13th-century
structure in 1760**

Because its bakeries have
traditionally supplied Sevillans
with their bread, the town is
nicknamed 'Alcála de los
Panaderos' (Bakers).

ITALICA

After defeating Hasdrubal's
Carthaginian forces at nearby
Carmona in 206BC, the Roman
Scipio Africanus founded a
settlement for his legionaries on
this site some 9km northwest of
Sevilla. It was among the
earliest Roman towns in the
peninsula and it rapidly grew in
size and importance.
Excavations revealed a large,
elliptical amphitheatre, forum
and extensive villas with good
mosaics. The amphitheatre
could seat 40,000 people and
the substantial remains include
those of the animal pits and
underground passageways.
   There is a small museum on
the site, but much of the
material found here is in
Sevilla's Museo Arqueológico,
and a good deal disappeared
into private hands. The site
received much attention as part
of the regional brush-up for
1992. Each summer the I*tálica
Festival Internacional de
Danza* (Itálica International
Dance Festival) is held here
under the auspices of the
Diputación de Sevilla and the
Luis Cernuda Fundación.

SOTOGRANDE

MAP REF: 108 B1

Bordering Málaga province's Costa del Sol and in most people's minds forming part of it, Sotogrande is an extensive area of luxury residential development, which includes a number of golf courses. Polo is one of the other sports for which there are good amenities. An attractive marina development in modern Mediterranean style is the latest focus of attention.

TARIFA

MAP REF: 108 B1

Continental Europe's most southerly town is also, almost certainly, its windiest. Winter blasts from the southwest or northeast reach 120km/h and the average annual wind speed is 35km/h. That is why Spain's experimental windpower station has been located near Tarifa. And it is why Tarifa has become a mecca for boardsailing enthusiasts. Mostly young, athletic and carefree, they come from all over the world and their presence has transformed Tarifa from a dull outpost town into a bright and lively place, which makes headlines when some international windsurfing competition is in progress or when another record is shattered. North of the town stretch long, wide beaches backed by pinewoods. Here there are campsites, hostels, hotels and eating places as well as windsurfing schools and shops for all the latest gear, some of which is of local origin and has been marketed successfully around the world.

The military still occupies the small island where a scouting

Arcos de la Frontera, most westerly of the *pueblos blancos*

party from North Africa landed in 710 before the Moors invaded near Gibraltar the following year. Restored town walls and the solid, 10th-century castle testify to Tarifa's strategic importance ever since. The castle retains the tower from which in 1294 Guzman *El Bueno* (The Good) threw down his dagger and shouted to a besieging army of Moors who held his son as hostage, 'let my son be killed with an honourable weapon'. Guzman had been charged with defending Tarifa, which had been captured from the Moors two years previously, and he sacrificed his son rather than surrender. He was relieved by reinforcements and rewarded with a title and large tracts of land. Within the castle precinct, the Iglesia de Santa María (Church of St Mary) was built upon a mosque and incorporates columns of a Roman building.

Nearby Some 22km to the north-west are the ruins of *Bolonia,* where streets, temples, a theatre, public bath, market and fish factory of the Roman town of *Baelo Claudia,* dating from the 1st century AD, have been excavated and can be visited. For archaeologists its necropolis is the second most important such site, after that of Carmona, yet discovered in Spain.

Moorish-looking battlements in Tarifa, just across from Africa

GIBRALTAR

The Rock, which covers most of the British colony's 750 hectares of territory, is not as solid as reputed. Its Jurassic limestone is pitted with caverns and some 50km of man-made tunnels. The population is a mix of English, Spanish, Maltese, Italian, Indian and Arabic origins among whom the majority refuse the integration that Spain seeks. Britain claims it is up to the Gibraltarians to decide their future, and thereby retains territory ceded to it in 1713 under the Treaty of Utrecht, which was ratified by another agreement in 1783. Franco closed the border in 1969, which caused economic hardship on both sides. It was opened again in 1985 and talks between Spain and Britain continue. The airport is an especially thorny issue. Gibraltar seeks to be an important financial centre and to attract tourism. Some financial scandals and few attractions – the beaches are not recommended – make both quests more difficult. There is a cramped and untidy mix of Arab, Regency and uninspired modern architecture.

Gibraltarians are more concerned with trade and finance and waving the Union Jack than with cultural pursuits; the colony is probably mainly of interest to British residents and tourists in Andalucía who are nostalgic for home-from-home ways and products.

Windsurfing off Tarifa

FERRIES TO NORTH AFRICA

Spain, too, has pockets of territory attached to another country: the port cities of Melilla and Ceuta are Spanish enclaves on the Moroccan coast and are campaigning to be recognised as another of Spain's autonomous regions. Melilla was taken for Spain by the Duke of Medina Sidonia in 1496; Ceuta was taken from the Arabs by Portugal in 1415 and, after the final separation of Spain and Portugal in 1640, passed to Spain. Melilla, which has some 60,000 inhabitants, retains its monumental aspect and is connected by ferries with Almería. Slightly larger and more developed for tourism, Ceuta is connected by ferry services, including fast hydro-foils, to Algeciras and Tarifa. Ferries also operate from these ports, as well as from Gibraltar, to the exotic Moroccan city of Tangiers. Tour operators offer one-day or longer excursions. For many visitors to Andalucía, a brief sojourn on African soil adds another dimension to their holiday.

PUEBLOS BLANCOS

As if a giant's hand had sprinkled salt over the hills and valleys, Cádiz province sparkles with white towns and villages. Some, which were for a time on the frontier between Christian Castile and the Moors' *Al-Andalus*, had 'de la Frontera' added to their names. Together they are an important tourist attraction in the province, and an effort has therefore been made in preserving much of their traditional appeal and keeping them white and clean. Arcos de la Frontera (see page 15) is the most prestigious of *los pueblos blancos* and receives many tourists. Running south from Arcos along the *Ruta del Toro*, the C343 leads through undulating pastures and fields of cereals, sunflowers and beet to Medina Sidonia astride its hill. To the east, Alcalá de los Gazules and Benalup de Sidonia are two villages that seldom see tourists. Further along the C343 atop a limestone promontory is Vejer de la Frontera, where strict urban regulations have not allowed modernity to intrude upon streets and buildings that strongly evoke their Moorish origins and make this a delightful *pueblo blanco* in which to spend some time, perhaps at the charming Hospedería del Convento de San Francisco.

From Arcos the C344 runs east to Grazalema via El Bosque, and to the south lies Ubrique – picturesque and interesting places in stunning scenery (see page 21). South of Ubrique and back in bull-rearing country, the white cubes of Jimena de la Frontera are profiled against a hill topped by castle ruins. British escapees from the coast have formed a community here and run a few of the local businesses.

Along a tortuous track off the road to the coast is what remains of Castellar de la Frontera. Alternative lifestylers from all over Europe moved into this village when its occupants abandoned their isolation and hard life in favour of settling in Nuevo Castellar. A ruined castle broods over the untidy utopia, which does not fit into the *pueblo blanco* image.

Marina at luxurious Sotogrande

•*MALAGA*•

Andalucía's richest province, providing some 30 per cent of the region's income, has just over 8 per cent of its territory and 17 per cent of its population. Some 55 per cent of the province's people live in the capital port-city, which is second in size to Sevilla. Five *comarcas* (administrative districts) constitute the rest of the province: Antequera, Coín, Marbella, Ronda and Vélez-Málaga.

Much of Málaga province's territory is hilly and mountainous. Many of the lower slopes are terraced and yield olives and almonds, while some of the higher slopes are forested. The valleys are intensively farmed, as are parts of the coastal plain, which lies in varying widths behind the 160km length of the Costa del Sol. Beyond the mountains in the *comarca* of Antequera is rich arable land for larger-scale agriculture. Although hindering the wider practice of such agriculture, the mountain chain is the province's great fortune, for it provides the coastal zone with the favourable micro-climatic conditions that have fostered the development of the mainstay of the province's economy – mass tourism and foreign residential development along the Costa del Sol. The 'Coast of the Sun' has two distinct parts. East of the capital city and running to the border with Granada province, the coast-line along the region of La Axarquía still has farmlands abutting the sea in places, as well as some traditional fishing hamlets, and its resorts are relatively low key and slow paced. West of the city an almost continuous 'lateral city' including resorts like Torremolinos and

Marbella stretches to the border with Cádiz province. Here is all the variety and contrasting razzmatazz that the world knows as the Costa del Sol.

Europe's package-holiday industry fired a demand for rampant development to provide pleasure and release in the sun from life's dull routine for many millions of Europeans. Large numbers of people from other countries also acquired second homes in which to spend holidays. Very significant, too, was the emigration to Málaga province of retired people on fixed incomes,

for whom the local cost structure at the time was as much an attraction as the climate. Britain provided most of the tourists and settlers in the sun. A building boom erupted and continued though most of the 1970s and 1980s. Málaga province absorbed a very large proportion of foreign investment in real estate in Spain: in 1989, Marbella alone accounted for 18 per cent of the national total. More than 100,000 foreigners, mainly British, German, Dutch and Scandinavian, are officially resident in Málaga province (the real figure is much higher) and 90 per cent of coastal real-estate developments are bought by foreigners, more than half by Britons.

While construction firms and property developers had a bonanza, there was ugly over-development in some parts, which a central government hungry for foreign exchange was unwilling to control. Local authorities had neither the plans nor the money to provide an adequate infra-structure. Nor did they have enough officials with foresight and environmental awareness. Many small property owners were eager to sell their land at previously unimaginable prices, and people entered the tourism service industry without any training. It was not a recipe for long-term success.

The bubble burst at the end of the 1980s and affected mainly the budget end of the market in all of Spain's resort areas; the pin that pricked it was said to be the faltering British economy, and the consequent dearth of tourists and fresh investment from that country. It was a simplistic and incomplete reasoning since numerous other factors were involved. Not least was a growing

Substantial farm on the fertile plain of Antequera

The bridge spanning Ronda's precipitous gorge

negative reaction to slovenly development, environmental and noise pollution, poor infrastructural provisions, crime levels, indifferent service and prices catching up with the rest of Europe. Not much can be done about the latter factor, but public authorities in Andalucía and Málaga province have responded well in confronting the others. A new breed of officials is about: better-trained people with deeper insight and greater foresight.

Much has been done to improve the infrastructure along the coast by widening and rebuilding the previously dangerous N340 coastal highway, building town by-passes, sewage and waste water treatment plants, and regenerating beaches. In regard to stopping pollution of the Mediterranean, Málaga province claims to be doing more than anywhere else along this threatened sea's coastline. Now the concentration is less on the British market and on breaking records year after year on the number of visitors. 'Quality tourism', which means higher-spending people, is the new key phrase, and part of the fresh drive is to promote the *Costa del Golf* as well as the many other excellent sports facilities. Twenty-seven golf courses are available and by 1995 there may be 40. Twelve marinas in Málaga province serve sailing and boating enthusiasts. Tourist promotion is also more closely identifying the Costa del Sol with the rest of Andalucía, as a well-serviced residential belt with easy access to the region's fascinating interior and its monumental cities and towns.

Property developers, too, have moved their attention inland. It can only be hoped that they will be held on a tight leash so that their fine-sounding 'rural tourism' does not repeat the ravaging

experience along parts of the coastline.

Málaga's airport has been greatly improved, mainly with the building of a new, international terminal to service 11 million passengers a year, the projected number for the year 2000. The city's railway station has also been renovated. A four-lane toll expressway stretching 52km from Málaga to Estepona is planned. East of the city, an expressway from Rincón de la Victoria to Nerja is on the drawing-board. Throughout Andalucía, other new roads are being built and existing ones are being upgraded. Health services in the province have been improved

with the opening of new hospitals in the capital and in Marbella, and the provision of more first-aid centres along the coast. Málaga's Technology Park is the flagship emblem of the policy to make the province somewhat less dependent on tourism and foreign residential development. Increasingly, agriculture is yielding better returns from the growing of new crop types.

In spite of the phenomenal development that this once-marginalised province has seen over three decades, there are still parts relatively untouched by progress. The province has its share of picturesque villages like Casares, one of the most-photographed places in all of Spain, and the timeless hamlets of La Axarquía. El Torcal's lunar landscape contrasts sharply with the thickly wooded Sierra de Grazalema running into Cádiz province. Two monumental towns, Antequera and Ronda, retain an unhurried small-town pace, although the latter receives hordes of day-trippers. Behind lie the wooded folds of the Montes de Málaga, west of which is the province's Lake District. Málaga province is much more than only its capital city and the Costa del Sol.

• ALORA •

Citrus groves and fields of mixed cultivation fill the fertile Río Guadalhorce Valley, in which Alora is the main town. Before the Moors and Christians settled here, Phoenicians, Romans and Vandals had known the area. New, tall buildings have reduced the town's Moorish aspect, although this is still evident in the cluster of white cubes and narrow lanes below what remains of the Moors' *alcazaba* (castle) on the south side of town.

Within Alora's fortified walls, a cemetery's whitewashed rows of tiered niches look like squared honeycombs, and are tended by old women dressed in black. There are wide views southwards along the valley and northwards to a curve of mountains. Locals are proud that their town's church, which took almost the whole of the 17th century to finish, is the largest in Málaga province after the city's cathedral.

Las malaqueñas, the province's version of flamenco, originated in Alora (map ref: 108 C1), which hosts a flamenco festival in June. It is mostly because it is a gateway to nearby places of interest that Alora has travellers passing through or stopping a while.

Nearby The Puente de Molina (bridge) across the river at the foot of the village of Ardales was first built in Roman times. Ruins of the Moors' fortress remain atop a hill. Below it is a 15th-century Mudéjar church whose tower rises high above the whitewashed houses stepping down the slope.

The Parque de Ardales was created as a recreational area, and has become very popular with *Malagueños* seeking leisure and sport away from the crowded coastal areas. The Río Guadalhorce and other rivers feed three large reservoirs, which spread out among pine-covered hills. At the entrance to the park there is an information centre and along the lakeshore are picnic and camping sites, places for boating and fishing (black bass, carp and pike), and restaurants that get very busy over weekends during the warm months. Other parts of the park are also popular with hikers and climbers. One area, near the dam wall and hydraulic works, has the refined look of shores along lakes in Switzerland.

Bobastro
Omar Al-Hafsun, a Christian convert and rebel against the rule of Córdoba in the 9th century, was successful in bringing large areas under his control. On the high, flat and impregnable mountaintop he built his capital, of which only scrappy walls remain. There are also caves, which were inhabited in those times. A short walk leads to a unique example of a Mozarab church carved out of the rock.

Garganta de El Chorro
The Garganta (throat) is a deep cleft of some 180m in a mountain mass through which the Río Guadalhorce passes. A rickety footbridge hangs high above the impressive gorge. It is part of the Camino del Rey (King's Path), a catwalk clinging precariously to the cliffside, which was used by King Alfonso XIII when he opened the Guadalhorce irrigation works in 1921. There is access to the catwalk across the railway bridge, but it is not advisable for the uninitiated to attempt walking along here.

The village of Ardales

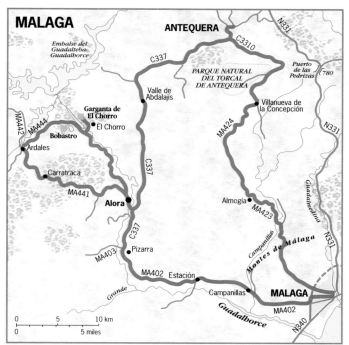

would not allow the match, and pursued by them the couple reached the summit of the peak from where, clinging together in an embrace, they jumped so that they could be united in death and achieve what prejudice had prevented them from being in life.

From Antequera follow signs to El Torcal along the C3310.

Parque Natural del Torcal de Antequera
In this almost lunar landscape, an area of deep ravines where great limestone boulders have formed bizarre shapes, you can experience a serenity and closeness to nature unimaginable along the Costa del Sol (see page 46).

The narrow MA242/3 twists down to Málaga past the villages of Villanueva de la Concepción and Almogía, and through the green hills of the Montes de Málaga.

MOTOR TOUR

This full-day tour from Málaga takes in a wide variety of scenery, some of it unexpectedly spectacular, and allows some time for sightseeing in Antequera. To make it more leisurely, think of staying overnight in Antequera's Parador de Turismo.

From the western edge of Málaga follow signs to Campanillas. After passing through industrial zones, the MA402 follows the course of the Río Guadalhorce to Alora (see opposite). From here, follow the twisting MA441 road signposted Ardales, to Carratraca.

Carratraca
A new highway now passes below the town, easing access to it, but the old road is more scenic. The mineral spa is likely to become more popular.

A short distance further on is Ardales.

Ardales and Parque de Ardales
The village of Ardales, with its population of 3,000 presents a picturesque sight as it rises up a hill topped by castle ruins.

Within the Parque de Ardales, the most spectacular views of lakes and mountains can be enjoyed by taking a track to the right just before the El Mirador restaurant.

Bear left on leaving the park, watching for the sign to the Ruinas de Bobastro on the right and go uphill for 6km.

Bobastro and Las Mesas de Villaverde
Turbines from the El Chorro dam hydroelectric works pump water up to the reservoir on the summit during times of off-peak demand for electricity in Málaga. At times of high demand, water rushes down to generate an increased supply.

Return down the hill and bear right along a narrow road through rugged country to Garganta de El Chorro (see opposite). Cross the dam wall and from behind the railway station take an unmetalled road for a slow drive through countryside that tourists seldom see.

Valle de Abdalajís
A bleak rock-face, in which there is a shrine to the Virgin, rises above the slumbering village. The area has become a popular venue for hang-gliding enthusiasts.

Follow signs to Antequera along the C337, through more enchanting scenery.

Antequera
Many travellers miss out on visiting this monumental town (see pages 46-7). Dominating the landscape east of the town is La Peña de los Enamorados (The Lovers' Peak), about which a sad story of love is told. From a distance, some people see its outline as resembling a couple embracing. Taysona was the daughter of the mayor of Archidona and a Moslem; her lover was a Christian. Their families

·ANTEQUERA·

Some 45km from Málaga along an impressive new highway, Antequera lies on the northern slopes of the coastal mountain range and overlooks a very fertile valley where cereals are the main crops. Antequera, busy as a market and commercial centre, does not cater very much for pleasure travellers except for having a modern and well-priced Parador de Turismo where the local cuisine can also be enjoyed.

Antequera's strategic importance has been recognised since people first settled in Iberia, and the town has unusual and important prehistoric monuments. After the Christians captured it in 1410, Antequera (map ref: 108 C1) was a crucial base for the assault on the Moorish kingdom of Granada. From this time, the town began to be endowed with a rich patrimony of religious, civil and private buildings, which makes it such a worthwhile stop.

El Conjunto Dolmenico, on the town's eastern edge, has two constructions dating from around 2000BC. These dolmens are thought to be tombs of leaders who were buried with their possessions. The one known as *Menga* is the biggest and best maintained of its type yet discovered anywhere. Built of 31 stone slabs, some weighing 180 tons, it is 25m deep and 3.75m high. A similar but smaller construction is called *Viera*.

La Alcazaba (the castle), on the hill above the town, was built by the Moors in the 14th century on the ruins of a Roman castle. Gardens are surrounded by the remaining walls, of which the most prominent feature is the Torre del Papabellotas belfry. The 'Tower of Father Acorns' is so

called because the sale of a cork-oak plot funded its building in 1582.

Real Colegiata de Santa María la Mayor (Royal Collegiate Church of St Mary), below the Alcazaba, is a large church completed in 1550. It is a National Monument and has recently been restored. Its Plateresque façade bears some resemblance to a Roman triumphal arch. Arranged in the form of a basilica with three naves, the interior is huge and bare below finely worked Mudéjar ceilings. Across the square, a view of the town below is framed by the Arco de los Gigantes (1585).

El Museo Municipal (Municipal Museum) is housed in the Palacio de Nájera, a rich family's home of the 18th century. The small but excellent museum has one of the most beautiful bronze statues of

Roman Spain, that was ploughed up in a local field in the 1950s. *El Efebo* is the life-size figure of a garlanded boy, made in the 1st century and probably copied from a Greek work done 500 years earlier. Among other interesting exhibits is a fine woodcarving of St Francis of Assisi by Pedro de Mena (1628–88), Granada's master sculptor.

Nearby The Parque Natural del Torcal de Antequera, 13km south of the town, comprises 1,200 hectares of limestone highland, which wind and water have shaped into fascinating formations of passages, bridges, hollows and weird forms, among which people identify all sorts of things. Hiding among them are rabbits, weasels and foxes; birds of prey fly above; wild irises and many herbs grow among labiates, phlomis, ivies and scattered holm oaks. There are marked paths for walkers: yellow for easy walks of one to two hours; red for more difficult walks of around three hours. A reception centre is open during peak holiday periods.

Laguna de Fuente de Piedra, 23km northwest of Antequera, is the largest saltwater lake in Spain and, with the Camargue in France, is Europe's remaining refuge for nesting greater flamingos. Huge flocks arrive in spring, when the water is at their preferred level of around 80cm, and stay until September. Other birdlife includes mallards, coots, black-headed gulls, kestrels, owls, stilts, red-crested pochards and shovelers. The area has been fenced in and access is controlled by the AMA (Andalucían Environmental Agency). Its reception centre is accessible from the village of Fuente de Piedra.

TOWN WALK

This walk round Antequera takes in some prominent churches and noble mansions as well as the Alcazaba and shopping streets.

Reconstructed Moorish archway in Antequera's castle walls

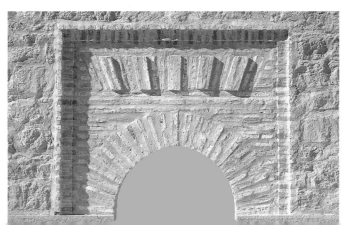

ANTEQUERA

0   300 metres

exemplifies Antequera's particular version of the baroque style. The adjoining Carmelite school is housed in a 16th-century palace showing Renaissance and Mudéjar elements.

Go ahead along Calle Calzada.

8 Another National Monument, the late-Gothic Iglesia de San Zoilo (Church of St Zoilo) was ordered by Ferdinand and Isabel and completed in 1515.

Turn left into Calle Diego Ponce and you pass: the Iglesia de Madre de Dios, an example of the Andalucían rococo style of the 18th century; the municipal market; and some examples of fine 18th-century mansions now in need of repair. Along Calle Canteros you reach Alameda de Andalucía and turn left into Calle Infante Don Fernando, the town's main street, with the Iglesia de los Remedios and the Palacio Consistorial (town hall).

9 This complex dating from the 17th century was the church and convent of the Franciscans, whose themes are depicted in tempera within the church, a National Monument, dedicated to the town's patron saint, Nuestra Señora de los Remedios. The

Start in the Plaza San Sebastián and note its elaborate 16th-century fountain.

1 The 16th-century Iglesia de San Sebastián has an imposing Renaissance façade and a tower that is a mix of Mudéjar and baroque styles.

Go up the Cuesta de la Paz and past the 17th-century Iglesia de Santo Domingo to turn right into Calle Pasillas.

2 A rich local family had the Mannerist-style Palacio de las Escalónas built in the 16th century. Three-level galleries overlook gardens evocative of Moorish times.

Go left into Calle Uveos to reach Plaza El Portichuelo.

3 Two baroque constructions of the 18th century form the plaza. The Iglesia de Santa María, substantially rebuilt after damage inflicted by Napoleon's forces, has the image of Santa María de Socorro, a favourite of *Antequeranos*. The small chapel of Santa María la Vieja looks like many of the roadside shrines found in the New World. From the adjoining Plaza Jesús there is a view up to the Alcazaba.

Go right along Calle Herradores, past whitewashed houses and through the Arco de los Gigantes to a plaza, from which there is a fine view west towards La Peña de los Enamorados.

4 The recent restoration of the Real Colegiata de Santa María la

Mayor (collegiate church) was done within a craft training and employment project.

5 A few parts of the Alcazaba, like the Torre Blanca, remain from the Moors' construction.

Through the Arco de los Gigantes go right down Calle Colegio to Plaza El Carmen. A gate in the old wall, Postigo de la Estrella, is on your left. Along to the right is

the Iglesia del Carmen (Church of the Carmel).

6 The Carmelite convent completed in 1633 has gone. Its remaining Mudéjar church, a National Monument, is being largely reconstructed.

From Plaza del Carmen go down to Plaza las Descalzas.

7 The façade of the Convento de San José (Convent of St Joseph)

Antequera has a history going back to prehistoric times

convent, with a neo-baroque façade, is now the town hall and has a notable cloister.

Go along past a choice of shops and you return to Plaza San Sebastián. Just down Calle Encarnación is the 16th-century Carmelite convent that gives the street its name and opposite is the Palacio de Nájera.

MUSIC AND CELEBRATION

When the Catholic Monarchs, Ferdinand and Isabel, began banning ethnic minorities and the Inquisition continued the persecution of all who did not embrace the Catholic faith, bands of Jews, Moslems and gypsies sought refuge in isolated areas, where they mixed and shared a common cause of survival. Three advanced musical cultures combined and expressed the anguish of persecution.

The sound of Spain: a flamenco guitarist in performance

FLAMENCO

The deepest form of flamenco, *jondo* or *grande*, stays truest to its origins. Its seriousness and melancholy is not unlike that in the original blues of the black people of America's South, which also originated under oppression. Although not wholly so, this most authentic flamenco, which is as much an art of emotional expression as a musical form, is still to a large extent the preserve of the marginalised gypsy community.

Less profoundly moving and easier to perform is *flamenco intermedio*. Another derivative, *flamenco chico*, is lively, amorous or sensuous and often ranges from gaiety to fleeting sadness and back again. Some are accompanied by dance and are named after their places of origin, like the *sevillanas* and *malaqueñas*.

Commercialised flamenco, of the sort which is presented in *tablaos* (performances) for tourists, is most often an amalgam of the three other types and, although it can be good and entertaining, it can sometimes be a crude mockery of a noble folk expression.

Flamenco has four components: *cante*, singing; *baile*, dancing; *toque*, guitar-playing; *jaleo*, accentuation of the rhythm by hand-clapping and foot-tapping.

Each can be performed separately, but the fullest emotional and visual impact is made when all are being performed.

Aficionados will quickly recognise in the flicking of a wrist, the timing of a chord or the emotion of a wordless song if the performer has *duende*, an indescribable attribute, more important than technical ability judged by conventional standards, which every outstanding performer of flamenco must have.

The triangle formed by Sevilla, Cádiz and Jerez de la Frontera is considered the homeland of flamenco. In these cities, and in others, there are annual festivals where the top performers appear.

During the Franco years, when a trend towards popular songs with a touch of flamenco was officially encouraged because it was considered innocuous, flamenco degenerated, but in recent years there has been a revival of general interest and diversification of the form. Throughout Spain, people are perfecting their *sevillanas* in dance academies and disco-thèques. Accomplished performers like Paco de Lucía and El Camarón have combined flamenco with other musical forms, such as Latin American and rock. Flamenco rock is now well established with a number of chart-topping bands.

CELEBRATIONS

Hardly a day passes when there is not some celebration somewhere in Andalucía. Many of the traditions centre on religious festivals. Often, however, the religious content is overwhelmed by a greater enthusiasm for having a good time. All places will have one or more *fiestas* a year in honour of patron saints, whose images are borne aloft in processions. *Verbenas*, usually in the open air and with much music and dance, are the celebrations on the night before a saint's day. *Romerías* are pilgrimages to outlying chapels, churches or hermitages by crowds in local dress and usually with a *cabalgata* (cavalcade) of brightly decorated carts and horses. Many places also have an annual, week-long *feria*, which includes processions, fairgrounds, flamenco performances, other cultural events, various competitions, bullfights, fireworks and more. Some have a strong agricultural content. Harvest festivals are held in a mixed mood of thanksgiving and anticipation. On the sea, fishing boats move in lighted processions to honour their protector, the Virgen del Carmen.

Carnaval in Cádiz during the week before Lent is among the most flamboyant in Europe. Groups and bands called *chirigotas* and *comparsas* wear outlandish costumes and perform specially composed songs, which are laden with irony. Sevilla mounts Spain's most spectacular celebration of *Semana Santa* (Holy Week), and Málaga is a close second, in a display of religious devotion verging on the pagan. From Palm Sunday to Easter Sunday the processions of some 60 *cofradías* (brotherhoods) pass slowly through dark and ominously quiet streets with their elaborately carved and decorated *pasos* (floats), on which revered images of Christ and the Virgin are borne. Muffled drums beat sonorously and zealous bystanders, or professional singers, call out haunting *saetas* in devotion and praise of the images. The smell of incense and candlewax hangs heavily in the air. The deepest passions are reserved for late on Thursday night through to the dawn of Good Friday.

Sevilla's week-long *Feria de Abril* began as a livestock fair last century and is now among the world's most colourful celebrations of spring. It is a high-society parade and a time for showing off by the rich and influential. It is a time for having

the right invitations and connections if you want to be at the heart of the celebration. But, even without these, other *Sevillanos* and visitors still have great fun during the *feria*. Some of the many *casetas* in the huge fairground are open to the public and inside these temporary constructions the wine flows freely, food is abundant, and the music and dancing go on until the early hours. Each day Spain's top *matadors* kill 12 bulls in the Maestranza ring. Another highlight is the *paseo de caballos*, when men and women in their finest *Andaluz* dress parade on horseback or in fine carriages. Later in the month, during the *Feria de Caballo* in Jerez de la Frontera, colourful costumes and beautiful beasts are again on display (see page 25).

El Rocío is Spain's largest *romería* (pilgrimage to a shrine). On the Wednesday before Whitsun, over one million pilgrims, on horseback, in brightly decorated carts and carriages, in cars or on foot, start from Sevilla and other points to make their way to the tiny hamlet of El Rocío in Huelva province. After merrymaking on the way, they arrive on the Saturday and that night the image of the Virgin, *La Blanca Paloma,* is paraded among the massed crowds and competing *cofradías* in a frenzy of excitement verging on hysteria, which can be an awesome experience for outsiders.

More comprehensible in modern times are the well-lubricated festivities during the *Festival de la Vendimia* in Jerez de la Frontera during September. The first juice of the grapes is blessed during this harvest festival and, during much sampling of the product and ceaseless flamenco, there are cavalcades, bullfights and a variety of competitions.

All dressed up for the Spring parade

ESTEPONA

MAP REF: 108 B1

Some 80km west of Málaga, this coastal town has so far been less changed by tourist and residential development than the other main towns of the western Costa del Sol. Agriculture, which is still so important to Estepona's economy, is being stimulated by town-hall initiatives. More profitable avocados, mangoes, chirimoyas (custard apples) and other sub-tropical fruits are increasingly replacing lemons, the previous mainstay. Further inland, the rearing of goats and the production of cheese from their milk is more important.

San Isidro Labrador, the farmers' saint, is the town's patron and his feast day is enthusiastically celebrated in May. An active fishing port adjoins the Puerto de Estepona marina complex, which has a concentration of eating places and nightspots and is the location for a lively street market on Sunday mornings.

Estepona's resident population of some 25,000 is tripled in high summer when holidaymakers fill more than 50 urban and tourist complexes, which are mostly low-rise and on the seaward side of the 23km stretch of the N340 highway within Estepona's municipal limits. They include Costa Natura, Spain's first 'village' for nudists. Montemayor is Estepona's fifth golf club and more are planned.

Parts of the old town, especially between Calle La Terraza and Avenida de San Lorenzo, retain whitewashed buildings with flower-decked balconies, grilles over windows, bright doorways and street names in ceramic tiles. Pretty Plaza de la Flores is usually bright with blooms. Close by is the Torre del Reloj (clock-tower), a remnant of a 15th-century church. Los Remedios, an 18th-century church, dominates the Plaza de San Francisco. The old town is also the area to find a few interesting arts and craft shops, boutiques and charming restaurants, among which La Pulga Que Tose (The Coughing Flea) is one.

Nearby Fifteen kilometres along the road to Jubrique is a turning into the woods of the Sierra Bermeja, where the *pinsapo* fir grows on the higher reaches and streams run through wooded glades. Walking paths are signposted. On a clear day, North Africa can be seen from the highest point of Alto Los Reales, 1,450m.

MOTOR TOUR

Whether setting off from Estepona or Marbella (see pages 54–5), make an early start for this full-day tour, which takes in Ronda, striking countryside and historic *pueblos*. These timeless land-scapes backing the Costal del Sol are the essence of rural Andalucia.

The popular village of Mijas is 425m above sea-level

On the eastern edge of San Pedro de Alcántara take the C339 for a leisurely drive of about one and a half to two hours along a good road with impressive views. For much of the way the rugged slopes of the Serranía de Ronda rise on the right, and the valley of the Río Guadalmina lies to the left.

Ronda

Compact, historic and monu-mental, this is one of Spain's most spectacularly sited towns and the cradle of modern bullfighting (see pages 58–9).

Leaving Ronda take the C341, signposted Algeciras. For much of the way the scenic road runs along a ridge between the valleys of the Guadiaro and Genal rivers.

Gaucín

The village of crowded, white-washed houses and narrow lanes is attractive, and equally so is its surrounding patchwork of fields. From the partially restored Castillo de Agulla (Agulla Castle) there are views to the coast and Gibraltar. The Fonda Nacional has been used since the early 19th century as a stopover on the then-arduous journey from the coast to Ronda, especially by British travellers from Gibraltar.

Follow signs to Manilva: the narrow MA539 meanders down to the Río Genal and up beyond it through very peaceful countryside. After some 16km bear left to Casares.

Casares

Perched on and tumbling down its rocky spur, which is crowned by the ruins of a Moorish castle, this is one of the most attractive and most photographed villages in Spain. And it is among the most frequently visited from the Costa del Sol. A statue in the main square commemorates Blas Infante, who was born in Casares in 1885. He was a leader of Andalucía's nationalist movement and was killed by Franco's supporters.

Return to the MA539 and go left, soon passing through an area of vineyards.

Manilva

It is known for producing good eating grapes and a *vino de terreno* (local wine) with a kick in its tail. Local *bodegas* sell it and in some the grapes are still pressed by foot.

Go west when reaching the N340 and shortly turn off to Puerto Duguesa.

Puerto Duguesa

This is yet another examples of Málaga province's self-contained residential and marina developments.

Return eastwards to Estepona or Marbella along the N340 coastal highway.

Donkeys will take you for a ride around Mijas

FUENGIROLA-MIJAS
MAP REF: 108 C1

On the site of present-day Fuengirola the Romans had a settlement known as *Suel*, which was called *Sohail* by the Moors.

The modern name was most likely derived from *Font-jirola*, a fountain at the foot of Sohail Castle, on the western edge of town, which was first built by the Moors in 956 and was destroyed after the Christian conquest of the area in 1485. The present structure is being converted into a cultural centre. Fuengirola gained its independence from Mijas in 1841. Before the tourist boom Fuengirola was a poor and tatty fishing village on an unwanted coast. Mijas, clinging to the hillside some 620m above sea level, was a tumbledown farming village with a poor economy.

Most of Fuengirola's long beachfront of more than 7km is backed by a promenade and a line of high-rise blocks. In the large area run by Mijas, which reaches the sea along the 12km stretch of Mijas-Costa, foreigners resident in many spreading developments already outnumber the municipality's Spanish residents. An extended urban mass is growing from sea to mountain with clumps of green spaces, mostly provided by golf courses. Mijas already has eight courses and more are planned. Package tourism predominates in Fuengirola, which appeals mainly to young families and older people, the latter throughout the year. Residential tourism is more

the order within the area of Mijas, but a lot of short-stay, self-catering apartment accommodation is appearing along its coast.

Fuengirola's Plaza de la Constitución is dominated by the main church. Some nearby streets retain vestiges of their past. A replica Roman façade in the Plaza de Castilla in Los Boliches is built of marble blocks from Roman times. *Andaluz* artists have done large murals on blocks of buildings, which have brightened up the town. In Mijas, rides around the modernised village can be taken in a horse-drawn carriage or on a donkey. The small Ermita del Puerto (Hermitage of the Gate) chapel is on the mountainside above the town. Near the main car park is the cave-like shrine of La Virgen de la Peña (Virgin of Sorrow), patroness of Mijas. A mobile museum has an odd collection of minute and unusual things. There is an unusually square and tiny bullring, with a small collection of bull-fighting memorabilia. The main church has Mudéjar elements and, in front of it, the *mirador* (viewpoint) affords extensive views across Mijas Campo to the coast and Fuengirola. A museum of popular arts has tools, photographs and the like from the village's past. A small, open-air auditorium hosts events during the summer.

• MALAGA •

More than half a million animated *Malagueños* and a constant flow of visitors and people passing through make Málaga a very bustling city. Modern districts have spread rapidly, older ones are being regenerated and international high-tech corporations are being attracted to Andalucía's Technology Park. The city's name is derived from *Malaca*, which the Phoenicians called their second-most-important trading port on the Iberian peninsula. Here they set up a fish-salting industry; *malac* means 'to salt'. For the Romans, too, it was an important colony. Until it fell to the Catholic Monarchs in 1487, it had during Moorish times been the main port of the kingdom of Granada.

Backing the city are the Montes de Málaga, which form a barrier keeping out cold winter winds from the north. During the last century, foreigners began to appreciate Málaga's gentle winter climate and it became known as a therapeutic and exotic place in which to escape from cold northern climes. The English, especially, favoured the city and many were laid to their final rest in the English Cemetery. They also favoured the lusciously smooth and sweet Málaga wine.

Although it is the capital of the Costa del Sol, one of the world's premier tourism zones, Málaga (map ref: 108 C1) itself retains much of its Andalucían character and has made few concessions to attracting tourists to stay. Most come on day excursions from the resorts.

Malagueta is the city's main seaside leisure district, and its beach has been enhanced by widening and by modern amenities. A part of the port is being developed as a leisure amenity. The seashore on the west side is also being improved and will be backed by a large park.

LA ALCAZABA

Moors began construction of their fortress in the 8th century on the ruins of a Roman one and used Roman columns to support some of their horseshoe arches. A double rampart runs up the hill connecting it with the Castillo de Gibralfaro, also Moorish but built on foundations of a Phoenician construction.

The layout of the Alcazaba as seen today is largely as it was ordered by a king of the region of Granada in 1057. Within double fortified walls and defensive towers a palace was surrounded by patios, pools and gardens. Abandoned during the 18th century, substantial reconstruction of the precinct was undertaken in 1933. Palace rooms retain Moorish features and house an archaeological museum with an assorted collection from the past. A Roman amphitheatre is preserved near the entrance to the Alcazaba.

LA CATEDRAL

Málaga's cathedral has not had a happy history since building started in 1528. Soon afterwards lack of funds stopped work; in 1680 an earthquake caused substantial damage; work continued between 1719 and 1782, sporadically and in different styles; one tower, *La Manquita* (The One-handed), was not completed because funds were diverted to support the American War of Independence; and during the Civil War, Republican forces killed its priests and sacked its treasures. Pedro de Mena, the Granadian sculptor, gave the cathedral its most outstanding feature when, in 1662, he completed the choir with 40 exceptionally detailed statues of saints.

MUSEO DE BELLAS ARTES

Around a graceful patio are 20 rooms with exhibits dating mainly from the 16th to the 20th century. Leading artists like Morales, Ribera, Murillo, Zurbarán, Alonso Cano and Pedro de Mena are represented here at the Fine Arts Museum. There is a strong collection of works by the 19th-century Málaga School and works by Picasso's teacher, Muñoz Degrain, as well as sketches by Picasso between the ages of 10 and 14. Ceramics, silverware, furniture and notable Roman mosaics are also displayed.

TOWN WALK

This route through Málaga takes in the principal places of interest and the shopping areas.

Start from Plaza de la Marina, which has an underground car park, and go west along tree-shaded Alameda Principal, passing the statue of the Marqués de Larios, whose cash donation made possible the reconstruction of the city centre in the 1880s. Turn right into Calle Torregorda.

1 An 11th-century Moorish entrance, Puerta de Atarazanas, gives access to a bright and busy food market *(mercado)*.

Some of the handsome buildings in Málaga

Exit at the opposite end and continue ahead to Pasillo de Santa Isabel, turning right to no 7.

2 In what was a 17th-century inn run by Franciscans, the Museo de Artes Populares (Museum of Popular Art) has a very varied and comprehensive collection of exhibits, including tools, carts, dolls, ceramics, posters and more, giving an insight into the folk art, crafts and traditions of Málaga province.

Go right on leaving, first right into Calle Cisneros and on to Plaza de la Constitución.

3 On the north side, the Casa del Consulado has a baroque portal; adjoining it, the Iglesia del Santo Cristo de la Salud displays typical elements of the Spanish mannerist style.

Go right into Calle Marqués de Larios, Málaga's main shopping street. Follow it down one side and return up the other to go right into Calles Strachan and Salinas to reach Plaza Obispo.

4 The Cathedral has recently received the attention of restorers. On the principal floor of the Museo Episcopal (Episcopal Palace), which has a fine patio and grand staircase, is a display of religious art and objects (see opposite).

Walk down the street on the left of the cathedral to see the elaborate portal on that side and, opposite it, that of the Iglesia del Sagrario. Return to continue

Málaga Cathedral: started in 1528, but never quite finished

along Calle Lario to Plaza del Siglo and follow signs on the left to Pasaje Chinitas.

5 This narrow lane and similar ones around it, typical of old Málaga, are lined by eating and drinking places and a wide choice of shops.

From Plaza del Siglo take Calle Victoria, then turn left into Calle Sant Augustín.

6 The Museo de Bellas Artes (Museum of Fine Arts) is housed in a 16th-century palace with a severe exterior and watchtower, which is a reminder that it was built as much for protection as for comfort (see opposite).

Exit right and into Calle Granada to reach the Plaza de la

Merced, recently renovated and busy in the warm months. The obelisk commemorates General Torrijos and other Liberals who were shot after Spain's War of Independence (the Peninsular War).

7 The Casa Natal Picasso (Picasso's birthplace) is a cultural centre of the Picasso Foundation.

Leave by way of the Plaza María Guerrero and turn right into Calle Alcazabilla, following signs to the Alcazaba.

8 In a redevelopment of this area the Casa de Cultura is being removed to reveal more of the Teatro Romano (Roman Theatre).

From the Alcazaba a path leads up the hill. Unsavoury characters have caused trouble for tourists here in the past.

9 The Castillo de Gibralfaro has recently been restored. It got its name from *Gebel-faro* which means mountain of the lighthouse. The Parador del Gibralfaro is in a peaceful setting and affords good views across the city.

Go back down the path and through the Jardines Puerta Oscura to a roundabout graced by the Renaissance-style Fuente Genovesa. Turn right into the shady Paseo del Parque.

10 Many of the 2,000 examples of flowers and trees that grow here are identified on ceramic tiles.

From here return to the Plaza de la Marina.

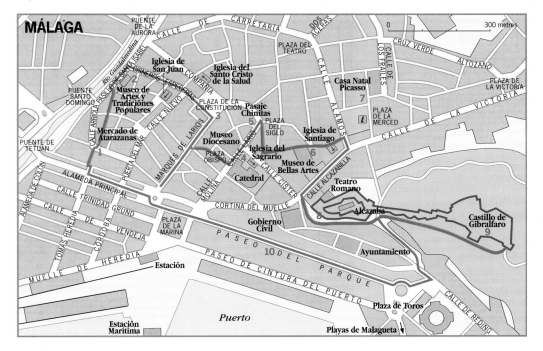

•MARBELLA•

The transformation of a poor town that had lived off iron mining, fishing and some agriculture began after 1953, when Prince Alfonso von Hohenlohe of Liechtenstein bought a small beachside farm and began to develop it. It opened as the Marbella Club and his friends arrived to stay, play and party. From then Marbella started to become the place for some of the world's rich and famous to spend their summers.

The N340 highway runs for 26km through Marbella's municipal district, which includes the village of San Pedro de Alcántara (or just San Pedro as it is often called). A resident population of 80,000 is greatly swelled by seasonal visitors, especially in the summer. Like a white rash, developments of luxury apart-ments and villas have spread across the land between sea and mountain. More and more pockets of barren land have been turned into golf courses and Marbella (map ref: 108 B1) is the centre of the 'Costa del Golf', which has Europe's largest offering of courses.

Puerto Banús and two more marinas are packed with luxury cruisers and yachts. Facilities for other sports and fitness training, and for convalescence and medical treatment are excellent. Some hotels, restaurants and nightspots are of top world standard. In short, Marbella is Spain's, and perhaps Europe's, top seaside resort in respect of its year-round climate and the variety and quality of entertainment and facilities on offer.

MARBELLA'S OLD TOWN

The Plaza de los Naranjos (Orange Tree Square) has long been the centre of the old town, which has been renovated without spoiling

it. Here, and at Puerto Banús, 6km to the west, the mixed bag of people that Marbella attracts congregate.

Besides a big choice of bars, restaurants, shops and art galleries along flower-bedecked and pristine lanes and plazas, the old town has a few places of note showing different styles: Moorish in the Casa del Corregidor

(although it carries the later date of 1552); late-Gothic and baroque respectively in the hospitals of San Juan de Dios and Bazán; Renaissance in the fountain on the Plaza de los Naranjos. The Bázan hospital is being converted to become the Casa de Cultura, which will host exhibitions and other cultural events. The small chapel of Santiago is from the 15th century; the main church, La Encarnación (the Incarnation), is dated 1505. Remains of a castle and town walls first built by Moors in the 9th century are at the old town's northeastern edge.

PUERTO BANUS

Andalucía's first village-port became the model for many others and is a big tourist attraction. Besides the luxury yachts, boutiques, bars, restaurants and nightspots in the complex and adjoining developments of Benabola and Gray d'Albion, there are the 'beautiful people' to gawp at and there is always a chance to catch a glimpse of somebody famous or infamous.

SAN PEDRO DE ALCANTARA

A political party is agitating for the separation from Marbella of this slower-paced village, 8km to the west of its parent. Redevelopment plans for its stretch of beach include a sports port.

PUERTO CABO PINO

At the eastern boundary of the Marbella municipality is this

Out of the rat-race: watching the world go by outside a bar in attractive Puerto Banús

attractive and compact marina and residential complex. West of it and backed by low dunes stretches an undeveloped beach favoured by nudists.
Nearby Benahavís, set in delightful scenery, is a growing centre for 'residential tourism' and a favourite excursion for lunch, 8km inland from the N340 coastal highway. A number of foreign-owned eating places and some interesting art and crafts shops cater for visitors.

Istán is only 18km inland from Marbella and offers escape from the hurly-burly of the coast to a world apart. On the way, there are views of the reservoir of La Concepción, which feeds Marbella. Little has changed in the village's layout of crooked streets since Moors founded it in the 9th century; water burbles from many

Take a breather from the bustle of Marbella among the palms of Parque de la Constitución

fountains; citrus groves line the valley.

La Sierra Blanca is a mountain massif, which helps give Marbella a microclimate a little milder than its neighbours, and forms part of the Reserva Nacional Serranía de Ronda hunting reserve.

Beyond the Refugio de Juanar hostelry, where game dishes are usually on the menu, is a *mirador* (viewing point) from where, 1,000m up, there is a panoramic view towards Marbella and, sometimes, across to Africa. Walkers can follow marked paths leading to Istán or Ojén. Access to the reserve is just beyond the Puerto de Ojén on the Marbella to Coín C337 road.

The elegant and exclusive Marbella Club Hotel

• NERJA •

Nerja is some 50km east of Málaga in La Axarquía region. It can justifiably claim to be the most attractively situated of all the Costa del Sol's resort towns. Perched on top of sea cliffs, its newer parts stretch inland to nestle in the foothills of the Sierra Almijara. Like Estepona, Nerja has so far maintained a more equitable balance between its traditional economy and the foreign tourism phenomenon.

In the 10th century a Moorish farming estate named *Naricha* was founded here. Silk and sugar production were its main activities. Today, close to and spreading on either side of the town, there are still sugar plantations, but the sugar factory is abandoned. Vegetables are grown in a patchwork of fields and terraces, where oxen are used for ploughing and irrigation methods bequeathed by the Moors supply water.

In 1812, during Spain's War of Independence, a British naval squadron allied with the Spanish forces destroyed Nerja's two castles, one near today's Balcón de Europa and the other on Torrecilla beach. A British invasion, with equally friendly intent but more substantial impact on the locals, started in the late 1960s when Nerja (map ref: 108 C1) was targeted for development for 'residential tourism'. The British predominate among the

community of foreign residents, seasonal visitors and package-holidaymakers. Many businesses, from plumbers to pullers of draught ales, are British-owned.

While on a tour of the region in 1885 to show sympathy following an earthquake, King Alfonso XIII stood on Nerja's promontory and grandiosely declared it to be the 'balcony of Europe'. The Balcón de Europa, a paved area lined by open-air cafés, is at the centre of the town's outdoor life. From here you can enjoy spectacular views of the rocky coastline. Below it are two attractive coves. A collection of shops, bars and restaurants catering to visitors is found in the area of Calles Pintada and Cristo. On the eastern side of town a modern Parador de Turismo is set in spacious gardens on the cliff above long and well-serviced Burriana beach.

Nearby The village of Competa, perched on a mountain spur with its honey-coloured, baroque church prominent among the cluster of white buildings, presents an attractive aspect on the approach. Creative people and others escaping from colder climates or the busy Costa del Sol have bought and renovated village houses and outlying *cortijos*. They are mostly British and Danish and have tended to fit into village life rather than change it to their ways. Local agriculture is based on the grape. At weekends, its bars and simple eating places are popular with day-visitors, and Competa enjoys a reputation for its strong *vino de terreno* (local wine – 18 per cent), which everybody enjoys for free during

The Ermita de las Angustias (Hermitage of Anguish), Nerja

CAVES

An ensemble of statues near the entrance to the Cuevas de Nerja depicts the group of young boys who in 1959 accidentally entered this huge cave network while hunting for bats. The caves were immediately recognised as being of great significance, not only for their size but because they yielded proof that Cro-Magnon man had lived in the area more than 20,000 years ago. A few finds are on display. More than half of the cave system is not open to the public, and hidden in some upper galleries are rock paintings of a variety of animals. Paintings of dolphins are the only ones from the Palaeolithic area yet found anywhere. Visitors follow an easy path through what many people consider the most impressive and best-lit caves in Europe, and which are often called 'nature's prehistoric cathedral' because there are stone 'organ pipes' rising upwards: small 'side chapels' are protected by limestone 'railings', and deep 'crypts' lie below the rocks. The temperature stays at a steady 21°C.

Each summer a music and dance festival is held in the first chamber, which has been converted into an auditorium with seating for 700. Next comes the Hall of Ghosts, named after a rock formation that looks like a shroud-covered figure. Largest of the chambers is the Hall of Cataclysms, which reaches a height of some 60m. Some major geological movement must have caused the shattering of formations that now lie as debris on the chamber's floor. Here can be seen what the *Guinness Book of Records* (1989) claimed to be the world's widest column, shaped by the merging of a stalactite and a stalagmite.

At Rincón de la Victoria, near Málaga, the Cueva del Higuerón was sculpted millions of years ago by marine erosion. Palaeolithic paintings and proof of its use as a Neolithic necropolis have been found.

the *Noche del Vino* (Wine Night) on 15 August.

Few visitors to Nerja do not make the 6km trip inland to the popular village of Frigiliana, which appears above green terraces as a brushstroke of white against the grey slopes of the Sierra de Tejeda. Frigiliana has previously won a national award as one of Spain's prettiest villages and it is proudly maintained to remain as such. Housewives appear to be constantly polishing their pristine abodes and sweeping their patch of cobbled, stepped streets. In the 16th century the population of Moors who had converted to Christianity joined the rebellion against the forces of Philip II. Decorative tiles in some of the streets vividly tell stories of the village's unsuccessful resistance under the *morisco* leader, Hernando el Darra. A leaflet with translations can be collected at El Jardín, a pleasant bar and restaurant located at the top of the town, from where there are fine views. A few more simple restaurants and places selling genuine crafts and local produce,

The gleaming white houses of pretty Competa

including the tasty *vino de terreno* and *miel* (honey), cater for the village's many day-visitors.

Just east of Nerja, Maro is a coastal village not yet marred by excesses of tourist development. Since it was the Roman settlement of *Detunda*, its fertile fields and terraces stepping down to the sea have been intensively worked to produce a variety of crops, as they do today. Sections of Roman aqueducts remain among fields where coins and tombs from those times have also been revealed. A Roman-style aqueduct nearby was a much more recent construction by a sugar entrepreneur. A campsite, unpretentious hostels and eating places cater for people wanting less costly and quieter holidays. From Maro's *balcón* there are views eastwards to Granada's mountainous coastline.

Nerja is well situated for sightseeing in La Axarquía, an enchanting mix of old and new with a lot of natural beauty (see page 63).

The Playa de Burriana, one of Nerja's excellent sandy beaches

· RONDA ·

Ronda's strategic position and the fertile plains that stretch away from the town made it attractive to a succession of people. Palaeolithic people lived in its surroundings; Celtiberians called it *Arunda;* Romans renamed it *Munda;* Moors brought it great prosperity and it was for a time capital of an independent kingdom. In 1485 it was taken by the forces of the Catholic Monarchs, who ordered the construction of its principal church on the site of the main mosque.

Above steep cliffs, Ronda (map ref: 108 B1) straddles a high ridge, dramatically cleft in two by the deep Tajo gorge of the Río Guadalevín, which is spanned by the spectacular Puente Nuevo bridge. From the west the view of Ronda is unforgettable and it has beguiled and inspired many writers and artists. Most visitors first approach the town from the south, to come across the remains of its ancient walls and two well-preserved gateways. The Puerta de Almocabar was built by the Moors in the 13th century as an access to their *alcazaba* (fortress) and town. The Puerta de Carlos V (Gate of Charles V) is a Renaissance construction of the 16th century. Beyond them is La Ciudad, the oldest part of Ronda. On the other side of the Tajo is the newer district of El Mercadillo, which is fringed on the north by a modern urban sprawl.

PLAZA DE TOROS

Ronda's bullring was inaugurated in 1785, and is 66m wide with fully covered seating. Originally, members of a chivalrous order, Real Maestranza de Caballería, used it for equestrian training and

The finely decorated tower of Santa María la Mayor in Ronda

fighting bulls on horseback. Francisco Romero first started fighting on foot and using the cape and sword. His grandson, Pedro Romero (1754–1839), who killed 6,000 bulls without once being gored, perfected the techniques of fighting on foot and is regarded as the father of modern bullfighting. He and the Ronda bullfighting scene were subjects of paintings by Goya. At the end of August there are *corridas* (bullfights) commemorating Pedro Romero, in which costumes from that time are worn. *Aficionados* of the ritual

find much of interest in the bullfighting museum located under part of the terraces.

PUENTE NUEVO

This 18th-century bridge is 98m above the Tajo gorge at its highest and narrowest point. Its architect fell to his death while inspecting the work. The bridge's middle section was once used as a prison. Horses killed or maimed in bull-fights used to be thrown into the gorge.

Nearby To the north, Ronda Viejo (Old Ronda) was the Roman settlement of *Acinipo* and retains an amphitheatre; Setenil is a small town where overhanging rock faces form the roofs of some houses and shade the narrow streets. To the southwest, the Cueva de la Pileta (Pileta Cave), upon which a farmer stumbled in 1905, was inhabited by Palaeolithic man. The paintings here are among the most treasured in Spain.

TOWN WALK

The walk takes in the districts of both La Ciudad and El Mercadillo. Along cobbled streets you will see decorative wrought-iron work for which Ronda is well known.

From the Plaza de España, where there is a tourist office, cross the Puente Nuevo and go left into Calle Santo Domingo.

1 Although its name suggests it was the house of a Moorish king, La Casa del Rey Moro was built in the 18th century for a wealthy *Rondeño* family. Its garden is very attractive. A stairway, La Mina de Ronda, goes down to the river. The Moors used Christian slaves to carry water up these steps when the town was besieged.

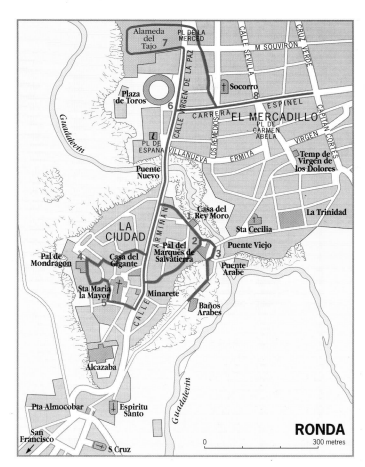

(prayer niche), a delicate arch and a minaret, which was topped by a Renaissance belfry. Much of the church that the Catholic Monarchs had ordered was rebuilt after an earthquake in 1580. Gothic and Renaissance are the predominant styles, augmented by Mudéjar and baroque decoration. From the balcony, an unusual feature on a church, the ruling classes used to watch spectacles in the plaza, which is now lined by the town hall, two convents and a boys' school on the site of the Moor's alcázar.

Exit into Calle Armiñán and go left to cross the Puente Nuevo and Plaza de España into Calle Virgen de la Paz.

6 Spain's oldest, widest and most illustrious are the superlatives claimed for this bullring, the Plaza de Toros, which can be visited.

Ahead, go left into attractive gardens.

7 Fines for blasphemy and indecent behaviour provided funds for the completion of the Alameda del Tajo (park) in 1806. Wide views of the surrounding landscape are seen from the high balcony. During the Civil War, Republicans threw more than 500 people suspected of supporting Franco's rebellion over its edge.

Exit into the Plaza de la Merced

Continue a short way along Calle Santo Domingo.

2 Another 18th-century palace that features a notable façade with a sculptured balcony and fine examples of Ronda's wrought-iron work is the Palacio del Marqués de Salvatierra (Palace of the Marquis of Salvatierra). Guided tours can be taken through rooms of the privately owned mansion.

Go on and left through the Puerta de Felipe V, built in 1742 in honour of Spain's first Bourbon king, and down the incline.

3 The Puente Viejo (Old Bridge) was built in 1616; on its right, the Puente Arabe is a Moorish construction. In a fair state of preservation are the Baños Arabes (Arab baths), which were built in the 13th century.

Return through the Puerta de Felipe V and go left up Calle Marqués de Salvatierra, then right into Calle Armiñán to pass on the left the Minarete de San Sebastian, a remaining minaret, and the Casa del Gigante, a much-reformed Moorish palace, which both date from the 14th century. After the latter, turn left following signs through alleys to the Palacio de Mondragón.

4 Except for its foundations and underground passages leading to where the *alcázar* once stood, not much remains of the original palace that the Moorish king of Ronda built here in 1314. Notable now are its Mudéjar towers,

Renaissance portal and some baroque features. Inside, where archaeological finds are displayed and cultural events are held, fine Mudéjar coffered ceilings can also be seen.

Follow signposted lanes, through Plaza Mondragón, to the front of the Colegiata de Santa María la Mayor .

5 Evidence of a 13th-century mosque is retained in a *mihrab*

Skyline view of tiled roofs in spectacular Ronda

and go right into Calle El Niño to cross the Plaza del Socorro.

8 Nicknamed la Bola, Carrera Espinel, a pedestrianised street, is at the heart of Ronda's main shopping area.

Walk along it, and adjoining streets, as you will, and then return to Plaza de España.

TORREMOLINOS/ BENALMÁDENA

Starting just 3km west of Málaga airport and sprawling for 13km on either side of the N340 coastal highway are the highly developed resorts of Torremolinos and Benalmádena. It is now difficult to imagine that not very long ago Torremolinos was a poor fishing village and Benalmádena was a simple village just a little way inland. In 1932 Charlotte Alessandri bought a piece of land in Montemar just west of Torremolinos village, which was then included in Málaga's city limits. When asked what she was going to do with her land, she replied, 'I'm going to plant tourists.' The cultivation of her crop was interrupted by the Civil War and World War II.

After a Spanish aristocrat, the Marqués de Nájera, settled in Torremolinos (map ref: 108 C1), some wealthy Spanish families began holidaying here and ex-colonial officials from other European countries retired where the warm climate, low costs and the autocratic regime of Franco reminded them of their previous postings. A cosmopolitan mix of creative people and bohemians followed and through the 1950s and early-1960s 'T-town' was one of the most hip, happy and hectic playgrounds on the world circuit of 'in' places. It was a punchy mix of wealth, eccentricity, creativity and mindlessness. When European holiday operators targeted Torremolinos as a prime location for package tourists, they did not foresee how much the mass arrival of short-stay visitors would change the character of the place. Hordes of pale strangers invaded the intimate haunts of resident lotus-eaters, who began abandoning their paradise.

Torremolinos derives its name from the old watchtower that still stands sentinel above El Bajondillo beach, and which once protected the numerous water-fed flour-mills (*torre* means tower, *molinos* means mills). In 1930 natural springs were diverted to supply nearby Málaga and the mills fell into disuse.

The resort is split into three principal areas. The town centre contains the main shopping zones, restaurants and evening bars. Pedestrianised Calle San Miguel is its main artery and ends in the Cuesta del Tajo, a steep winding walkway, which leads down from a 14th-century Moorish watch-tower through the old fishing quarter of El Bajondillo to the beach area. Along it, the 16th-century La Bóveda flour-mill has been converted into a restaurant and flamenco venue.

The beachside areas of El Bajondillo and Playmar have most of the big hotels and apartment blocks and the best of the watersports and other beach-fun facilities. On the west of the resort, La Carihuela and Montemar have more large hotels, many fish restaurants and another concentration of nightspots.

Development of Benalmádena Costa grew as an extension of Torremolinos, and it includes the little hamlets of Arroyo de la Miel and Benalmádena.

Although there are a few luxury establishments, Torremolinos and Benalmádena were developed to satisfy the lower-cost end of the European package-holiday market. There was little planning control and much of the development was done on the cheap. They became brash foreign enclaves where millions of people from dull northern cities could afford good times in the sun on short annual holidays.

As their costs started to rise, local businesses had less funds to maintain or improve their establishments; buildings became tattier and services declined. Spain's general downturn in tourism badly affected resorts like these. Local people are battling to generate a revival.

There is a lot on offer: wide, safe and well-maintained beaches; a big choice of accommodation at fair prices; many restaurants of every sort and price category; very lively and varied nightlife; fun attractions at water parks and the leisure complex of Tivoli World; and many sports facilities. With its Conference Centre and supporting infrastructure, Torremolinos seeks to attract another type of tourist. Very often it is people who don't know these resorts who snobbishly deride them.

Málaga is near by, and much of Andalucía can be discovered on day trips.

Calle San Miguel, Torremolinos

MOTOR TOUR

Just inland from the resorts there is a much slower pace of life and attractive countryside, some of it dramatically beautiful, but 'rural tourism' is fast causing changes. This route, starting in Benalmádena, takes in villages, mountain scenery and monu-mental Ronda, and returns via Marbella and Fuengirola.

Take the MA408 from Benalmádena, which winds along the
mountainside above the coast.

Mijas
Here is the most explicit example
of what 'rural tourism' may do to
many other inland villages (see
page 51).

Go along the MA485 for 17km.

Alhaurín el Grande
Surrounded by an unappealing
modern spread, its old town
retains some charm and there are
traces of its Roman and Moorish
settlement.

For some 8km the C344 crosses a
protected plateau.

Coín
With 22,000 inhabitants this is a
busy market town encircled by a
productive area for olives, cereals,
citrus and other fruits. Terracing
and irrigation networks are a
legacy of the Moors. Churches
raised after the Christian
Reconquest of 1485 show
Renaissance and Mudéjar features.
A shady promenade along the
main street is at the centre of the
town's social life.

From here it is 28km back to the
coast at Marbella on the old
C337, but this suggested route
continues along the C344 and
into the mountains.

Tolox
There's little in the hillside town,
but up a small valley and beside a
river is the Balneario de Fuente
Amargosa, whose mineral waters
are supposéd to be helpful for

lung and kidney ailments (see page
45).

After Alozaina the countryside
gets more rugged as the road
goes up into the Sierra de las
Nieves (Snows) and through the
passes of Jorox and Las Abejas.
On the left, the peak of Torrecilla
rises to 1,919m. After the
mountain-encircled village of El
Burgo, there is the Mirador del
Guarda Forestal, where a
limestone statue of a forest
guard and a boy looks across a
stunning vista. The pass of Puerto
del Viento (The Wind) is almost
1,190m above sea level, and
beyond, across a plateau, is
Ronda, some 80km from Coín.

Ronda
Compact, historic and monu-

**Tivoli World, amusement park
near Benalmádena**

mental, this is one of Spain's most
spectacularly sited towns and the
cradle of modern bullfighting (see
pages 58–9).

Take the C339 for a leisurely
drive along a good road. For
much of the way, rugged slopes of
the Serranía de Ronda rise on the
left and the valley of the Río
Guadalmina lies below on the
right. The N340 coastal highway
is joined on the outskirts of San
Pedro de Alcántara, from where
it is 50km to Benalmádena via
Marbella and Fuengirola (see
pages 54–5 and 51 respectively).
For another interesting inland
tour which takes in the town of
Antequera, see page 45.

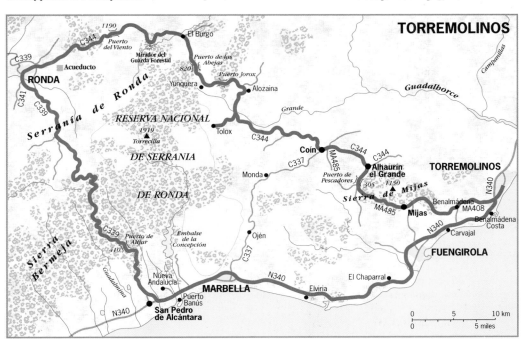

TORROX

MAP REF: 108 C1

Only 4km from the coast, the old
town has been little assailed by
the modern development that it
has allowed on its share of the
eastern Costa del Sol. Torrox
Costa has been fashioned into a
dense amalgam of big apartment
complexes and Moorish-style
developments, and the long
promenade, which backs a wide
beach, is lined by bulky blocks.
The styleless architecture of a
building outburst in the 1970s
has been replaced by more
imaginative designs.

Foreign owners of apartments
are predominantly German, and
bars, restaurants, nightspots and
shops mostly cater to their tastes.
Many businesses close during the
off-season.

VELEZ-MALAGA

MAP REF: 108 C1

Vélez-Málaga, third-largest town
of the province, is the capital of
its extensive *comarca* and the La
Axarquía, a distinctive area of the
province. The important Greek
settlement of *Mainake* was sited
close to the present town.

Agricultural lands separate Vélez
from its seaside suburb of Torre
del Mar and it is with agriculture,
as well as the administration and
servicing of its *comarca*, that the
town is most involved. The area's
fruits, vegetables, oils and other
products are distributed from large
warehouses. A factory processes
the local sugar cane and there is
some light industry in furniture,
metal decorative items and
ceramics.

A restored 13th-century Moorish

**Torre del Mar offers huge beaches
and moderate prices**

alcázar (fortress) dominates the
skyline. To one side is the oldest
barrio of Arrabal de San Sebastián,
which has changed little in 500

**A colourful corner in Vélez-
Málaga's old town**

The promenade and apartment
blocks of Torrox Costa

years. Near by, another medieval
quarter has houses with large
overhanging eaves – an
architectural detail inherited from
Asturian immigrants who
repopulated the town in the 16th
century. Most notable among
other buildings is the Mudéjar
Iglesia de Santa María la Mayor,
which was started after the town's
capture in 1487 from the kingdom
of Granada, for which it had been
a long-held bastion.

With a large proportion of
permanently resident people, and
still being very much a preserve of
Spanish holidaymakers, although it
is also popular with Germans,
Torre del Mar has a noticeably
different ambience to other Costa
del Sol resorts. Little attempt is
made at attaining a glamorous
status, and the provision is of
honest value in unpretentious
apartments and catering places
that ordinary families can afford.

Away from the long, wide beach,
which has good watersports
facilities in summer, other water
fun can be enjoyed at the Agua
Velís aquapark and at Fuerte El
Dorado there are Wild West
performances to entertain
children. Puerto de la Caleta has
modern amenities for leisure
sailors.
Nearby To the east, Algarrobo
Costa is also developing as a
summer resort based on apartment
and villa accommodation. The
adjoining Mezquitilla retains more
of its fishing-hamlet character.
Both places belong to the town of
Algarrobo a little way inland.

LA AXARQUIA

This southeastern part of
Málaga province, in which
some 30 villages and towns are
situated, is bordered by the
coast running from the capital
city to Maro, just beyond Nerja
(see pages 56–7). Its boundary
then turns inland to make a
rough semicircle along the
mountain ridges of the sierras
Alhama Tejeda and Almijara and
back to the coast through the
eastern edge of the Montes de
Málaga. Metals mined in the
mountains attracted Greeks and
Phoenicians to establish trading
settlements. Romans settled
more permanently and many
places have yielded evidence of
their sojourn.

Seven centuries of Moorish
domination gave the region
much of its present character.
Fertile lands along the coast and
in the broad valley of the Río
de Vélez became prime
production areas for grapes,
cereals, fruits, silk and sugar
cane, and on terraced hillsides
olives were harvested. Most of
these crops are still being cultivated today and the majority of
small, rural communities started
as prosperous Moorish farming
estates.

During the Christian
Reconquest, La Axarquía was
the scene of an overwhelming
Moorish victory in 1483.
Although the Moors were
defeated four years later, the
conflict did not finish then. In
the 1560s the Moorish
Rebellion of Las Alpujarras
spread through La Axarquía,
and Frigiliana was the final
bloody battleground (see page
57). All who had not converted
to Christianity were expelled
and the area was repopulated
by immigrants from northern
Spain, who knew little of the
local economy, and there was a
gradual decline in prosperity.

TOURING LA AXARQUIA

Tourist authorities have
designed five routes along
which to explore La Axarquía
by car. The routes are colour-
coded and signposted along the
roads. Tourist offices will
supply more details and a map.
Each itinerary loosely follows a
theme: the Sun and Avocado
Route follows the rich flatlands
of the Río Vélez valley; the Sun
and Wine Route takes in the
principal wine-producing
villages, including Frigiliana and
Competa (see page 57); the
Mudéjar Route goes to small
villages of the Sierra de
Almijara, which have examples
of this architectural style; the
Raisin Route lies to the west of
the Río Vélez among the lower
hills; and the Oil and Mountain
Route passes through the
higher villages and olive-
growing areas in the north.

La Axarquía is a good area for
walkers. Villages are not far
apart and the meandering roads
do not have heavy traffic. There
is a network of age-old tracks
through the agricultural
flatlands and over hills. From
most of the villages there are
paths that link up with others
or minor roads so that it is
possible to take circular walks.
Villagers will often help with
directions.

One example of a hike is to
take the road heading northwest from Vélez-Málaga and at
Tapiche to turn left to
Benamocarra – a distance of
under 12km. From here a track
leads southeast and down to
the Almayate, from where other
tracks can be followed back to
Vélez; or from Torre del Mar,
some 3.5km from Almayate,
there is a regular bus
connection with Vélez.

**The Moorish fortress dominates
the skyline of Vélez-Málaga**

CORDOBA AND JAEN

Together these two landlocked provinces cover 31 per cent of Andalucía's territory, and they are almost equal in area: Córdoba with 13,718sq km and Jaén with 13,498sq km. The combined population of the two provinces is 1,345,000 and the density of Jaén province is slightly lower than that of Córdoba province. Some 30 per cent of the people live in the two provincial capitals. Both provinces are bordered by the Sierra Morena in the north and have mountains of the Sistema Subbética running across them on a southwest to northeast axis. They also share the Río Guadalquivir, which rises in Jaén province and runs for 130km through Córdoba province. Another feature common to both provinces and immediately noticeable to the traveller is their *olivares,* the seemingly endless plantations of olive trees.

The lower-lying area of Jaén province is in two parts: Las Lomas, where the major crops are cereals, olives, fruit and vegetables, as well as small-scale vine growing; and La Campiña, where the olive tree is ubiquitous. Lead mining and the metal industry have traditionally been the main industrial activities apart from the production of olive oil. Córdoba's larger agricultural area of La Campiña also produces cereals and olives, as well as legumes. Viticulture is more widespread than in Jaén, and the production of wines with the Montilla-Moriles denomination is an important contributor to the province's economy. Of its industries, iron and steel are the most important. In the mountain regions around Peñarroya and Pueblonuevo, mining has been an age-old activity.

Jaén has always been a cross-roads zone, and its name derives from the Arabic *Geen,* meaning 'on the route of caravans'. As it has been for successive civilisations,

the Desfiladero de Despeñaperros is for today's road and rail builders the best natural pass through the Sierra Morena, and therefore the gateway to Andalucía. At nearby

Navas de Tolosa, Christian Castile had a decisive victory over the Moors in 1212, which gave spirit to their reconquest of *Al-Andalus:* the city of Córdoba fell to them in 1236 and Jaén in 1246. Ibn el Ahmar fled from Jaén to found the Nasrid dynasty of the kingdom of Granada. Centuries before, Roman legions had won a major battle against the Carthaginians close to present-day Linares. And in 1808, during Spain's War of Independence, Napoleon's occupying forces suffered a significant defeat at the Battle of Bailén. In Jaén city a monument commemorates past battles.

In that city's offices of provincial authorities, thoughts are not of the past, and efforts are directed at losing the province's image as an area through which today's caravans of heavy lorries and freight railcars rush but where nobody stops. Foreign investment in industry and agriculture is being sought and found. To leisure travellers their message is that Jaén is the Reserve of Inland Tourism and in this respect the province undeniably has a lot going for it.

The towns of Baeza and Ubeda have examples of Gothic, Renaissance and baroque architecture that few places in Europe can match, and which anybody with an interest in monumental architecture should not miss. The Parque Natural de las Sierras de Cazorla, Segura y Las Villas, with its stunning scenery and recreational facilities, is another prize jewel in a crown that is studded with three more natural gems, the Parques

The Río de Aguas running near the pretty town of Sorbas

Naturales of Sierra de Andújar, Sierra Magina and Despeñaperros. Add to the list a number of good-looking towns huddling below impressive castles and some attractions in the capital itself, and it is understandable that people who have spent time in the province leave wondering why they had never heard of it before.

Bronze Age man had used the Guadalquivir to transport the minerals he mined. In the 2nd century BC the Romans captured what had been an important Iberian town, and their *Corduba* became the capital at the centre of their province of *Baetica* and the biggest city in the peninsula. During the period of Visigothic rule, Córdoba was of less importance, but under the Moors, especially from 756 to 1031, it again rose to greatness, this time to become the largest and most civilised city in Western Europe.

After the Christian Reconquest, its fortunes sank once more as the most accomplished of its people deserted. A revival came when Spain was at the height of its power in the 16th century and there was a spate of building. The attention was temporary and the once-great capital of Romans and Moors entered a centuries-long slumber, during which its monumental buildings crumbled.

However, not all of monumental Córdoba was wasted by neglect or looting, and much of what remained has had the attention of renovators. Almost continuously they are painstakingly busy on the city's pride and joy, La Mezquita, the great mosque that alone justifies a visit to Córdoba. Much

else to see, grand and of golden-coloured stone or pretty and blindingly whitewashed, stands awaiting visitors to the city.

And within the province, which tourists have not frequented much, Priego de Córdoba in the southeast is a treasure house of baroque architecture, which should not be missed off any itinerary. Near by is the Parque Natural de las Sierras Subbéticas, and adjoining the park area to the northwest are the vineyards that supply the wine towns of Montilla and Moriles. For a high price or by means of good connections, people join *monterias* (large, organised shooting parties) in the Sierra Morena, where deer and wild boar are the trophies.

The people of Jaén and Córdoba provinces are regarded as a sober lot by Andalucíans from the coastal provinces, less spontaneous in showing emotions and in having fun. By some, the people of Jaén are considered

more Castilian than *Andaluz*. And that is not flattering. The city of Córdoba has a cultural life and a small clutch of restaurants and bars that are by no means dull. And in May it lets its hair down for a month of continuous celebrations.

Like the rest of Andalucía, these two provinces are on the move and the areas in which they are successful are often surprising – medicine, for example. Remembering that Abulcassis, one of history's most innovative surgeons, was born near Córdoba in 936, it is less surprising to find that Córdoba's Reina Sofia hospital is today in the vanguard of organ transplants. More difficult to grasp is that the Colegio Universitario de Jaén is doing crucial test work on inhibitors for the duplication of DNA, which could help in the treatment of cancer and viral diseases like Aids.

The attractive town of Montilla

ALMODOVAR DEL RIO
MAP REF: 108 B2

Its fairy-tale castle, first built by Moors, was extensively restored early in the 20th century and rates among the most impressive fortifications in Spain. The nearby village of Posadas got its name from having had, since ancient times, a number of *posadas* (inns) along the road between Córdoba and Sevilla. La Breña reservoir is a scenic and peaceful spot favoured by fishermen.

ANDUJAR
MAP REF: 108 C2

From the Roman epoch Andújar retains a bridge across the Guadalquivir and remains of town walls. From later times, there are some notable religious and civil buildings, among which the Iglesia de Santa María is the most out-standing. It has a Renaissance façade and Mudéjar tower, and, inside, it treasures paintings by Pacheco and El Greco. Oil production – sunflower and olive – is important and the town also has factories producing furniture and ceramics. Marmolejo is a nearby spa for kidney and liver disorders.

NUESTRA SEÑORA DE LA CABEZA

Within the municipal limits of Andújar and in the foothills of the Sierra Morena, is the sanctuary of Nuestra Señora de la Cabeza (Our Lady of the Head), which was founded in 1227. The original Gothic structure has had much remodelling. The Virgin, whose small image is venerated in the Capilla Mayor, is the patron of the town and of the provincial diocese. On the last Sunday of April each year, she is the object of an animated *romería* (pilgrimage), the second largest in Andalucía, when over half a million people make their way to the shrine in colourful procession.

During the Civil War, 'Nationalist' (rebel) troops and a few civilians resisted 'Republican' (government) forces for eight months in defence of the sanctuary until their Capitán Cortés was killed and no more than 30 starving men were left. The story of this useless valour and war's waste is related on a stone tablet outside the church.

Delivering the milk by mule and cart in Baeza

BAEZA
MAP REF: 108 C2

Historically and architecturally, Baeza is twinned with Ubeda just 9.5km away across the ridge of Loma de Ubeda (see pages 80–1). Sightseeing in the two towns is among the most rewarding experiences awaiting travellers in Andalucía. Roman *Vilvatia* became a prosperous Visigothic city, and for a while Baeza was capital of a Moorish *taifa* (small

Baeza's Plateresque town hall

kingdom). The town's endowment of fine religious and civil buildings, even those serving very ordinary purposes, began after it was taken for Castile by Ferdinand III in 1227, and reached its high point in the 16th century. In ambience and physical aspects, Baeza and Úbeda are rather more soberly Castilian than typically Andalucían.

First port of call should be the tourist office in the Casa del Pópulo, originally a civil court building, which has a 16th-century Plateresque façade. The Plaza del Pópulo, which has two arched entrances, is graced by the Fuente de los Leones (Lions' Fountain), on which an Iberian-Roman statue is said to be of Imilce, wife of Hannibal. Distinguished by a good-looking gallery, the Antigua Carnicería (Old Butchery) is a Renaissance building from the mid-16th century. In the adjoining Plaza del Mercado Viejo, the double-arched gallery of the baroque Casas Consistoriales Bajas (Lower Town Councils) faces the galleried front of the Alhóndiga (Corn Exchange), which is connected to the Pósito (Communal Granary), where grain was stored to meet shortages. A Renaissance building with baroque elements served as the University, and Juan de Ávila (1500–68), mystic and writer, was its first rector.

The *Andaluz* poet, Antonio Machado (1875–1939), taught French here from 1912 to 1919 and is remembered by a simple monument in the double-arcaded patio. Dating from the late 15th century and studded with diamond-point motifs is the flamboyant Gothic façade of the Palacio de Jabalquinto which also has a fine Renaissance patio and a baroque staircase.

Another architectural ensemble surrounds the Plaza de Santa María. The sombre façade of the 1660 Seminario de San Felipe Neri (Seminary of St Philip) faces the cathedral, and between them is a fountain in the form of a triumphal arch, which bears the coat-of-arms of Philip II. Gothic Renaissance and Mudéjar styles combine in the cathedral, which was built on the site of the main mosque. Its oldest part, the west front, includes a portal of Arab inspiration and a large rose window. Mudéjar chapels in the cloister are decorated with Arabic characters. Notable also are the baroque altarpiece and a huge monstrance of chiselled silver.

Adjoining the cathedral is the Gothic building of the Casas Consistoriales Altas, on which there is the coat-of-arms of Juana *la Loca*, the 'mad' daughter of the Catholic Monarchs. There is a concentration of other noble palaces in Calle de San Pablo, among which the Casa Cabrera, with a 16th-century Plateresque façade, is most notable. A good many more fine mansions are spread throughout the town.

Previously the palace of justice and prison, the Ayuntamiento building (town hall) is considered the most accomplished expression in Baeza of the work of architect Andrés Vandelvira and his school (see pages 80–1), and of the Andalucían Plateresque style. Coats-of-arms of Philip II and of the town feature among those between the ornate balconies and human figures decorate the cornice. Near by is the impressive southern façade of the 17th-century Hospital de la Concepción (Hospital of the Conception), which was inspired by that of the neighbouring Convento de San Francisco (Convent of St Francis). An earthquake, the War of Independence and dissolution of the monasteries in the 19th century contributed to the convent's falling into ruin.

The transition between Renaissance and baroque styles can be seen in the Convento de la Encarnación (Convent of the Incarnation), which was founded for the Barefooted Carmelites at the end of the 16th century. It was here that San Juan de la Cruz completed his *Spiritual Canticle* (see pages 80–1). A Plateresque façade adorns the Templo de Santa María del Alcázar y San Andrés (Temple of St Mary of the Castle and St Andrew). The Virgen del Alcázar is the town's patroness. Ferdinand III had instituted a military-religious brotherhood of Baeza's nobles in this church.

Baeza was known as the 'royal nest of hawks' and its valiant captains were exhorted to stain their swords with blood of the Moors of Granada. More than two centuries later, Isabel the Catholic had the town walls torn down as part of an effort to stop feuding nobles. Surviving parts are the Puerta de Úbeda, some adjoining ramparts and the keep of El Torrico.

Andújar – olive groves as far as the eye can see

•CAZORLA•

An ancient settlement and then a Roman town, Cazorla was the see of San Isicio, one of the seven apostles who arrived to evangelise Iberia. Five religious orders founded monasteries in a place whose isolation encouraged contemplation. One of their buildings now serves as the town hall. Below the crag of Peña de los Halcones, the town is a charming labyrinth of layers and winding streets where the sound of water is ever present. Remains of old castles still stand guard and ruins of the Iglesia de Santa María, designed by Vandelvira, now serve as an auditorium.

Cazorla's accommodation and eating places are simple and get very busy during holiday periods as the town is the principal gateway to the Parque Natural de las Sierras de Cazorla, Segura y Las Villas, a protected wilderness area of stunning beauty. These mountains cover a larger area, but only their parts within Jaén province are, since 1986, under the protection of AMA (see pages 70-1). With around 214,000 hectares, this is Spain's biggest natural park, of which around a third has been a national game reserve since 1960.

Cazorla (map ref: 109 D2) has been declared a Biosphere Reserve by UNESCO and a Special Protection Zone for Birds by the European Community. Most of the park is over 600m above sea level and the highest point of Empanadas reaches over 2,107m. The climate is continental and average daily temperatures in winter are below freezing.

A mosaic of ecosystems covers this large area. Below rock faces and soaring crags most of the slopes are heavily forested with pines; olives cover some lower slopes. Fast-flowing streams race through deep gorges and tumble over rapids and waterfalls.

Andalucía's great river, the Guadalquivir, rises within the park; so does the Segura, which runs eastwards to the Mediterranean.

Large numbers of deer, wild boar and mountain goats roam the park; mouflon (mountain sheep) have been successfully introduced; otters are also plentiful. The Valverde lizard, peculiar to the region, and the bearded vulture are among rare species of the many birds, small mammals, insects and butterflies that have been recorded in the park. Its own strain of violet and geranium are features of the park's varied flora. Cave paintings and traces of later Iberian settlements are evidence of early human activity.

Some 90,000 people live within the park – in towns, villages and scattered *cortijos* (farmhouses) – and its economy has been based on three products – timber, sheep and olive oil – while hunting and fishing, for food and sport, have also been important money-earners. With tourism approaching one million visitors annually, there is a threat to the traditional economy and labour force as well as to the ecological balance. Organic farming is among the solutions that AMA and others are promoting.

The top place to stay within the park is the Parador del Turismo del Adelantado, and there are other very pleasantly situated hotels, rustic hostels, family guesthouses and idyllic sites for camping. AMA issues permits for youth groups to use 14 designated camping areas called *Campamentos Juveniles*. Booking of any accommodation well in advance of the Easter and summer holiday periods is usually essential.

QUERCUS, a cooperative society formed by young naturalists and professional guides, provides a number of highly recommended services to enhance visitors'

Pinsapo pine in the Parque Natural de las Sierras de Cazorla

enjoyment and appreciation of the park. Excursions of half-day or full-day duration by four-wheel-drive vehicles, with some parts covered on foot, take in the most 'essential' sights of the park. Horseback excursions of similar durations, cover smaller distances. Experienced riders can hire horses by the hour. Walking treks along forest paths, in the company of guides who know and love the area, are the best way to get to know the park, and interfere with it least. 'Photographic hunts' are led by people who know just where and when to find the park's fauna and most representative flora. Guides can also be contracted to accompany parties who wish to have tailor-made excursions or to pursue particular interests.

QUERCUS has an office in Cazorla town and in the park. There is a choice of detailed maps, which show all roads, forest tracks and paths, most scenic spots, villages, campsites, refuges, etc. AMA publishes a range of useful leaflets and there are commercially produced guidebooks. All this material is very helpful for planning walking or cycling excursions.

Two motors tours from Cazorla take in principal sights. A short day tour goes via the hamlet of La Iruela to enter the park at the Burunchel control point. After the Mirador del Caudillo, from where there is an extensive vista, a road leads up to the Parador del Turismo. Further along is the Puente de Herrerias, supposedly built in one night to allow Queen Isabel to cross. A signposted track leads to La Cañada de las Fuentes, source of the Guadalquivir. Following signs to Pozo Alcón, the road weaves below the peak of

Cabañas (2,028m). A right turn leads to Tiscar, a spectacularly sited hamlet with a popular sanctuary. Beyond the park boundary Quesada lies among an expanse of olive trees and its Museo Zabalete shows works of this local artist. It is a short distance back to Cazorla.

A longer circuit takes in most of the park's length and picturesque towns of the northern part. After the Mirador del Caudillo, go first left and along the young Río Guadalquivir to the Centro de Interpretación de la Naturaleza, where you can obtain all the information you need about the park. The Museo de Caza displays hunting trophies. The Jardin Botánico concentrates on the park's flora. Ahead, the river enters the Embalse del Tranco de Beas, first of many dams along its course. At the Parque Cinegético, animals gather to eat the food provided for them. After crossing the dam wall and hydroelectric plant the road leads to Hornos, huddled below its ruined castle. Continue to Segura de la Sierra and enjoy the wide view from its restored castle. Via the villages of Orcera and La Puerta de Segura, connect with the N322 and follow signs for Jaén. From Villacarrillo take the road signposted Cazorla.

Fire is always a danger in the Cazorla nature park

BATTLEGROUNDS OF JAEN

Near today's industrial town of Linares, then called *Cástulo,* Roman armies had a decisive victory over the Carthaginians in the Second Punic War. It was to Porcuna, where there are remains of a Roman bridge, that Julius Caesar later travelled directly from Rome to organise the army that was to defeat his rival, Pompey. Much later, Boabdil, King of Granada, was to be imprisoned in a fortified tower of Porcuna. On 16 July 1212, Christian armies defeated the Moors at Las Navas de Tolosa.

The Gateway to Andalucía through the Sierra Morena is the very scenic pass of Despeñaperros. The name translates as 'thrown-down dogs' and, according to legend, Moors were thrown down the dizzy heights after battle. The large fortification of Baños de la Encina had been completed in 968 to protect the Moors' trade route between Cordoba and Toledo. During the Reconquest, Christians won and lost the place six times. At the Battle of Bailén in 1808 General Castaños beat the French General Dupont and turned the tide in Spain's favour in her War of Independence against Napoleon. The victor's remains lie in the town's Gothic church.

A typical *cortijo,* or farmhouse – one of many scattered through the Cazorla nature park

WILD ANDALUCIA

Andalucía ranks among the world's regions that nature has most variously and generously endowed. In what ecologists claim is a rather delayed appreciation of its great natural gift and a late realisation of the need to secure its survival, Andalucía now gives protection, in varying degrees, to 82 natural areas covering some 14,835sq km. That amounts to 17 per cent of the region's territory, which is well above the European average. The Agencia de Media Ambiente, AMA, is the environmental agency of the Junta de Andalucía, which administers the nature areas. It has offices in all provincial capitals, where information can be sought. AMA's most delicate task is balancing the interests of ecology, economic development and tourism. There are many new laws and policies to protect the environment, but, sometimes unfairly, pressure groups criticise what they see as a lack of commitment to effective enforcement and implementation, and they claim the scale is weighted in favour of economic interests. Most of AMA's field-workers have an infectious love and enthusiasm for their work.

Fascinating rock formations in El Torcal park

MOUNTAIN AREAS

Spain is one of Europe's most mountainous countries, and Andalucía contributes a good proportion of the high land. West of the Cazorla nature park (see pages 68–9), along the region's northern boundary are the Sierra Morena or 'Dark Mountains', so called because of the dark woods that cover their slopes – holm, gall and cork oaks, as well as different kinds of pines.

Five nature parks are dotted through this low range, where the highest peak is around 1,300m. Some 40 wolves in danger of extinction survive in the parks of Selladores y Contadero and Sierra Carde a Montoro on the borders of Jaén and Córdoba provinces: another 15 in Córdoba's Sierra de Hornachuelos park. Around 1,100 of the remaining Spanish lynx also survive across the Sierra Morena.

Hunting has become a commercial activity in these mountains and wild boar, stags, roebuck and mule deer are the targets.

A number of nature parks cover parts of the Sistema Penibética along the south of the region. In the west they include those of the Sierra de Grazalema and Sierra de las Nieves in the area of Ronda, where the *pinsapo* pine, a relic of ubiquitous forests of the Tertiary period, grows above heights of 1,000m. There is also Los Alcornales in the east of Cádiz province, where the economic exploitation of thick forests of indigenous cork oaks is controlled and where deer roam further south than anywhere else in Europe. Science-fiction films have been shot against the weird limestone formations of the El Torcal park near Antequera.

Crowning Granada and Almería

provinces is the Sierra Nevada natural park, which covers some 170,000 hectares, and has two distinct zones. Below the peaks of Mulhacén and Veleta, Mediterranean vegetation gives way to alpine and tundra types and there are deep glacial lakes and slopes that in winter become runs for Europe's most southerly ski resort. On the southern side of the massif is the haunting enclave of Las Alpujarras, typically Mediterranean and hinting of Africa (see pages 90–1). Some 60 plant species belong exclusively to the Sierra Nevada; more than 4,000 mountain goats nimbly tread the higher slopes, while badgers and wildcats wiggle around the lower ones.

Other mountainous areas under protection include the Montes de Málaga, the Sierra Subbética in Córdoba province, the Sierra de Huetor, Sierra de Baza and Sierra de Castril of Granada, the Sierra María in Almería and the Sierra Magina in Jaén, where 18 species of birds of prey have been identified. Almería's Parque Natural de Sierra de Gato-Níjar, whose mountains are of volcanic formation, also encompasses some of the region's most beautiful coastline.

WETLANDS AND COASTAL ZONES

Doñana in Huelva province is the only one of Spain's National Parks within Andalucían territory, and it has the strictest protection of all natural areas in the region (see page 20). AMA safeguards an area surrounding the park where the woodland is similar to that which moving dunes often cover within the park. Funds from the European Community are being applied to implement a more promising ecological/development plan for this humid zone, which is so crucial to Europe's migratory birdlife and varied resident animals. Marshes in the estuary of Huelva's Río Odiel, others near Cádiz and Barbate, as well as a number of lakes in the southwest corner of the region also teem with birdlife. Many other lakes and reservoirs throughout the region support aquatic life. Near Antequera, the Fuente de Piedra salt lagoon is one of two places in Europe where the greater flamingo nests. Pink flamingos and other birds also stop over in the salt marshes of Cabo de Gata. It is a misconception that all of Andalucía's coastline has been developed, and nature-lovers can find many parts where typical Mediterranean plant and animal habitats flourish. In the west, the Atlantic creates a different seashore and attendant flora, and frequent strong winds drive oceanic birds on to the land.

FLORA

With its geographical diversity and many microclimates, Andalucía offers botanists a bonanza, which is at its biggest in spring and has another fresh breakout in autumn. Wild irises, narcissi, crocuses, squills and asphodels burst forth in early spring; bindweed, buttercups, birthworts, salvias and mallows brighten open ground and fields; among the *maquis* vegetation of herb bushes, gorse, broom, heather and dwarf fan palms, bright clusters of different cistuses and rock rose appear. In autumn, squills and snowdrops are among the flowers from bulbs and tubers that resist the summer drought. Different types of pine and oak are the most ubiquitous trees of the region. Cork oaks, whose fleshy bark is harvested every 15 to 20 years, remain productive for up to 150 years. There is a rich variety of growth under the cover of forests, and especially under pines in areas of limestone many different strains of wild orchids grow in profusion.

FAUNA

Andalucía provides a habitat for 14 of the 19 zoological species in Spain that are threatened with extinction: 10 species of bird, including the imperial eagle, black swan and white-headed duck; two species of freshwater fish; two mammals – the lynx in the wild and the monk seal, which is being safeguarded in captivity. In addition to its resident, typically Mediterranean birdlife, in spring and autumn most of the migratory birds that breed in Western Europe can also be spotted within the region, especially at its eastern and western corners. Eagles rule the skies – golden, short-toed, booted and, more rarely, the imperial. Other birds of prey include peregrines, kestrels, buzzards and different owls. Griffon and huge black vultures also soar above. By contrast, a profusion of butterflies flutter among the flowers and herbs. More than half-a-dozen different snakes slither along the ground and bask in the sun, a variety of lizards dart between rocks, and in a few places camouflaged chameleons clamber along twigs. Rabbits, hares, foxes, boar and different deer are among the other furtive creatures of Andalucía's wildlife.

Cactus purchena (prickly pear), widespread in Andalucía

• CORDOBA •

Packed with impressive monuments and picturesque corners where echoes of the past are strong, Córdoba quickly transforms its visitors into lifelong admirers. Most of the city sits on the Río Guadalquivir's northern bank with mountains not far behind. Considered as sober and conservative by flamboyant *Sevillanos* or *Malagueños*, but repeatedly electing a communist mayor, the 300,000 *Córdobeses* can be justly proud of their city's glorious past. It was Rome's administrative centre for the rich province of *Baetica*, and the West's biggest and most cultured city during the Moslem caliphacy. Proud they can be, too, that Córdoba was the home town of the philosophers Seneca, Averroës and Maimonides, all honoured with statues, and that it was for long a place of cooperation across racial and religious divides. Rightly, many *Córdobeses* express the opinion that their city requires more time to savour than most tourists allow themselves, or are allowed by tour operators.

La Mezquita is the greatest legacy and biggest tourist-puller in Córdoba (map ref: 108 C2). The magnificent mosque is one of the largest in the world and ranks among its finest architectural treasures. It was begun in 785, and through four stages of building reached its present great size by 990. Aisles and cross-aisles are formed by lines of arches, which are two-tiered to raise the height of the ceiling. Their striped pattern effect was made by alternate use of stone and brick. Supporting pedestals, columns and capitals in porphyry, marble and jasper are of varying styles, as material to build the mosque was taken from different Roman and Visigothic buildings, including the Visigothic basilica on whose site the mosque was built.

The *mihrab*, which effectively amplified the voice of the prayer leader, is an exceptional achievement of imagination and craftsmanship in Moorish art. Its shell-shaped ceiling is carved from a single piece of marble. An octagonal cupola and Byzantine mosaics adorn the *maksura* antechamber, which was used by the caliph and his retinue. Some 300 chandeliers and 1,500 lamps lit the interior. Daylight filtered in where the north front was open to the tree-filled Patio de los Naranjos (Courtyard of the Orange Trees), the courtyard of ritual ablution, above which rose the minaret, subsequently transformed into a baroque tower.

After Ferdinand III captured the city in 1236, Christian chapels were built against the mosque's walls, and some of its 856 interior columns were removed. During the 16th century, against the opposition of the town council, the cathedral chapter began building a Gothic church within the mosque, which, as it took 243 years to complete, acquired decoration in later styles. It can, at best, be described as a mistake. When Charles V realised what he had permitted, he exclaimed, 'You have built here what you or others may have built anywhere but you have destroyed something unique in the world.'

La Judería, the medieval Jewish quarter northwest of the mosque, has one of Spain's two remaining synagogues that retain their original structure. La Sinagoga (Synagogue) on Calle Judíos, which a Hebrew inscription dates as being built in 1315, has a plain exterior, but inside are the remains of fine Mudéjar decoration. In jasmine-filled Plaza Tiberiados there is a 1960s statue of Maimonides. On a plaza named after him and in a house believed to have belonged to his family, there is now the Museo Municipal de Arte Taurino (Municipal Museum) in which one of the most famous Córdoban bullfighters among many, Manolete, is much revered. Adjoining, El Zoco is a centre where craftspeople produce both traditional and modern pieces. On Plaza Angel Torres, the Casa del Indiano is an example of Córdoba's noble private mansions. Plaza Levi, which has the municipal tourist office, is a pleasant place for a rest and drink.

Within La Judería and the rest of Córdoba's oldest part, narrow *calles* and tiny plazas are lined by more fine mansions and other buildings whose *cancelas* (wrought-iron gates) lead to cool, beflowered patios where fountains play. Do not miss Calles Manriquez and Albucasis, and Calleja de las

A few of the hundreds of arches in La Mezquita

Flores, the 'little street of flowers'. Cervantes mentions the Posada del Potro (Inn of the Colt) in *Don Quixote*. It is now an arts and crafts centre. The Museo Municipal de Bellas Artes (Fine Arts Museum), small but interesting, has wide-ranging works by Córdoban artists and the better-known Zurbarán, Goya, Murillo and Valdés Leal. Very popular is the Museo Julio Romero de Torres, which takes its name from the early 20th-century artist who painted scenes of Córdoba and of its dark-eyed women. In the Museo Arqueológico (Archaeological Museum), a handsome building, is a rich collection from prehistory to baroque. Wrought-iron balconies hang on the brick façades of the arcaded Plaza de la Corredera, built in the 17th century and once the scene for bullfights and other spectacles. A colourful market is held here in the mornings. In the building below the clock-tower is a municipal market.

The gardens of the Alcázar – ideal for a relaxing stroll

TOWN WALK

Start at La Mezquita.

1 On its west side is Calle de Torrijos, where there is a tourist office.

2 The Palacio de Congresos is an exhibition and congress centre whose Gothic-Plateresque portal once gave entrance to a church on the site of a Visigothic palace and the Moorish alcázar.

Wander as you will through La Judería and the rest of the old part, taking in places of interest mentioned above.

3 La Judería and the Old Quarter is the area with the most typical

bars, eating places and craft shops. Brightened by flowers through the year, it is especially so during May, when there are competitions for the most beautiful patio and many private places are open to the public.

Arrive at Plaza de la Corredera and leave it by the northwest corner to reach Calle Capitulares.

4 Columns of a Roman temple rise next to the very modern Ayuntamiento (town hall), which stands above a ruined amphitheatre.

5 The most complete of Córdoba's churches from the time of Fernando III, the Iglesia de San Pablo (Church of St Paul) has a Romanesque-Gothic portal and a Mudéjar coffered ceiling.

Turn right along Calle de San Pablo.

6 The Palacio de los Villalones (Palace of the Villalones) is a handsome Renaissance palace.

7 In contrast the Iglesia de San Andrés (Church of St Andrew) displays a flamboyant Gothic façade.

Go left into Calles Hnos López and Enrique Redel to reach the Palacio Viana.

8 The plain outside of the Palacio de los Marqués de Viana (Palace of

the Marquis of Viana) belies the interior delights of this palatial town house, whose earliest parts date from the 15th century. Fourteen plant-filled patios are surrounded by rooms in which one can still imagine the life of an aristocratic family. Furnishing and exhibits include Córdoban leatherwork, old ceramic tiles, arms, china and porcelain, fine carpets and a variety of art works.

Go into Calle Morales and Plaza de Santa Marina at the heart of the bullfighters' quarter of La Marina.

9 The Gothic Iglesia de Santa Marina (Church of St Marina) has three portals in the Fernandine style.

Go via Plaza Conde de Riego to Plaza de los Dolores.

10 Eight lamps (*faroles*) light the image of Cristo de los Faroles in one of the *Córdobeses*'s best-loved plazas.

Go along Calles Carbonell y Morand and right into Claudio Marcelo.

11 Plaza de la Tendillas, Córdoba's main commercial district, is to the north and west of here.

Calle Jesús María and a succession of signposted streets lead back to La Mezquita and the end of this walk.

Take a ride in a pony and trap to see the sights of Córdoba

MOTOR TOUR

From Córdoba it is 42km to Montilla along roads NIV and N331, passing the small towns of Fernán Nuñez and Montemayor.

Montilla
It is best to phone ahead to check about visiting one of the town's *bodegas*: Alvear (tel: 650100) is the biggest (see page 78).

About 8km on is Aguilar.

Aguilar
First settled by the Greeks, the town has an octagonal plaza and some notable churches, including the baroque one of its Carmelite convent.

Continue for 21km.

Lucena
Small factories and craft industries give this town a work-a-day air and you may want to do some craft shopping here (see page 78).

Head southeast for a further 21km on a minor road.

Rute
This white town of some 10,000 inhabitants nestles snugly in the foothills of mountains of the same name. It is best known for its many distilleries making aniseed liquors. The *ermitas* (hermitages) of Carmen and San Pedro (St Peter) hold images that are much revered locally.

Follow signs to Priego de Córdoba for a drive of 30km through highland landscapes. A longer route takes in the town of Iznajar, perched above a large reservoir.

Parque Natural de las Sierras Subbéticas de Córdoba
Comprising some 31,568 hectares across the three sierras of Rute, Cabra, and Horconera, this protected area is at the geographical heart of Andalucía. At 1,570m, the peak of La Tinosa is the highest in Córdoba province. Vegetation varies from evergreen oak, quejigos (an oak species), scrubland of broom, rosemary and thyme to reforested areas of pine and cultivated, or abandoned, olive and almond trees. It is the habitat of royal and partridge eagles, peregrine falcons and tawny vultures.

ALCAZAR DE LOS REYES CRISTIANOS

Built in the 14th century as a palace of the Christian kings, it was from here that the Catholic Monarchs planned their final assault on Granada. Here, too, Isabel finally gave Christopher Columbus her support for his first voyage. It has attractive water gardens, a display of Roman mosaics and wide views from its towers.

PUENTE ROMANO

The bridge has 16 arches and has been restored many times since its construction by Roman engineers. Halfway across the bridge, passers-by cross themselves at a figure of the Archangel Rafael, Córdoba's patron saint, who is also commemorated on the northern bank by the Triunfo de San Rafael column. Near by, the Puerta del Puente is a 16th-century gateway by the Córdoban architect Hernán Ruíz, who also worked on the cathedral. Downstream are the remains of three Arab mills.

TORRE DE LA CALAHORRA

Across the bridge is a 14th-century guard tower where a diorama show, wax figures and models depict the life and history of Arabs, Jews and Christians in Córdoba and *Al-Andalus.*

Nearby Las Ermitas (Hermitages) have a serene location in the Sierra de Córdoba, where you can take quiet meditative strolls and enjoy side views across the city and La Campiña, the Córdoban plain, beyond. Hermits have lived in these hills since the 4th century.

MEDINA AZAHARA

The splendour of the Córdoban caliphate can be peacefully contemplated among the ruins of a once-fabulous palace city on a hillside 8km west of Córdoba. Abderraman III ordered its construction in 936 and named it after his favourite wife, Zahra (flower). It took 10,000 men with 1,500 mules and 400 camels some 25 years to build the complex, which occupied 120 hectares. It could house 20,000 people and included a harem of 6,000 women and barracks for 12,000 bodyguards, with stables for 1,000 horses. Local hills supplied the marble for most of the complex's 4,000 columns but some came from as far away as Carthage. The palace-city was three-tiered: the top level contained the *alcázar* of the caliph and his retinue; on the middle level were administrative buildings; the mosque, gardens and market filled the lowest level. Medina Azahara's glory was shortlived. Berber mercenaries ransacked the complex in 1010 and through the centuries its treasures were pillaged and materials were taken to build elsewhere, including the Reales Alcázares in Sevilla.

Rediscovered in the last century, the site has seen some careful restoration work, which continues. An idea of its former glory is revealed in restored sections of the royal apartments.

Priego de Córdoba

Splendidly situated on a bluff, this town has a very rich endowment of fine architecture (see page 79).

Drive along the 24km of road to Cabra, re-entering the natural park.

Cabra

Next to the castle, a Christian reconstruction of the Moors' citadel, is the baroque Iglesia de la Asunción y Angeles (Church of the Ascension and Angels), built on the site of a mosque. With its steep, winding streets, the Cerro de San Juan district retains the feel of Moorish times. Another baroque church, San Juan Bautista (St John the Baptist) has Visigothic origins. La Fuente del Río is a beauty spot at the source of the Cabra River. From the Ermita de la Virgen de la Sierra (Hermitage of the Virgin of the Mountains) there are good views of the mountains.

Doña Mencia, Zuheros and Luque are three white villages, each with ruined Moorish fortifications, on the 25km route leading to the H432; Baena is 7km from the junction.

Baena

This is the main centre in Córdoba province for olive growing and processing. On top of its hill, crusted with white houses, is the 16th-century Iglesia de Santa María la Mayor (Church of St Mary). The churches of San Bartolomé (St Bartholomew), San Francisco (St Francis) and Madre de Dios (Mother of God) are also notable. At the convent of the latter, nuns sell their cakes. The town is

Torre de la Calahorra, Córdoba

famous for its Holy Week celebrations.

It is 55km to Córdoba past the towns of Castro del Río and Espejo with its towering castle owned by the Duke of Osuna, one of Andalucía's biggest landowners.

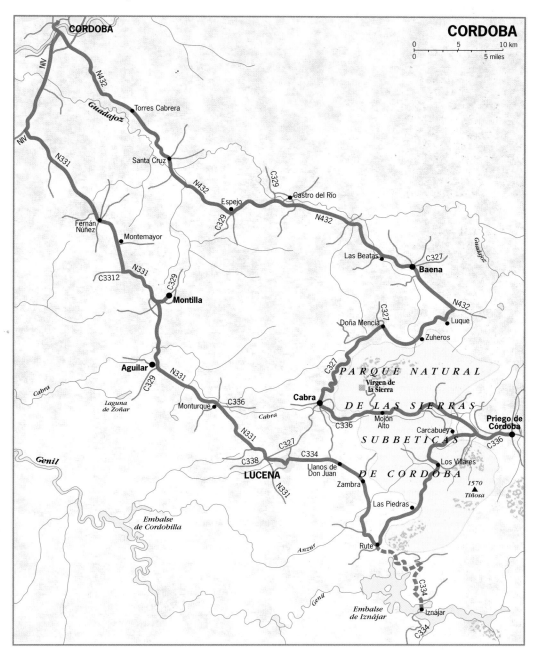

·JAEN·

It is a mistake of many visitors to Andalucía to exclude this provincial capital from their itineraries. One of many good reasons for visiting Jaén is to enjoy an overnight stay in a luxurious reconstruction of a Moorish *alcázar* (fortress) and to sample local dishes in its splendid dining-hall. Another very good reason for stopping over is to see the large and well-preserved Arab baths.

Silver-mining was the main attraction for Carthaginians and Romans, who built settlements at what the latter called *Auringis*. The Moors named their town *Geen*. In 1246 Ferdinand III of Castile captured the town, which became an important bastion in the last years of the Reconquest. The Castillo de Santa Catalina was extended during this time. Its nucleus has been restored and is open to visitors.

Modern Jaén (map ref: 108 C2) retains the feel of a market town serving its agricultural province and diversions are few. Among its industry is, appropriately, the production of four-wheel-drive vehicles and agricultural machinery.

Los Baños Arabes (the Arab baths) date from the 11th or 12th centuries and were probably later used by Christians until the 15th century. They were rediscovered in 1913, and the 14-year restoration, completed in 1984, gained an 'Our Europe' award from the organisation concerned with the protection of Europe's cultural heritage.

El Palacio de Villardompardo was built over the site of the Baños Arabes in the late 16th century for a viceroy of Peru. It has been beautifully restored and very well adapted for use as museum space. The Museo de Artes y Costumbres

Populares rates among the best-arranged museums of popular art. The Museo de Arte Naif (Museum of Naive Art) has ideally lit rooms on four floors, where walls are packed with works in this genre. La Magdalena, the quarter in which the Palacio de Villar-dompardo is located, has other notable buildings along its cobbled alleys. El Real Monasterio de Santo Domingo (The Royal Monastery of St Dominic) was built on Moorish palaces in the 15th century and has a very attractive patio. The tower of the Iglesia de San Juan (Church of St John) houses the city's official clock. La Iglesia de la Magdalena (Church of the Magdalen), built on a mosque and, probably, an earlier Roman structure, has a tower that is a modified minaret, a patio that was the mezquita's ablution area, and a main façade that is 15th-century Gothic.

The cathedral, which took over 300 years to complete, is best viewed from high ground to the south. It has Gothic and later elements, but is mostly a substantial example of the Renaissance style of the architect, Andrés de Vandelvira, who also designed many of the buildings in monumental Baeza and Ubeda. Among its treasures, but only to be seen in the Capilla Mayor on Fridays, the Santo Rostro relic is

claimed to be a veil which St Veronica used to wipe the face of Christ.

For history buffs The archaeo-logical section of the Museo Provincial has a collection of Iberian ceramics regarded as among the most notable in Spain. The 1920s buildings incorporates 16th-century elements in its façade and patio.

GITANOS

As elsewhere in Europe, Spain's gypsies live on the margin of society and are mostly immune to integration. Breaking out from their community and gaining acceptance in the mainstream often comes with the expression of some creative talent or fiery flair, and *gitanos* are among the leading professional exponents of flamenco and the *corrida* (bullfight). The claim by Spain's chief of national security that 70 per cent of the country's illicit drug distribution is through the hands of gypsies confirmed for many people their prejudice against a community that they consider idle, immoral and dependent on crime. Mancha Real in Jaén province has a history of racist action against gypsies, and in 1991 it flared again when houses of gypsy families were set alight. Under the protection of the Civil Guard the houses were restored by the Cruz Roja while non-gypsies jeered.

Castillo de Santa Catalina, which adjoins the Parador de Turismo

MOTOR TOUR

From Jaén follow signs to Córdoba and Torredonjimeno along the N321, and from the latter to Martos, 24km from Jaén.

Martos
Olive-growing and its subsidiary and supporting industries sustain Martos, which is claimed to be

Jaén cathedral façade

Spain's largest olive-production centre. The neat and prosperous-looking town is dominated by its twin-towered church and Castillo de Peña.

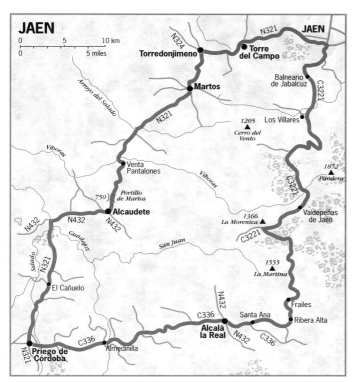

JAEN

0   5   10 km
0   5 miles

N324

Torredonjimeno

N321 Torre del Campo JAEN

Balneario de Jabalcuz

Martos

Arroyo del Salado

N321

1205 ▲ Cerro del Vento Los Villares

C3221

Víboras

Venta Pantalones

Víboras

1872 ▲ Pandera

C3221

N432 750) Portillo de Martos

N432 Alcaudete

1366 ▲ La Morenica Valdepeñas de Jaén

C3221

San Juan

Guadajoz

1555 ▲ La Martina

N321

El Cañuelo

Saladillo

N432

N432 Frailes

C336 Santa Ana Ribera Alta

Alcalá la Real

N432 C336

Priego de Córdoba C336 Almedinilla

N321

Continue on the same route for 24km to Alcaudete.

Alcaudete

Its castle dominates the town, whose Iglesia de San Pedro (Church of St Peter) and Convento de Santa Clara (Convent of St Clara) are examples of Mudéjar craftsmanship.

Take the N432, signposted Córdoba, before turning on to the N321 for Priego de Córdoba, a distance of 27km.

Priego de Córdoba

Splendidly situated on a bluff, this town, one of the region's little gems, with its dazzling white houses and tiny winding streets, has a very rich endowment of fine architecture (see page 79).

Go along the 336 road for 27km.

Alcalá la Real

The crown of Castile considered Alcalá as the key to Andalucía. Although its hill fortifications and main church are in ruins, this officially designated artistic and historic town is attractively maintained. Most notable are the main plaza, where there is an unusual lunar clock, the palaces of Abada and Tercia, and the old hospital in Calle Rosario.

Return to Jaén along minor roads via Frailes, Valdepeñas de Jaén and Olivillas, a distance of 74km.

LUCENA

MAP REF: 108 C2

During the period of the Córdoban caliphate, this was a Jewish town, virtually independent, which thrived as an important trading centre. The Iglesia de Santiago (Church of St James) is believed to occupy the site of the synagogue and Talmudic school. Persecution forced the Jewish population to flee to Toledo in the 12th century. Hebrew words are retained in the vocabulary of the town's potters and some of their designs also retain Roman and Moorish inspiration. Others among Lucena's many craftspeople work in copper, brass and bronze and in numerous factories on the outskirts where furniture is made.

Boabdil, the luckless last King of Granada, was captured here in 1483 and imprisoned in the town's Torre de Moral. Not far away at Iznajar, in 1861, landless peasants rose against the monarchy and landowners and proclaimed a republic in a revolt that was promptly and ruthlessly crushed.

MONTILLA

MAP REF: 108 C2

Montilla perches on two high points in rolling countryside where Julius Caesar routed the sons of Pompey, and which since the 8th century BC has yielded grapes for wine-making. La Escuchuela is a picturesque quarter through which to wander. Some handsome manorial houses line Montilla's streets. Among them is the Casa del Inca (House of the Inca), which was home in the 16th century to Garcilaso de la Vega, a writer of Spanish-Incan descent who informed Spaniards about the Incan Empire. There are a number of fine churches, including Santa Clara. Most visitors are attracted by a tour of one of Montilla's *bodegas*.

Near by, La Rambla has more than 50 ceramics workshops and a parish church with lavish Plateresque decoration.

MONTILLA-MORILES WINES

A local tale tells of a soldier, Pieter Siemens, who some time in the 16th or 17th century introduced vine stocks from the Rhine Valley. This variety became known as Pedro Ximénez, and is now the predominant grape grown in the vineyards within an area bordered by Lucena, Puente Genil, Fernán Núñez and Baena, which includes Montilla and Moriles, the two towns that give their name to the area's *Denominación de Origen* (DO). Previously the bulk of the area's wines went to Jerez de la Frontera for blending and onward sale as sherry. *Amontillado*, the name for a medium dry sherry, is derived from Montilla. *Fino*, the dry white wine that is the favourite tipple of *Córdobeses*, has an alcoholic strength of between 14 and 16 per cent, and unlike that of Jerez is not fortified by the adding of other alcohol. In contrast to Jerez, vinification takes place in large earthen-ware or cement containers, *tinajas*. Then, like Jerez, maturation takes place in oak barrels, using the *solera* system of blending, by which wine passes down from one barrel to another so that consistency of taste and quality is maintained. Alvear, founded in 1729 and among Spain's oldest *bodegas*, is the largest operation in Montilla and has some 21,000 *solera botas* containing close to 10 million litres of wine. This company has spearheaded the successful effort to get greater recognition for good traditional wines, which have long been in the shadow of sherries. In recent years, the DO of Montilla-Moriles has also used modern technology to produce light white wines, whose popularity is growing fast. Early September sees the lively celebration of a harvest festival.

Tinajas – **wine jars used in Montilla**

MONTORO

MAP REF: 108 C2

The sleepy white town sits on five hill crests above a bend in the Río Guadalquivir, which is crossed by a fine 16th-century bridge. This, like the Plateresque façade of the Ayuntamiento (town hall), once a palace of the Dukes of Alba, and that of the Iglesia de San Bartolomeo (Church of St Bartholomew), is a reminder of an importance long since gone. **Nearby** At Pedro Abad, the construction of the first mosque to be founded in Spain since Moorish times was begun in 1980, with funds contributed by Britain's Ahmadiyya community.

PALMA DEL RIO

MAP REF: 108 B2

In an area of citrus groves close to where the Río Guadalquivir enters Sevilla province, and with remains of fortifications raised by the Almohades, this is a prosperous-looking town that glories in being the birthplace of the waif, Manuel Benitez, who illicitly perfected his skills against the area's famed fighting bulls and went on to become the millionaire matador, El Cordobés.

Lucena's Jewish past has been overlaid by Christian culture

PRIEGO DE CORDOBA

MAP REF: 108 C2

Priego's people are justly very proud of their town. It ranks among the most beautiful in Andalucía and in the whole of Spain. Its situation, too, is both delightful and impressive. La Tinosa peak, snow-capped in winter, rises behind the town above the Río Salado, with commanding views over folds of hills and valleys in which Priego's cluster of many hamlets lie.

Some 14,000 people live in the town and another 10,000 occupy the hamlets and scattered houses. Areas not studded with olive trees produce cereals, vegetables and fruits, among which apples are the main crop.

A few clothing factories retain the area's textile tradition. It was the town's flourishing silk industry in the 18th century that gave it the wealth to raise the many fine buildings with which it is adorned today. The town's fortunes were also helped by a propitious union in 1711 between the Fernández de Córdoba family, the Marquesado de Priego, and Spain's rich and influential House of Medinaceli.

Priego was an 'in' place for the gentry and aristocrats to build palaces to join those of silk merchants. These fine folk ordered the construction of churches in which the munificence of their bequests would not be forgotten. Jobs were plentiful for the most accomplished sculptors, carvers and gilders in Priego's baroque outburst. Francisco Javier Pedrajas was responsible for much of the most outstanding work.

To him is attributed the extravagant ornamentation in the Iglesia de la Asunción's (Church of the Assumption's) Capilla del Sagrario, which has been declared a national monument. He was also responsible for the heavily styled and multi-coloured marble entrance to the Iglesia de la Aurora (Church of the Dawn) and for the conversion into baroque style of the Iglesia de San Francisco (Church of St Francis), which had previously been an austere convent. In these and other churches – San Pedro (St Peter), San Juan de Dios (St John of God), las Angustias del Carmen and las Mercedes – the interiors drip with baroque decoration and also retain artistic riches from earlier times. Priego's pride includes two fountains, which have also been honoured as national monuments:

La Fuente del Rey (Fountain of the King) has three levels, some 130 spouts and a sculpture depicting Neptune and Anfitrite on a horse chariot; La Fuente de la Salud (Fountain of Health) has a small sculpture of the Virgen de la Cabeza.

Along Calle Río are a number of noble mansions displaying well-crafted ironwork, and houses from around the turn of the century. Niceto Alcalá Zamora, who in 1931 became President of Spain's Second Republic, was born at no 33.

The Alcazaba (fortress) survives fairly intact from when this was the Moorish stronghold of Medina Bagu. Strongly evocative, too, of those days, and one of the prettiest places imaginable, is the Barrio de la Villa where narrow, sinuous lanes are lined with spotlessly kept and flower-bedecked small houses. A commanding view of the surrounding countryside is seen from the Paseo Adarve. The Carnicerias Reales (Royal Butchery) is a 16th-century Mannerist building used as a local museum.

Beautiful Priego de Córdoba, one of the gems of Andalucía

•UBEDA•

Many an unknowing traveller in search of Andalucía's famed tourist attractions must have flashed past Ubeda, unaware of missing a place that rates inclusion among the region's top 'sights'. From the N322 highway the town presents an unattractive aspect of modern sprawl, which gives no hint of the splendid assembly of Renaissance architecture and other styles that constitute its core. The Parador del Turismo is a converted palace facing a plaza that is the town's glorious centrepiece.

The Moors surrendered their *Obdah* to Ferdinand *el Santo* in 1234, and some of his Castilian nobles began building residences in the town. As in Baeza, feuding among their descendants caused Queen Isabel to order the demolition of the town's fortifications in 1506. Francisco de los Cobos was born in Ubeda (map ref: 109 D2) in 1477, and while serving Charles V as secretary of state for 20 years amassed great fortune and influence. His nephew, Juan Vázquez de Molina, subsequently became secretary to Philip II. Their patronage of their home town was generous, and the architect Andrés de Vandelvira (1509-75) was largely responsible for its execution. He was influenced by the Italians and specialised in making Renaissance architecture more monumental and less superficially decorative.

An exploration of Ubeda should start in the Plaza de Vázquez de Molina, a monumental set piece. The Capilla del Salvador (Chapel of the Saviour), intended as the family pantheon, was part of a palace ordered by Francisco de los Cobos, since destroyed by fire.

Plaza de Vázquez de Molina, Ubeda's magnificent heart

Designed by Diego de Siloé and finished off by Vandelvira, with contributions from the French sculptor Esteban Jamete, it is one of the most outstanding examples of Spanish Renaissance architecture. Be sure to see also the portal on the southern façade. Adjoining the chapel, the Hospital de Honrados Viejos del Salvador was the retirement home for ex-priests and has an especially fine-looking patio. The palace of the first chaplain of San Salvador has a severe front, but its portal hides a delicate patio. In high-ceilinged rooms visitors can pass the night

as guests of the Parador del Turismo, which was opened here in 1930. Waking to a view of the honey-coloured plaza is unforgettable. On the same side of the plaza as the Parador is Vandelvira's Palacio de las Cadenas (Palace of the Cadenas) with the coat-of-arms of Juan Vázquez de Molina above the doorway. Classical styles are layered – Corinthian at the bottom, Ionic next and caryatids along the top. It now serves as Ubeda's Ayuntamiento (town hall), and many a large city must envy so fine a building. Opposite, the Iglesia de Santa María de los Reales Alcázares (Church of St Mary) is mainly 17th-century with 18th-century bell-towers, but its Gothic cloister incorporates the patio of a mosque. Adjoining, the Cárcel del Obispo (Bishop's Prison) is from the 16th century and now serves as the Palace of Justice. The Palacio de Marqués de Mancera (Palace of the Marquess of Mancera), a typical private palace from Ubeda's golden days, is now a convent. Completing the plaza is the Pósito, originally the communal granary.

The joy of walking through Ubeda's old centre is that around almost every corner another architectural delight awaits, and much of it is to be found in small elements and detailed work. The following are among places not to be missed: on the Plaza del Primero de Mayo, the Antiguo Ayuntamiento (old town hall) clearly shows Italian influence with its loggia and gallery; the Iglesia de San Pablo (Church of St Paul) is mainly of late-Gothic style, to which Vandelvira added Renaissance elements, and its original west wall shows the transitional Romanesque style; a memorial to San Juan de la Cruz (1542-91) stands in the plaza. Near by is the Oratorio bearing his name and a small museum with

OLIVES AND THEIR OIL

Greeks first introduced olives to the region; Romans planted large areas north of the Río Guadalquivir with olive trees; the Moors greatly enlarged the area of planting and, by terracing, extended it up unused hillsides. *Olivo* (the tree) and *olivar* (olive grove) are words derived from Latin. *Aceituna* (the fruit) and *aceite* (oil, in general) are derived from Arabic. Olive oil is *aceite de oliva* and Andalucía produces around 20 per cent of the world's total.

Jaén province is the biggest producer within the region, and with Córdoba province it shares the honour of having one of Spain's four *denominación de origen* areas, where consistent production of the best quality virgin oils is strictly controlled: the Sierra de Segura area in Jaén and the area of Baena in Córdoba. Virgin oil is from the first pressing and the best of it, 'extra virgin' or 'fine virgin', is from fruit milled immediately after being picked ripe. A tree is at its most productive between seven and 60 years, and an average yield is around 30kg per tree. The picking season of two months starts in December and, although mechanical vibrators are now used to shake fruit off the tree, harvesting and the rest of the oil-making process is very labour-intensive, which explains the product's relatively high price. At the *almazara* (mill) the olives are washed, then crushed by heavy wheels to leave a pulp, which is laid upon *capachos* (mats, traditionally of esparto grass). These are layered into a press where they are squeezed to release the oil, which is then filtered. The pulp may be pressed up to three times.

Nutritional science confirms what Andalucíans and other Mediterranean people have always known: using olive oil in cooking is better for health than using other vegetable or any animal fats. A liberal consumption of garlic is also scientifically proven to be beneficial to health. Memorial stones in the region's cemeteries show that many Andalucians live to a very ripe age.

relics and personal objects of the mystic and writer. The Palacio de Vela de los Cobos, another work by Vandelvira, features a corner balcony with a small white marble column and a delicate upper gallery. Plateresque decoration of the most elaborate confection covers the front of the Casa de las Torres (Tower House). What is considered to be Vandelvira's supreme work, and perhaps the finest expression of Renaissance architecture in Andalucía lies away from the old city centre. Diego de los Cobos y Molina, a Bishop of Jaén, ordered the construction of the Hospital de Santiago (Hospital of St James) in his home town and little was spared to make it a magnificent building. The combined beauty of the façade, patio, staircase and chapel leave an indelible mark in the memory.

On the opposite side of the town, beyond the Puerta del Losal, a remnant of the medieval fortifications, Calle de Valencia has many of the workshops making Ubeda's acclaimed pottery and esparto grass-work, and which carry on a tradition for which the town was also well known in Moorish times.

GRANADA AND ALMERIA

Andalucía's two eastern provinces have 24 per cent of the region's land area: Granada with 12,531sq km and Almería with 8,774sq km. Of their total population of some 1.2 million, around 33 per cent live in the two capital cities. Almería has a slightly lower population density than Granada.

Travellers through these provinces will not complain about a lack of geographical variety. The provinces share the eastern part of Andalucía's Mediterranean coastline and each has mountain ranges and narrow valleys within the Sistema Penibética as significant topographical features. Neither province has a major river, but each has smaller watercourses that feed intensively farmed valleys. The Vega de Granada, one of Spain's richest agricultural areas, has a higher average annual rainfall than the south of England; by contrast, during most years there is hardly any rain in the Parque Natural del Desierto de Tabernas of Almería province.

Among the coastal hills of Granada province there are valleys lush with tropical fruit trees; in parts of Almería province even the most drought-resistant vegetation struggles for survival. *Plasti-cultura* (farming under plastic) has had a boom time in Almería and the sea of plastic has spread across the eastern part of Granada's coastal plain.

Summer resorts in Almería province have been developed to meet the demands of Europe's package holiday industry; those along the much shorter coastal stretch of Granada province rely more on Spanish holidaymakers. Mojácar in Almería and Almuñécar in Granada have sizeable communities of foreign residents.

In winter, while people are basking in the sun along the seashore, others are also enjoying the sun and having fun in the snow at Europe's most southerly winter sports resort, just 40km inland below the high peaks of Granada's Sierra Nevada.

During the Bronze Age, Almería was an important mining area where lead, copper and silver ores could be easily extracted, and the latter was found in its pure state. Successive civilisations were attracted by the area's mineral wealth and mining of iron, lead, lignite and zinc remains of significance to the province's economy. Extraction of marble is another important economic activity and exports go as far as Japan.

The fishing industry, traditionally significant, has been hit by declining yields from the Mediterranean. Grapes, sugar cane, beetroot, olives, almonds, oranges, cereals, cotton and esparto grass are the province's principal crops, apart from the wide variety that is intensively grown under plastic. *Plasticultura* and mass tourism were the two factors that, during the 1970s, breathed life into the backward economy of the province.

Among Spaniards, Almería had

Trevélez in the Sierra Nevada claims to be the highest village in Europe

always been considered as 'that place down there' – arid, harsh and forsaken; all right for filming 'spaghetti westerns' or epics like *Lawrence of Arabia*, but for nothing else. More recently, however, the sun, which shone so fiercely for so many days, ceased to be the eternal curse of this isolated province. It could tan the skins of fortnightly waves of European sunseekers and it could give the light and heat to produce three crops a year of salads, vegetables, flowers and fruits for European kitchens. Here could be the 'California of Europe'; or is it to be 'Florida'?

Europe's space-shuttle project, HERMES, foresees Almería province as its home base. One of the world's most important experimental stations for solar energy is located in the province. Unpolluted air and skies that are clear on more than 200 nights a year were reasons for Germany's Max Plank Institute to site an advanced observatory high in the Sierra de los Filabres.

High technology and the future may have arrived in Almería province, but it is still easy to find communities where little has changed or to stray and come across almost absolutely nothing but one's own sharp shadow.

The largest Moorish fortress in Andalucía dominates the skyline of the port of Almería, which is delightfully provincial and gently paced. West of the city are the resorts of Aguadulce, Roquetas de Mar and up-market Almerimar, as well as the plastic-covered Campo de Dalias, which lies below the gaunt Sierra de Gádor. East of the city, the Parque Natural de Sierra de Cabo de Gata-Nijar is a preciously protected area of stunning beauty along its shores and across barren landscapes moulded by volcanic activity. Further along the east coast, beyond Carboneras with its ugly power station and cement works on the beach, is the resort area comprising Mojácar, Garrucha and

Playas de Vera. Northwest of Almería city, the citrus-covered valley of the Río Andaraz runs into the Parque Natural de Sierra Nevada, which includes Almería's portion of Las Alpujarras.

North of the city are the desertlands of Tabernas, and beyond the stark Sierra de los Filabres is the intensively farmed Valle de Almanzora. On the borders with the region of Murcia and abutting the Parque Natural de Sierra María are the two monumental small towns of Vélez Rubio and Vélez Blanco.

Granada needs less introduction. It has for long had a place in the popular consciousness of Spaniards. This was the last domain of the Moors in the Peninsula, and its Christian conquerors, the royal duo of Ferdinand and Isabel, through whom Spain was united, honoured the city as their burial place. The Moors bequeathed it their filigreed fantasy of the Alhambra, known far and wide as one of the world's most beautiful buildings. Through the centuries, writers have lauded the city, its Alhambra and its abundantly productive Vega. From the 20th century comes the deeply evocative poetry of Federico García Lorca, born in Fuentevaqueros, 20km from Granada.

Granada is Andalucía's 'brain factory', for it has Spain's third-biggest university, to which students come from all over the country and beyond. The university gets a very large slice of the region's budget for research,

and work on microbacteria and molecular genetics are significant areas in which it is applied.

Granada is among the most favoured places for foreigners wanting to learn the Spanish language and to participate in a wide variety of summer courses. In the city's streets there is always a parade of serious-browed foreigners and a babble of different tongues.

On the south side of the Sierra Nevada, which soars above the

The Moors' love of gardens seems to be reflected in this street with its floral cascades

city, Las Alpujarras is an area of stunning scenery and time-trapped hamlets. Further south, the Costa Tropical is both a holiday paradise and an intensively farmed area. West of the city stretch the rich farmlands of Granada's Vega. Northeast of Granada, Guadix is best known for its many cave-dwellings.

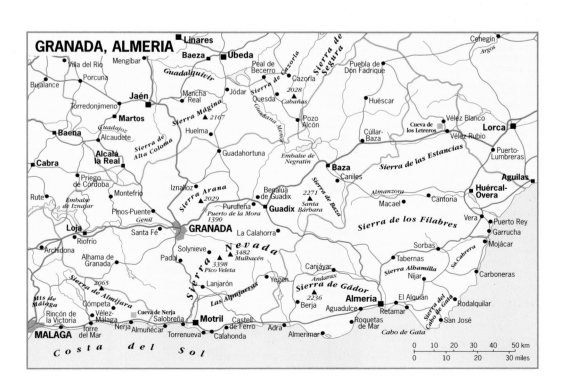

•ALMERIA•

Almería city enjoys a fine location at the centre of its wide *golfo* (gulf), defined by Punta Sabinal in the west and Cabo de Gata in the east. The very mild winter climate is secured by the Sierra de Gádor and Sierra Alhamilla behind the city, which protect it from cold continental winds. The Río Andarax, whose surface is usually dry, passes between the two mountain ranges and enters the Mediterranean on the city's eastern edge.

In the 10th century, the Moors rejected earlier Iberian and Roman settlements near by, and gave birth to Al-Mariyat by building a port at the mouth of the Río Andarax. When the Cordoban caliphate collapsed in 1031, Almería (map ref: 109 D1) became capital of a separate *taifa* (kingdom) for a time. Its population grew to some 300,000, a silk-weaving industry gained fame far and wide, ship-building was an important activity and so, too, was piracy. Following the Christian conquest of Almería in 1489, its fortunes steadily declined and in the 17th century the population was down to around 500. The opening of a railway in 1899 and growth of the province's mining industry, followed also by successful cultivation of eating grapes, revitalised the economy. Parts of the city destroyed during the Civil War by the shells of a German naval squadron were rebuilt without much style. Today's population of around 150,000 is engaged in a mixed economy, in which tourism and farming under plastic in adjacent areas are leading elements. Essentially, the city itself is a sedately provincial one, and it makes little concession to foreign tourism in its hotels and catering. In that lies much of its charm.

The extensive port area fronting the city is busy with cargo ships, ferries to North Africa and a fair-sized fishing fleet. It is an interesting place to stroll and to take in good views of the city and La Alcazaba, Andalucía's largest Moorish fortress. An attractive park is planned to cover the dry river-bed of La Rambla de Belén, to the east of which is the more modern district. Shops and pavement cafés line the shady Paseo de Almería, which runs north to Puerta de Purchena at the centre of the commercial district. Southwest of the Puerta and once within the city walls, La Almedina is the most attractive district with narrow streets, picturesque corners and monumental buildings. Below La Alcazaba is the quarter of La Chanca, where brightly coloured houses and cave-dwellings are homes of the fishing community and gypsies. Its Monday *mercadillo* (street market) is a noisy and colourful affair.

La Alcazaba dominates the city from its ridge on the western edge. Abderraman III ordered its construction in the 10th century and successive rulers enlarged the fortress so that it could house 20,000 people and include a palace, a mosque, reservoirs and decorative gardens. A third area was added by the Catholic Monarchs and it is the best-preserved part within the extensive sandstone ramparts on which restoration work began in the 1950s. In the 16th century, two earthquakes wrecked much of the fortress and from around 1800 it was abandoned. Gardens, scrubland and ruined stonework now lie within the well-restored ramparts, which are good viewpoints across the city and its surroundings. Near by, Cerro de San Cristóbal is an even better *mirador* (viewpoint).

For history buffs Almería's Museo Arqueológico (Archaeological Museum), located in the modern district, has an underrated assembly of exhibits dating from the Bronze Age to the Moorish period. Luis Sert, a Belgian miner and archaeologist, assembled much of this worthy collection.

Back to nature At the Centro de Rescate de la Fauna Sahariana in La Hoya, beyond and below La Alcazaba, endangered Saharan species like antelopes, foxes and vultures are being sheltered and studied. Enquire at the Tourist Office about visits.

Nearby East of the city, El Alquian is famed locally for its simple places serving fresh fish; Costacabana and Retamar are small-scale seaside residential developments; beyond lies Cabo de Gata (see pages 90-1). It is from the highly developed resort zones of Aguadulce and Roquetas de Mar, west of Almería, that most of the city's tourists come on day trips.

Massive walls of Almería's Moorish fortress, the Alcazaba

TOWN WALK

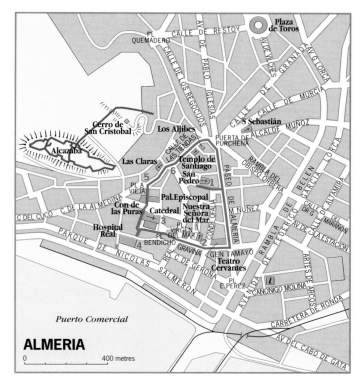

ALMERIA

0   400 metres

Puerto Comercial

Start from Puerta de Purchena and go along Paseo de Almería. A short detour along Calle Ricardos takes you to Plaza San Pedro and its church.

1 The construction of the Iglesia de San Pedro (Church of St Peter) on the site of a mosque was ordered by Ferdinand and Isabel, the Catholic Monarchs; destroyed by the earthquake of 1790, it has been well restored.

Return to Paseo de Almería and go along as far as the Teatro Cervantes, then right into Calle General Tamayo to reach Plaza de la Virgen del Mar.

2 The restored 18th-century Basilica de Nuestra Señora del Mar (Basilica of Our Lady of the Sea) is the sanctuary for an image of the Virgen del Mar, the city's patroness, apparently found on a beach in 1502.

Leave by Calle Gravina into the alleys of Solis and Cisneros to Plaza Bendicho, to be confronted by the mass of the cathedral.

3 Designed to be both a church and fortress, from the outside the cathedral looks much more like the latter, with tall windowless walls, embrasures and battlements. After the earthquake of 1522 had destroyed the principal church, Diego de Siloé was commissioned to design a replacement that could also be a place of refuge when Turkish and Berber raiders were threatening the population. The building was completed early in the 17th century. Inside, the predominant style is late-Gothic, although Plateresque decoration had by then been more widely adopted elsewhere. The most

notable features are the choir-stalls of carved walnut, paintings by Alonso Cano, a gold reredos depicting the life of Mary, a sculpture of San Indalecio, patron saint of the city, and a stained-glass window with another image of the saint.

From the cathedral take the alley of Duende to reach the old Hospital Real (Royal Hospital).

4 An 18th-century neoclassical front distinguishes this building.

Make your way back to the cathedral and neighbouring Convento de las Puras to enter La Plaza Admón Vieja.

5 Also known as Plaza de la Constitución, this porticoed square is among the city's most attractive sights.

From here you can make an uphill detour westwards to La Alcazaba. (It is advisable not to walk alone in this area.) Northeast of the plaza and past the 17th-century Iglesia de las Claras you enter Calle de las Tiendas (the Street of Shops).

6 This is one of the city's oldest and most characterful streets. Radiating from it are other pedestrianised shopping streets worth exploring. On the right are the 16th-century Templo de Santiago (Temple of St James) and Los Aljibes, water cisterns dating from the 11th century.

Ahead is Puerta de Purchena and the end of the walk.

The busy city and port of Almería at the foot of the ridge which bears the Alcazaba

ALMUÑECAR

MAP REF: 108 C1

Three necropolises have yielded evidence of the Phoenician and Punic settlement named *Sexi*. The Romans expanded its fishing and salting industry and an area of *salazones* (salting pits) has been preserved. So have channels and aqueducts which supplied the *salazones* with fresh water. A bronze statue commemorates the landing here in 755 of a survivor of the deposed Umayyad dynasty in Damascus who was to become Abderraman I, the first Emir of Córdoba. Moors strengthened the Roman fortifications and improved agriculture in the fertile valleys.

Today those valleys, as well as terraced hillsides, are yielding abundant crops of tropical fruits – avocados, chirimoyas, nisperos, mangoes and papayas. A profusion of exotic palms gives shade on the town's promenades, streets and squares, and a botanical garden displays some 400 varieties of subtropical plants.

Almuñecar is the showpiece of Granada's Costa Tropical, and nowhere else in mainland Europe will the traveller feel more like being in the tropics.

A picturesque old town huddles below castle ruins. Apartment blocks, mostly holiday homes for Spaniards, line three long beach fronts, and other beaches nestle in coves. Developments of villas, many of which are foreign-owned, are spread through the large municipal area, which includes the unspoilt satellite village and resort of La Herradura on a handsome horseshoe bay, as well as Marina del Este, Andalucía's prettiest pleasure port.

Farmhouse in the Alpujarras with an enviable view

ALPUJARRAS, LAS

MAP REF: 109 D1

Tightly folded landscapes of steep slopes and deep valleys extend for some 65km between the southern slopes of the high Sierra Nevada and the coastal ranges of the Sierra de Lújar, Contraviesa and Gádor: like a crumpled piece of cloth, a topography more African than Spanish has been embroidered here. During the period of the Nasrid kingdom of Granada, silk production and weaving gave wealth to the wild mountain region of Alpujarras, and within this natural bastion a large community of Moslems, although nominally *moriscos* (converts to Christianity), maintained their traditions long after their loss of Granada.

When in 1568 the use of Arabic and the practice of their customs was banned, they responded by crowning their own king, Aben Humeya, and rising in a revolt which spread beyond Las Alpujarras. Crushed by greater forces, some 50,000 *moriscos* were expelled from Las Alpujarras, which was resettled by people from Galicia, Extremadura and Castile who did not cope well with the new terrain, climate, crops and irrigation systems. Those systems are still in use today by peasants engaged in subsistence farming on small, scattered plots, where they work with old-fashioned tools and methods. They are among those with the lowest per capita income within Andalucía, illiteracy is at Third-World levels, a very high proportion of the younger generation emigrates and desertification threatens in parts. It is tempting to sell houses and plots to escapist foreigners or property speculators.

On the slopes of the Alpujarras. Many Moors fled to the region after the Reconquest

'THE HAIRY ONES'

Los peludos are what *Alpujarreños* call newcomers. An early arrival was Gerald Brenan, who dropped out of Britain after World War I and set up home in the isolated village of Yegen, where members of the Bloomsbury set visited him. He subsequently wrote *South from Granada*, which is regarded by some as essential reading about Las Alpujarras. In the 1970s, long-haired and brightly clothed foreigners began seeking an earthly paradise in Las Alpujarras; their care-not ways showed little respect for an adopted environment. Other newcomers are more thoughtful, and among them are creative people, some of whom have become active in reviving traditional crafts.

Not showing much hair are the Buddhist monks of O-Sel-Ling, 'The Place of Light', a meditation centre near Portqueira, which the Dalai Lama inaugurated in 1982. Five years later, Osel, son of two of the retreat's founder members, was widely proclaimed within the international Buddhist community as the reincarnation of a Tibetan lama.

Solitude and meditation is not on the minds of 'yuppies' and trendsetters, for whom Las Alpujarras is a weekend alternative to their fashionable haunts in Madrid and other cities.

MOTOR TOUR

This tour takes in the heart of the Granadian Alpujarras, where the scenery is the most stunning and the villages are the prettiest. Fill up your tank – the only petrol stations are at Lanjarón, Orjiva and Cádiar – and drive with special care on the narrow roads.

Lanjarón
The gateway to Las Alpujarras is known throughout Spain because of its bottled mineral water. Around 400,000 litres of purified water from some 40 springs, fed by the Sierra Nevada's snows, are bottled daily. Spa facilities operate between May and October.

Turn left just before Orjiva and soon the folding landscapes are in view on the right.

Pampaneira, Bubión and Capileira
Stepped up the side of the Pampaneira valley, with the high peaks of Veleta and Mulhacén as a backdrop, this trio of villages receives most visitors, and a sign at Pampaneira exhorts travellers to 'stay and live with us'. Many have, and also at Bubión, the middle village, and Capileira, the highest of the three at 1,436m above sea level. Houses have been turned into craft shops, art galleries, eating places or smart nightspots, and at Capileira one house has become a small museum. The Villa Turística at Bubión has modern, self-catering accommodation.

Continue from Pampaneira above the valley of the Río Trevélez, past productive patches of farmland and through evergreen groves. Just beyond Portugos, the Fuente Agria spouts water very rich in iron.

Trevélez
The village, itself situated at over 1,560m, has a claim to being Spain's highest municipal area. Another claim is to having the perfect conditions for curing *jamón serrano*, and hams are trucked in from other parts to earn the pricier Trevélez tag.

Along the road at Juviles, Muley Hacen, a king of Granada after whom the peak is named, hid three black diamonds and, so the story goes, whoever discovers them will be crowned king or queen of Granada. The road rises to Berchules and then drops to Cádiar where in December 1568 Aben Humeya was proclaimed king of the moriscos. The road skirts the arid slopes of the

A display of wickerwork in Almuñécar's market

coastal range above the valley of the Río Guadalfeo and past sleepy Torvizcon. Return to Lanjarón via Orjiva.

CYCLING, HIKING AND HORSE-RIDING

This is a delightful area in which to get around in more energetic ways. The motor tour route is also a popular circuit for cyclists undeterred by hill climbs. Hikers will find that on the northern side villages are not far apart and, in addition to road connections, they are linked by shady paths used by peasants and their animals. From Capileira there are organised horse-back excursions of different durations. Simple *fondas* (inns) have cheap accommodation and there is a camping site at Trevélez.

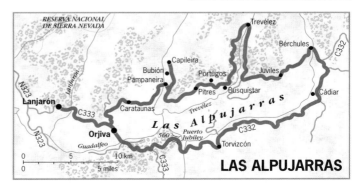

LAS ALPUJARRAS

POPULAR ARCHITECTURE

As with much else about Andalucía, there are stereotyped images of the region's popular architecture, which in turn has given an image of 'typical' Spanish architecture. In reality, there is a diversity that reflects the adaptation to the region's variety of geography and climate. The imprint of the long Arab presence in the region is strongly seen in much popular architecture.

Roman domestic architecture had centred on the atrium, and Arabs perfected the patio as the private place for the conduct of family life. Use of lime is another linking feature, and its widespread application in fairly recent times was both for reasons of hygiene and to reflect the sun and thereby keep dwellings cooler. Sometimes a different colour is highlighted as a decorative feature. Everywhere, colour is added by a profusion of ceramic pots, flowers and creepers. Wrought-iron work in *balcones* (balconies), *rejas* (window grilles) and *cancelas* (door grilles) are attractive additions to many less humble buildings. *Azoteas* (flat roofs) contrast with sloping ones covered in reddish-brown pantiles.

Potted flowers transform a simple balcony into a garden

96

Village *calles* (streets) are narrow so that the sun's rays do not touch the cobbles, and many *plazas* (squares) are arcaded or tree-lined to offer more shade. Small street altars, other religious motifs, fountains, communal washing troughs, ceramic tiles with street names or commemorative tiles and statues of local figures are other decorative features of villages.

There is a distinctive Berber look to the hamlets and villages of Las Alpujarras that mostly cling to south-facing slopes. Flat roofs are made with *launa*, a clay formed from the decomposition of slate, and the roof of one house may be a terrace for the house above. Smoke twirls up from short, cone-shaped chimneys. Houses' upper floors have verandas with wooden balconies, and are often connected across narrow alleyways, giving more shade and an attractive,

disordered shape to a village's layout. Produce from surrounding terraces and fields left out to dry on roofs and balconies add splashes of colour. Cows or pigs are kept on the ground floor. Slate decorates cornices and solid stone walls are whitewashed. The same flat roof and basic cube shape of these dwellings is also seen in the houses of Almería's desert and coastal regions.

Andalucía has some 10,000 cave-dwellings and over 90 per cent of them are in Granada and Almería provinces – in the vale of Guadix, the plateaux of Baza and Huéscar and the Almerian valleys of Andarax and Almanzora. Here, there is impermeable ground in hillsides or hillocks that is easy to excavate, and the climate is dry with big temperature variations between day and night and from one season to another. Inside the dwellings, the temperature remains even and they require little heating in winter. Usually they are built around one square room. Adding a room takes less than a week, and is relatively inexpensive. Ventilation and lighting are given by skylights. Above the caves, television aerials sprout from the earth next to whitewashed chimneys. A small, fenced area, *la placeta*, is defined in front of a lime-washed façade, which contrasts with the ochre-coloured earth. As with other properties, owners of cave homes have property deeds, and they are provided with electricity, water, sanitation and road services. Contrary to popular belief, it is not only gypsies who live in caves.

Andalucían elements mix with those of Castile in the popular architecture of the Sierras de Cazorla y Segura of Jaén province. Steep streets are lined with houses, sometimes of three storeys, on which stonework may be featured among the whitewash. Because of the harsh winter climate, chimneys are plentiful, door and window openings are few and small, and the tiled roofs are more steeply pitched to allow snow to slide off. Large drying-rooms at the top of houses are a characteristic feature. Villages in the Los Pedroches area of Córdoba province also show influences from Castile, like impressively solid woodwork, large granite stones used as jambs and lintels, and silver or white-painted window grilles. Long, narrow chimneys emerge from double-pitch gables.

In the Sierra de Aracena of Huelva province, aspects from Extremadura are included in the popular architecture and, as in adjoining Sevilla province, there is widespread use of box-windows with sills, grilles and upper dust ledges. Characteristic, too, are wide upper verandas and ensembles of double and single pitched roofs with overhanging eaves, which descend as far as common walls and create semi-enclosed areas for each house.

In Huelva's Parque National Coto Doñana are examples of very different folk dwellings, which hark back to Neolithic times. A rectangular pine frame is fitted with fine rush matting to create side walls, and they have a double pitched roof. Two such *chozas* (shanties) – one as the kitchen and living space, the other as bedrooms – make up the home and a third may house animals. During warm months, most of the activity takes place under the shade of a trellised area. A hedge, often of heather, encloses a family's domain within a collection of others, which comprise the *rancho* (village). Such primitive structures are also found in other parts of Andalucía, where they are used by shepherds or for keeping livestock or storing farm equipment.

In areas of Andalucía, like Las Campiñas of Sevilla and Córdoba, where the Mediterranean trio of wheat, vine and olive flourishes, Romans created large farming estates managed from an extensive villa. The formula remains in today's *latifundios* (large estates) where spreading *haciendas* or *cortijos* (farmhouses) retain features from the Roman villa, like a central courtyard, a big hall and attic areas. The main entrance is a large gateway, sometimes topped by a bell-tower; studded doorways, boxed and grilled windows embellish the large façade, topped by pantiled roofs. In some places, stark whitewashed walls are relieved by soft colours along the foundations, on cornices and around windows; sometimes the whole façade is painted. Adjacent working buildings like *lagares* (press houses) are no less handsome. The humble house of a peasant is usually a narrow whitewashed building with small openings for doors and windows and a single-slope pantiled roof. A vine or flowering creeper covers a trellised area for summer living. A dome-topped oven and, sometimes, a simple well are conveniently close by.

It is, perhaps, in *Los Pueblos Blancos* (the White Villages) of Cádiz and Málaga provinces that the stereotyped idea of Andalucía's folk architecture is most a reality. Here as elsewhere, it is the spectacular placing of an urban ensemble in a stunning landscape that creates a harmony of breathtaking beauty.

Sloping pantiled roofs over white-walled houses form a harmonious assemblage

remaining clumps of the once-widespread 'jujube' trees.

As it is a stopping-off point for migratory birds where some 150 species of birdlife have been identified, the area is also a favourite place for birdwatchers. Among those they watch for are trumpeter finch, Dupont lark, partridge eagle, avocet and stork. Flocks of up to 2,000 flamingos gather in the salterns. Salt extraction, fishing and the gathering of aromatic herbs and heart of palm, as well as the development of small-scale tourism, are the area's main economic activities.

Brightly painted fishing boats lie on the long beach at the simple village of Cabo de Gata, and saltpans, the other source of income, are near by. Across the mountains, San José lines a horseshoe bay and has low-key residential and tourist development, which includes a sports port. Near by are delightful beaches of fine sand and shallow, clear water: Playa Genoveses is long, wide and backed by pine and eucalyptus trees and has a campsite; Playa Monsul has four cosy coves.

At Rodalquilar there are ruins of buildings from the time when this was a gold-mining centre. La Isleta de Arráez, Las Negras and Agua Amarga are simple seaside villages living off fishing and their basic amenities, including delightful beaches, which satisfy escapist holidaymakers.

FOR WALKERS AND CYCLISTS

In the villages of San José, Las Negras and Agua Amarga, information centres can provide details on the park's flora, fauna and amenities and suggested routes for walks, including some through parts where walkers must remain on marked paths.

From Almería, a one-day circuit

A sunlit corner of Berja, at the foot of the Sierra de Gádor

BAZA
MAP REF: 109 D2

Below its mountain and facing its *boya* (plain), which spreads to the large expanse of the Necratin reservoir, Baza is now skirted by Autovia '92, but is worth stopping at to catch the flavour of an agricultural and market town untouched by tourism. A Moorish air persists in the quarters of Santiago (St James) and San Juan (St John). Renaissance is the style in the churches of Santa María (St Mary) and Santiago, in the Enriquez Palace and in the Caños Dorados fountain. Baroque mansions line some streets.

A longtime rivalry with Guadix comes to a head each September in the Cascamorras festivals, when a man of that town is foiled in his attempts to steal Baza's image of the Virgin and Child by being drenched in used engine oil. In 1971 a necropolis yielded *La Dama de Baza*, a painted stone sculpture, which is held in Madrid's archaeological museum as one of Spain's most outstanding examples of Iberian art.

CABO DE GATA
MAP REF: 109 D1

The natural park covers 26,000 hectares and includes strips of the sea so as to protect marine life in some of the clearest and least polluted waters of the Mediterranean. Understandably, this is a favourite area of divers and underwater photographers. The varied coastline has long beaches backed by permanent dunes, wide bays, isolated coves, steep cliffs and salt pans.

A stark mountainous spine of barren slopes and eroded rock, which reaches its highest point in the peak of Rellana at 479m, was formed by volcanic activity and shows evidence of ancient craters and lava formations. The mountains plunge to the sea at the *Cabo* (Cape), which is overlooked by the high points of San Miguel and Vela Blanca. Vegetation is adapted to conditions of high average temperatures and low mean rainfall and includes *palmito* (palm trees), lentiscus and wild olives. There are also *barron* (*Ammophila arenaria*) as well as

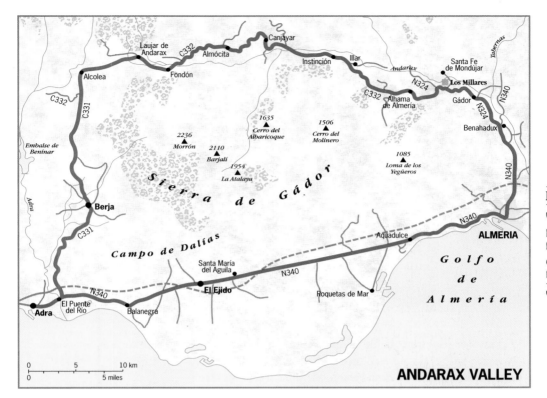

ANDARAX VALLEY

---

of some 80km for cyclists with mountain bikes can take in the small resort of Retamar, the village of Cabo de Gata, the salterns and the cape, Playa de los Genoveses, San José and the hamlets of El Pozo de los Frailes and Ruescas. Cyclists basing themselves in one of the villages have a choice of other round routes along empty roads and tracks. More information and cycle hire is available in the villages.

MOTOR TOUR

Starting from Almería, the route takes in a Bronze Age settlement, then goes through the green ribbon of the Andarax Valley and around the gaunt Sierra de Gádor to join the coastal highway.

After 12km on the N340 north of Almería bear left on to the N324 and just before the hamlet of Santa Fe de Mondújar turn right.

Los Millares
There is a reception centre at the excavation site, where a Neolithic community of around 2,000 people lived more than 4,000 years ago.

A little way along go left on to the C332, which rises among the terraces of trained vines producing the delicious eating grapes for which Almería has long been renowned.

Alhama de Almería
Used since Roman times and very popular with the Moors, the spa waters of this attractively situated town are especially recommended for rheumatic complaints.

The C332 road runs through the Andarax Valley where the greenery of citrus groves, vines and a patchwork of plots contrast with the starkness of hills. Canjayar and Fondón are probably the prettiest of the

peaceful farming villages along the route.

Laujar de Andarax
The main town of the Almerían part of Las Alpujarras is a popular Sunday excursion destination from the capital. El Nacimiento, the river source, is a particularly scenic spot.

Some 9km on, bear left on to the C331.

Berja
At the foot of the Sierra de Gádor, and with a balcony view to the Mediterranean, Berja has some good-looking town houses and pretty corners, and is a pleasant place in which to wander for a while. The cultivation of eating grapes for export is an important activity.

The C331 twists down to the N340 coastal highway. Go west for a short distance.

Adra
A colony of the Phoenicians, Greeks, Romans and Carthaginians, and one of the last places from which the Moors left Spain, Adra now stands among waves of sugar cane and plastic, and also lives off its fishing fleet and its simple, inexpensive tourist amenities.

It is 53km back to Almería.

Leaving the town of Berja. The coast is just a short drive away

•GRANADA•

'There is nothing worse in life than the pain of being blind in Granada', so goes the most repeated saying about the city. Arab poets unceasingly praised it, and among the store of eulogies that Granada has provoked are those of 19th-century Romantics like Théophile Gautier, Victor Hugo and Washington Irving. For its most famous son of this century, poet and playwright Federico García Lorca, 'Granada was a dream of sound and colours ... where the hours are longer and sweeter than in any other Spanish town'.

In the noise and traffic pollution of the city centre on an oppressive summer's day, first-time visitors to Granada (map ref: 108 C2) may feel they have entered a nightmare, not a dream. Although the centre has places of beauty and interest to discover and enjoy, it is essentially Granada's setting and Alhambra palace that have inspired its eulogisers. To understand why, visitors should go to the Mirador San Cristóbal on the road signposted to Guadix and Murcia. Below the viewpoint, the Albaicín quarter, town centre of Moorish Granada, spreads down the hillside, a woven mat of steep and narrow streets and jasmine-filled, small squares studded with secluded mansions and fine churches. Beyond the Río Darro and crowning the hill of La Sabika is the incomparable Alhambra palace complex, with towers and ramparts of the Alcázar in front of it and the gardens and palace buildings of the Generalife behind and to the east. Framing that splendid spectacle and heightening its impact are the snow-capped mountains of the high Sierra Nevada, on which the light plays games of changing hues and shadows. East of Albaicín, the hillside of Sacromonte is where most of the city's gypsy

population lived until recently in cave-dwellings. South and west from the *mirador,* the view stretches across the city rooftops with monumental buildings like the cathedral standing proud. Extending far beyond a ring of residential suburbs and industrial zones is the Vega de Granada, a plain so abundantly productive and closely linked with Granada's fortunes that its praises, too, have been sung through the centuries.

LA ALBAICIN

The pattern of streets and squares here in Granada's prettiest quarter has changed little since Moorish times. Many mosques were replaced by churches and convents, and where Moorish palaces once stood there are *carmenes,* the typically Granadian mansions with delightful gardens secluded by high walls and with towers from which to spy the world beyond. From less affluent homes the old-time residents, as well as newcomers who are buying up and renovating old properties, spill out to give the area its animated streetlife in the warm months and to patronise its many lively bars and eating places throughout the year. On the Carrera del Darro, El Bañuelo preserves Moorish baths from the 11th century in a building on which Roman, Visigothic and Caliphal capitals were reused. Next door, El Convento de Santa Catalina (Convent of St Catherine) displays Renaissance features and retains traces of a Moorish palace. La Casa de Castril, which has a Plateresque façade and a fine coffered ceiling in its main hall, houses the Museo Arqueológico Provincial (Archaeological Museum) displaying finds from megalithic, Phoenician, Visigothic and later periods. Further into La Albaicín, El Monasterio de Santa Isabel la Real has remains of a Nasrid palace beyond its Gothic-Isabeline façade. Behind this building, on Callejon del Gallo, Dar Al-Horra was the palace of Boabdil's mother, Aixa. Close by are some remnants of the walls that once enclosed La Albaicín.

El Sacromonte, 'the holy hill', is topped by the imposing Abadía (abbey), which hides a treasure of works of art and documents, and awaits much more restoration. Building was begun in the late 16th century on the site where remains of Christian martyrs, including those of Granada's patron saint, San Cecilio, were found. In a few caves dripping

The walls and towers of the Alhambra form a magical vista

with copper and ceramic
decoration, gypsies still present
their *zambras* of flamenco music
and dance. Straying foreigners
are plagued by pleas for money
and flamenco shows that are
tailored for tourists. However,
attending a genuine *misa de doce*
('midnight mass' meaning a
flamenco get-together) in the
company of an informed
aficionado will make a very
memorable night.

LA CAPILLA REAL

Ordered by the Catholic
Monarchs, Ferdinand and Isabel, as
their burial place in the city where
they had completed their crusade,
the Royal Chapel was begun in
1506 and finished in 1521. Its
northern façade, originally the
main one and later incorporated
into the cathedral, exemplifies the
Isabeline style; that is, flamboyant
Gothic with Mudéjar elements.
The façade that now gives access
to the Royal Chapel is Plateresque.
Inside, the royal tombs are
challenged for richness by a finely
wrought and gilded screen and the
sacristy's display of paintings from
Isabel's collection. The queen's
crown and the sceptre and

Ferdinand's sword are also on
show here.

LA CATEDRAL

Built on the site of Granada's
principal mosque, the cathedral
was begun in 1521, consecrated
40 years later and finished in the
early 18th century. It retains the
plan and height of the original
intention for a Gothic structure,
but is much more in the
Renaissance style, the creation of
its second architect, Diego de
Siloé. It is regarded as one of the
most outstanding examples of its
kind in Spain. The Puerta del
Perdón on the cathedral's north
side is especially indicative of
Siloé's interpretation of this style.
Among the ornate decoration of
the huge and gloomy interior are
sculptures and paintings by the
multi-talented Alonso Cano, who
was also responsible for the
cathedral's main façade.

EL HOSPITAL REAL

Also commissioned by the
Catholic Monarchs, the Royal
Hospital has notable Plateresque
decoration on its façade, a baroque
portico, delightful patios and
beautifully crafted ceilings. Now

Granada's Capilla Real

used by the university
administration, this handsome
building has through the years
been a hospice for the poor, a
hospital for venereal diseases, a
home for old people and an
asylum for the mentally ill.

EL MONASTERIO DE LA CARTUJA

The monastery was founded for
the Carthusian order in 1506.
Grotesque paintings of martyrdom
hang in the austere refectory and
chapter rooms. The church is an
extravagance of Spanish baroque,
which in the Sancta Sanctorum
(Holy of Holies) and sacristy
reaches an eye-straining
indulgence in marble, stucco and
woodwork inlaid with silver, ivory
and mother-of-pearl.

EL MONASTERIO DE SAN JERONIMO

The Monastery of St Jerome is
another fine Renaissance building,
to which Diego de Siloé
contributed the façade as well as
elements in the church and patio.
Gonzalo Fernández de Córdoba,
the Catholic Monarchs' *Gran
Capitán*, is buried in the church.

GRANADA'S GUILT

'The two rivers of Granada come down from the snow to fields of wheat.' Among wheatfields of the Vega, the village of Fuentevaqueros was the birthplace of Federico García Lorca. The house where he was born has been turned into a museum and so has the Huerto de San Vicente, a peaceful place where Federico later spent many summers with his parents.

Lorca was one of the brightest stars among Spain's Generation of 27 (1927), a group flowering of creative talent that Spain had not seen since its Generation of 98, the year of his birth. While at university in Madrid, where he studied philosophy, literature and law, Lorca was friends with other luminaries like Salvador Dalí and Luis Buñuel.

At the start of the Civil War, many of Lorca's fellow intellectuals who supported the Republic left the country or went into hiding. He returned to Granada believing he would be safe in his home town, which he felt regarded him as a 'small glory'. But not all *granadinos* glorified this *maricón* (homosexual) with Republican sympathies. On 19 August 1936, a gang of Franco supporters shot him at a place near the village of Víznar, which Moors had known as the 'spring of tears'.

Lorca's output included poetry of local and popular appeal like his *Canciónes*; works like *Poeta en Nueva York* (Poet in New York) were more difficult; in others like *Seis poemas gallegos* his social pre-occupations and a surrealistic use of language are more strongly evident. His dramatic works included farces, comedies and experimental works. It is probably for his tragedies like *Bodas de Sangre* (Blood Wedding, 1933) and *Yerma* (1934) that he is most universally known: a true tale of passion and revenge in Níjar (Almería province) inspired the first; some scenes in *Yerma* are based on the *romería* (pilgrimage) that takes place in the village of Moclín in October.

Lorca was pleased to be *Andaluz* and proud of his Moorish ancestry. His killing robbed the world of a young and brilliant talent.

Taking a break. Sightseeing in Granada requires stamina

TOWN WALK

Start at Plaza de Padre Suarez.

1 The 16th-century Casa de los Tiros retains parts of Moorish buildings and houses the city's museum of art and crafts as well as a tourist information centre. Also note the Casa del Padre Suarez with its Renaissance portal.

Go along Calle de Pavaneras to Plaza de Isabel la Católica, left into Calle de los Reyes Católicos, a main shopping street, and left into the first alley.

2 The Corral del Carbón is probably the city's most untouched original Moorish building from the 14th century, and has had quite a few different uses since first serving as a guesthouse. Local arts and crafts are now sold here.

Cross Calle de los Reyes Católicos to enter a maze of little streets.

3 The maze (La Alcaicería) was once the Moorish silk market and is now a hubbub of noise and colour with shops and stalls selling souvenir junk as well as some genuine arts and crafts.

Go out of the maze and into the light of Plaza Bib-Rambla with its bright flower-stalls; leave by Calle Libreros and ahead is a small square bound by the mass of the cathedral, the church of El Sagrario, the Episcopal Palace and curia. Before moving to the right into Calle Oficios, note the monument to Alonso Cano. Then you pass the Café Sevilla, long favoured by the local intelligentsia. Ahead, opposite the Capilla Real, is La Madraza.

4 This oratory with delicate decoration is a remaining part of the Arab university established here in the 14th century; the later building's baroque façade stands in contrast to it. Cultural activities are now presented here.

5 Recently renovated, the Cathedral and La Capilla Real are the essential downtown sights to which tourists flock (see page 93).

Go left when leaving the Cathedral and around it, past the Casa de Cabildos (chapterhouse) to reach and go right into Calle de San Jerónimo; it ends in Plaza Universidad, which is graced by the baroque church of Santos Justo y Pastor.

6 The law faculty now occupies the original Universidad (university), founded by order of Charles V in 1526. Other buildings of Spain's third-largest university are spread through the city. Many businesses around here cater to the needs and whims of students, whose presence enlivens the city so much.

Continue ahead to reach Calle San Juan de Dios; to the left is the San Jerónimo monastery and to the right the San Juan de Dios basilica and hospital.

7 The Monasterio de San Jerónimo is another of the city's essential sights (see page 93).

8 In the baroque Basílica y Hospital de San Juan de Dios (Church and Hospital of St John of God) is the tomb of St John, who founded the adjoining hospital for the poor, which still functions as such.

At the northern end of Calle San

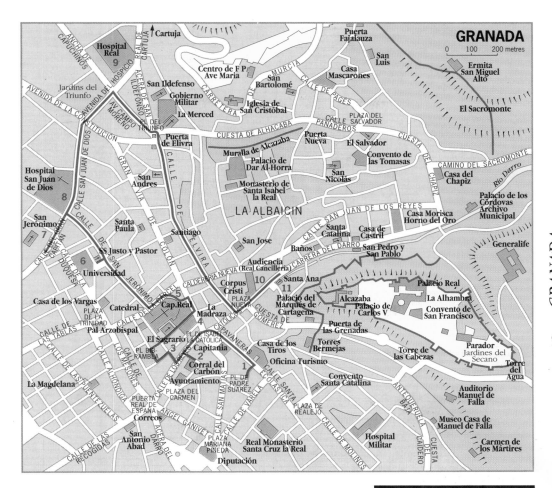

Juan de Dios, cross Avenida de la Constitución to the gardens of Fuente de Triunfo.

9 The Hospital Real is now used by the university (see page 93).

Leaving the Hospital Real, take Avenida Campo Moreno to Plaza del Triunfo; Puerta de Elvira is a remaining gateway from the walls that encircled La Albaicín. Go right into Calle de Elvira to reach Plaza Nueva and turn left.

10 Baroque elements are included in the front of the Real Cancillería (royal chancellor's) Renaissance palace, whose special features are a patio designed by Diego de Siloé and a coffered staircase.

11 The Iglesia de Santa Ana (Church of St Anna) has an interesting mix: mainly Mudéjar with a Plateresque portico and a tower with glazed tiles in the style of Moorish minarets.

From here you can make your way back to your starting point, wander at will through La Albaicín (see pages 92–3) or follow the signs to La Alhambra (see pages 96–7).

The Parador de San Francisco in Granada is a former convent

MANUEL DE FALLA

Spain's acclaimed composer was born in Cádiz in 1876 and for 20 years from 1919 he lived in Granada, which keenly considers him as its own. His *carmen* below the Alhambra is now the Museo de Manuel de Falla and the city's main concert venue has been named after him.

One of de Falla's best-known works is the music for *El Sombrero de Tres Picos* (The Three-Cornered Hat, 1915), a ballet based on a short story by a writer from Guadix, Pedro Antonio Alarcón. Another very popular work is the symphony for piano and orchestra, *Noches en los Jardines de España* (Nights in the Gardens of Spain, 1915). In 1922 he collaborated with Lorca in organising the *Festival de Jante Jondo* and from this time dates one his most important works, *El Retablo de Maese Pedro*. Widely regarded as his greatest composition is the *Concierto for Clavichord and Five Instruments* (1928). His distaste for Francoist Spain made de Falla move to Argentina, where he died in 1946.

·LA ALHAMBRA·

Visiting the Alhambra is reason enough for the traveller to come to Andalucía. It is the Moors' richest architectural bequest to Spain; the world's finest example of a medieval Arab palace; a small city, encircled by walls and towers, where the sound of water is ever present and delicate decoration survives as testimony to the finest Moorish craftsmanship. For its greatest admirers, the Alhambra is the eighth wonder of the world.

It is not the size or solidity of the buildings which impresses most: the halls are not very large and much of the construction was on weak foundations and with materials that could not have been expected to last for centuries. The impact is made by the wealth and variety of the ornamentation, using in the main such fragile materials as wood and plaster. That so much of the Alhambra survives to be appreciated today is in itself a wonder. Added to neglect over the centuries was damage caused by an earthquake in 1522, a gunpowder explosion in 1590 and efforts by Napoleonic troops in 1812 to despoil it. Some attempts at repair began in 1828 and from 1862 the intention became more wholehearted. Work continues.

When his seat of power in Jaén was captured by the Christians in 1246, Ibn el-Ahmar, who had inherited territory stretching from Algeciras to Almería, made Granada his new power base. Styling himself Mohammed I, he founded the Nasrid dynasty and, rejecting the court palaces in the Albaicín, his builders began moulding local clay to build his *al-hamra* (the red one) fortified palace. Shrewdly, he made pacts with Christian Castile, even helping in the capture of Sevilla, and he welcomed to his kingdom talented refugees from the Reconquest. So the Kingdom of Granada rapidly grew in size and wealth and Moorish art and culture in *Al-Andalus* reached its apogee. Yusuf I and his son Mohammed V, who together reigned from 1333 to 1391, ordered most of the Alhambra that remains today. Arabic calligraphy is the predominant decoration on the walls. A couplet boasts:

No greater mansions I see than mine
No equal in East or West.

And in many places is inscribed the motto of the Nasrids: 'No conqueror but Allah.' It was dissension among the Moors and intrigues of love which opened the way for the Catholic Monarchs' conquering of Granada. Abul Hassan (1462–85) had a son, Boabdil, by his first wife, Aixa, but a favourite in his harem was Zoraya, who had the support of the powerful Zegries family. Aixa's fears that her son's claims to the throne would be supplanted were shared by another powerful family, the Abencerrajes, who were to suffer the misfortune of having 36 of their members slain at the behest of Abul Hassan in a hall of the Alhambra that now bears their name. Spurred by his strong-willed mother, Boabdil (Abd Ala) did finally become king and it was his misfortune to hand the keys of the kingdom to the Catholic Monarchs on 2 January 1492.

The new rulers of Granada repaired and strengthened parts of the palace buildings and ordered the building of the Convento de San Francisco (Convent of St Francis), where their bodies lay until 1521. Today it is a delightful and heavily booked Parador de Turismo. Their successor, Charles V, decided to leave a greater, more incongruous mark among the

Moorish architecture at its most exquisite – the Court of the Lions

delicate Moorish buildings by commissioning a disciple of Michelangelo, Pedro Machuca, to design a Renaissance palace that, although not fully completed, is among the best examples of that style in Spain. The Moorish buildings have been described as effeminate, but the Palace of Charles V abuts them like a dominant male. At the end of the 16th century the Iglesia de Santa María (Church of St Mary) was raised on the site of the mosque on which the kings of Granada had surely also lavished wealth and fine craftsmanship.

At the western tip of La Sabika, the oldest buildings on the hill were constructed for military purposes and the palace of Mohammed I was probably here. Well restored, the fortress of La Alcazaba should be the first place to visit to get a view of Granada from La Torre de La Vela (Watch Tower) and, looking the other way, across the palace buildings of the Alhambra and towards the Generalife gardens and buildings.

There is not space to describe adequately the intricate craftsmanship and decorative beauty which visitors marvel at in the three-in-one palaces of Yusuf I and Mohammed V. The visit begins in the Mexuar, a reception hall in which justice was dispensed and which Charles V had remodelled to make it a chapel by adding an inner courtyard. Beyond that is the Cuarto Dorado, a waiting-room for those seeking an audience with the king. Its Renaissance ceiling was commissioned by the Catholic Monarchs. In the façade of the Palacio de Comares (Comares Palace) a doorway leads to the *serail*, centre of the Moorish court's diplomatic life. The rectangular pool of the large Patio de los Arrayanes (Court of the Myrtle Trees) is framed by two porticoes with seven arches supported by marble columns. Beyond the northern portico and the Sala de la Barca (Barca Gallery), and topped by the Torre de Comares (Comares Tower), El Salón de Embajadores (Hall of the Ambassadors) is the grandest of all the rooms in the palace. The high ceiling of carved cedarwood symbolises the seven Islamic heavens. The richness of the decoration on the walls, which incorporates Koranic inscriptions, plant motifs and glisteningly glazed tiles must have bewildered all who came to be received here by the king. At the southern end of

Intricate decoration on arches and walls of the Mexuar Patio

the patio, the Capilla del Palacio de Carlos V (Chapel of the Palace of Charles V) was later imposed.

Named after a cupola that was replaced by a baroque ceiling, the Sala de los Mocarabes (Mocarabes Court), leads to the Patio de los Leones (Court of the Lions), which is surrounded by halls comprising the private quarters. Twelve lions (perhaps of Phoenician origin), which are the focal point of its rectangular pool, gave this *patio*, probably the most photographed part of Alhambra, its name. There are displays of time-consuming craftsmanship, and a compulsion to linger in each of these *salas:* de los Abencerrajes; de los Reyes, and de las dos Hermanas.

In other corners and in other rooms, there is more decoration, man-made stalagmites, columns and arches so delicate you fear to touch them. Wander through the precinct slowly, take in the views from some of its 22 towers, smell the scents in the gardens of the Generalife higher up the hill, hear the tinkling of its waters. You will understand why Boabdil sighed and why Aixa scolded him for losing Paradise.

GUADIX

MAP REF: 109 D2

Red cliffs and barren highlands
overlook a fertile valley that has
seen settlement since the earliest
times. Silver, copper and iron
deposits were the main attraction
and the latter is still mined at
Alquife to the south. The Roman
town was called *Iulia Gemela
Acci,* from which the people of
Guadix get the name of *accitanos.*
Eroded hills around Guadix, and
nearby Purullena and Benalúa,
have for centuries been burrowed
to create the cave dwellings for
which the town is most well
known (see pages 88–9).

Guadix has a greater claim to
fame: it was here that St Torcuato,
one of evangelists sent to Iberia by
St Paul, set up his bishopric,
which is believed to be the first in
Spain. Torcuato, after whom many
local boys are named, died a
martyr, but bishops of Guadix
continue to enjoy certain
preferential rights among Spain's
bishops. One local boy, Pedro de
Mendoza, was a *conquistador*
who in 1536 founded a settlement
that became Buenos Aires.

Apart from the cave-dwelling
area of Barrio de Santiago (Ermita
Nueva), Guadix has other notable
sights. The cathedral was begun in
1549, using red sandstone and
following designs of the
Renaissance master, Diego de
Siloé, and was completed in the
18th century. Note the imposing
baroque façade, elaborate choir
seating and the small museum
with relics of St Torcuato. The
church of the Convento de
Santiago (Convent of St James), a
Mudéjar building, has a
Plateresque front, probably also
designed by de Siloé. The Alcazaba
of the Moors' town, *Wadi Asch*
(River of Life), was destroyed in
the 16th century and later rebuilt.
The Palacio de los Marqueses de
Peñaflor (Palace of the Marqueses
of Peñaflor), dating from the 16th
century, is the finest of the town's
noble houses.
Nearby The Balneario Alicún de las
Torres, 30km north, is open from
April to November for relaxation
or a choice of treatments in its hot
mineral water.

Eighteen kilometres southeast
of Guadix, the Castillo de la
Calahorra (Calahorra Castle)
dominates the landscape. Within
the sombre walls and towers is an
unexpected Italian Renaissance
palace completed in 1512 for a
bastard son of Cardinal Mendoza,
to whom the Catholic Monarchs
gave large tracts of land here.
Enquire locally about visiting.

The tower of the imposing
cathedral is a landmark in Guadix

LOJA

MAP REF: 108 C2

In the past the town, which
straddles the Río Genil between
two highlands, has been a strategic
guardian of the Granada-Málaga
route. Parts remain of the alcázar
(fortress), a key defensive position
for the kingdom of Granada,
which was captured in 1486.
Most notable of Loja's buildings
are two churches: the Iglesia de
la Encarnación (Church of the
Incarnation) with a Gothic central
nave, and the Iglesia de San
Gabriel (Church of St Gabriel)
to which Diego de Siloé contributed.

Just east of the town, the Río
Genil cascades through the scenic
gorge of Los Infiernos. West of the
town is its most recent claim to
fame: the new, five-star Hotel La
Bobadilla is a complex of
traditional-style buildings, in an
estate of 700 hectares, where
every luxury is provided. Its La
Finca restaurant rates among the
best in Spain. By contrast, at cheap
prices simple *mesones* in the
hamlet of Riofrío serve the freshest
trout imaginable; they are caught
from the bubbling stream or trout
farm dams.
Nearby Some 32km southeast,
Alhama de Granada perches
sleepily above a high gorge, like
Ronda on a smaller scale. Its 16th-
century parish church has a finely
worked ceiling. A bridge survives
from the time Romans favoured
the nearby springs gushing hot
mineral water, and Arab baths can
be viewed at the Balneario where
modern facilities, including
medical attention, are available
from June to October.

MOJÁCAR

MAP REF: 109 E1

There is a make-believe air about
the town that claims Walt Disney
as its son. So time-warped was
Mojácar within recent history that
up until the Civil War, women
walking the Moorish maze of its
hilltop streets covered their faces
at the sight of a man. In the 1950s,
a desperate mayor gave away
ruined buildings with the proviso
that they were promptly
renovated, and a mud-coloured
mess started to turn into the
pristinely white confection on a
spur of the gaunt Sierra Cabrera
that Mojácar is today.

Many of the early foreign settlers
were creative people, and the
town still has a large number of
active artists and craftspeople.
Others opened bars, restaurants
and service companies and
Mojácar became a fun-time foreign
enclave in what was Andalucía's
poorest, least known and most
neglected province. Property
developers and holiday operators,
mainly British, followed. Apart
from a large hotel in the town,
their activities are concentrated
along the stretch of Mojácar Playa,
where all the usual offerings of a
summer holiday resort are
available. Here, too, is a modern
Parador del Turismo, the best
hotel in the area.

Development is spreading
northwards up to the lower-key
fishing village of Garrucha, where
there is a small leisure port. Simple
fish restaurants line the waterfront

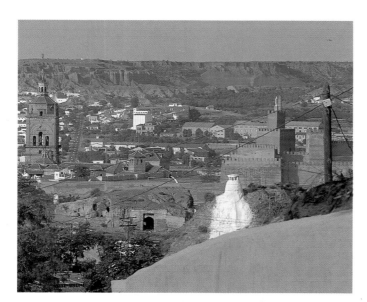

unlikely to remain so. Naturists have the choice of either an apartment complex or campsites lining the beach.

INDALO MAN

In this part of Almería, and especially in Mojácar, the name Indalo and the stick-figure image of a man holding aloft a semi-circle is seen everywhere. The semi-circle denotes a rainbow – the symbol of benevolence and plenty – and Indalo was an important god of the area's ancient inhabitants. He was credited with the power of being able to ward off evil. His image is used by the modern Indalian movement to project the history and culture of Almería province. A Neolithic painting of Indalo was found in La Cueva de los Letreros near Vélez Blanco.

road. Developments have also grown inland and that of Cortijo Grande, in a valley setting, has large luxury villas, a golf course and lawn bowling greens. From here, there are organised horse-riding treks through the stark country. Pampered relaxation in an enchanting farmhouse and gourmet country cooking can be enjoyed at the Finca Listonero. **Nearby** Vera lies in the fertile lands of the Almanzora valley and is an unassuming market town for the area, which has some distinguished buildings in its centre, notably a fortress-like Gothic-Mudéjar church. Shoe-making is an important local industry and Vera's pottery is notable for retaining Phoenician designs. Playa de Vera's long stretch of good beach is still relatively undeveloped, but is

The famous cave dwellings of Guadix, hollowed out from the tufa rock behind the town

TRADITIONAL CRAFTS

Another of the delights for travellers in Andalucía is the discovery that the region is still surprisingly rich in craft traditions that have been lost in many other parts of Europe. That is not to say that the traditional craftspeople of Andalucía have not greatly decreased in number and that the remaining adherents to old ways are not under threat. However, the threat appears less great than it was a decade or two ago, when, in a rush to appear modern and wealthier, there was a wholesale rejection of handmade articles in favour of mass-produced things, and synthetic materials were all the vogue.

The Church had long been the greatest supporter of many traditional crafts, for its buildings, images and clergy needed adornment by masters in stone, wood and metal, carvers, gilders, embroiderers and others. The aristocracy, too, provided work in the decoration of their palaces. Repairing historic workmanship still provides work for today's craftsmen. In the extensive recent programme of renovation in Andalucía there has been a great demand for their talents. In fact, the shortage of people in some crafts has delayed many projects.

Job-creation schemes have included the training of young people in traditional crafts while working on renovation projects. The regional government and some local authorities give some support, but no craftsperson would suggest that it is sufficient. However, there has been a revived interest in all things traditional, and popular crafts are fashionable again. Fresh blood has been injected by talented craftspeople among the region's foreign settlers, who have brought crafts from their native country or taken up local ones.

Most widely found are ceramic and pottery workshops, and in the most simple of them ovens are still wood-fired. Much of their output is inexpensive utilitarian items found in every Andalucían home, and which command high prices overseas. Many objects are gaudy and kitsch, supposedly satisfying the tastes of tourists for some 'typical' souvenirs. Some designs are inspired by those of previous inhabitants of the region – Iberians, Phoenicians, Romans, Arabs – and there is much variety in colouring and glazing.

Embroidery and lacework, done by nuns in convents, women at home or in small workshops, are also good buys throughout much of the region. So are items made from esparto grass, wicker and other fibres, which can range from intricately worked models to baskets, lampshades, tableware and furniture.

Leathercraft of very fine work-manship is still the speciality of a few places, and there are many workshops producing more ordinary items. As is to be expected in the land of flamenco, the making of guitars is a local craft. Handcarved pieces of Brazilian rosewood are included in the finest instruments.

Madonna and Child embroidered on a bullfighter's costume

Large craft shops in the cities may have items from a wide area, but often craft items are not sold beyond the place where they are made. Walking the back-streets of cities, towns or villages and coming across a small workshop provides the opportunity to watch a while; perhaps, to buy something made just for you. It is free and educational entertainment.

Following is a brief list of where to look for what.

ALMERIA

Esparto grass is plentiful in the province, and a variety of useful or decorative articles made from it is widely available. In the capital city they make wrought-iron items, guitars and embossed leather goods. Berja, too, makes embossed leather goods as well as pottery and *jarapas* (rainbow-coloured blankets). Ceramics and pottery, of distinctive styles, are the speciality of four towns: Níjar, (also known for its *jarapas* and textile mats and bags), Sorbas, Tabernas and Vera. Huércal Olvera produces lacework. Carvings in marble are done in Macael and nearby towns.

CADIZ

Throughout the province, horse-lovers should look for finely crafted leatherwork in the *Andaluz* equestrian tradition. Olvera is especially renowned for this. Near by, Algodonales enjoys a reputation for guitars. Grazalema has a working museum weaving woollen blankets and ponchos, which the town once exported as far afield as South America. In Ubrique, family workshops and small factories make good leather items – handbags, wallets, etc – and the *Piel de Ubrique* label is a guarantee of high quality. Some production is contracted by famous-name fashion houses. Arcos de la Frontera produces attractive floor rugs. Apart from its craft of making sherry, Jerez de la Frontera also has a reputation for good wickerwork. Dolls in traditional dress are the speciality of Chiclana de la Frontera. Around Tarifa a new craft industry serving the exacting demands of boardsailers has mushroomed.

CORDOBA

The capital is known for fine work in precious metals, especially filigree jewellery in silver, and its *Cordobanes* (embossed leatherwork) and other leather items. Fine guitars are made in a few workshops. Lucena has craftsmen working in copper, brass and bronze as well as potters continuing with Jewish and Arab designs. La Rambla has some 50 ceramics workshops. Fine wood-carvings are done in Priego de Córdoba.

GRANADA

A few workshops continue producing distinctive *Fajalauza* ceramics, named after an old gate of the city around which the workshops were grouped in Moorish times. Basic designs remain faithful to that period, as can be seen when comparing today's with those of the ceramic decoration in the Alhambra. Beaten copperwork, gold and silverwork and brass objects are other items to look for in the city. In Las Alpujarras there is small-scale production of tulle embroidery, lacework and handwoven fabrics.

HUELVA

Aracena is the province's main pottery centre and a few of its craftspeople, as well as those of Alonso and Puebla de Guzmán, also do fine embroidery work. Valverde del Camino specialises in leather footwear, especially boots, and copper objects. Along the coast, handicrafts include miniature ships, ships in bottles and a variety of souvenirs made from shells.

JAEN

Ubeda is the most rewarding town in the province for good craft items, which include ceramics, items of esparto grass, wrought-iron work and attractive candles. In the capital city, look for pieces of wood sculpture as well as esparto-grass items.

MALAGA

Most typical of the city's craft items are *barros malagueños*, earthenware figurines, which include the *torero* (bullfighter), *contrabandista* (smuggler) and *vendedor de pescados* (fishmonger). Ronda specialises in wrought-iron work. In country areas look also for carvings in olive wood. Craftspeople, including foreigners, have also set up shop in resort towns of the Costa del Sol.

SEVILLA

A few ceramic workshops in the city continue in traditional ways, making distinctive pieces and the famous Sevillan tiles. The city is also known for fine gold and silver jewellery, religious ornaments and various items of dress adornment related to the region's traditional dress and the bullfighting ritual.

Guitarist José Luis Postigo in his shop in Sevilla. Guitar-making is an Andalucían local craft

for Spanish people, although it is lively throughout the year. A walk through the old town and up to the castle is recommended. So is a drive along the shore to take in the beachfronts of Velilla in the east, to San Cristóbal and Cotobro to the west of the town (see page 86).

Back on the N340 going west, take the road down to Marina del Este and, on the way back, go down to the horseshoe bay of La Herradura. Return to the N340 and head back to Almuñécar, until traffic lights just before the petrol station. Make a loop here and head north, signposted Jete.

The Old Road to Granada

Bear in mind that in 755 Abderraman may have travelled this way when he was *en route* for Córdoba to become the first independent emir of *Al-Andalus.* The narrow road meanders through the lushness of the Río Verde Valley. Successful growing and export of chirimoyas (custard apples) and other tropical fruits transformed the local agricultural economy. The two villages of Jete and Otivar look unattractive from the road, but wandering through the steep streets will reveal some pretty aspects. A small road winds off and up to the village of Lentegí, where a simple life goes on much as it did when all three villages were owned by a titled family whose fine mansion still stands on a promontory commanding the valley beyond Otivar.

The 'main' road climbs around corners to the Mirador de las Cabras Montes, from where there are good views across the undulating landscape to the coast. Impressive road engineering and spectacular mountain scenery continues until a plateau covered in pines is reached. Beyond that, the road dips and rises through the folds of a plain where cereals grow.

Puerto del Suspiro del Moro (The Moor's Sigh)

Here the old road joins the new N323 Granada to Motril highway. In 1492 Boabdil had his last look at Granada from this high point and, so the story goes, was rebuked by his mother for crying like a child for the city he could not defend like a man.

The Sierra Nevada loom to the east and Granada is a few minutes away.

MOTRIL

MAP REF: 108 C1

The administrative town for the Costa Tropical hides no sights of any note and 45,000 *motrileños* are engaged in local government, service industries, agriculture and fishing. Motril's harbour serves Granada and its fishing port is one of the largest on the south coast. A beachside area, not yet much developed, includes a golf course. Sugar cane sways in surrounding fields and rum is made locally. There is also mixed farming and increasing areas are being given over to *plasticultura.*

Nearby To the west, among sugar-cane fields adjoining the sea, Salobreña is spectacularly sited on a high outcrop of rock topped by a restored castle, below which white cube houses huddle. Not interfering with the old town's charming aspect, modern apartment blocks line a long beachfront. Villa developments line the coastal highway west of the town.

East of Motril, Torrenueva, Calahonda and Castell de Ferro are traditional fishing and agricultural villages with unassuming and lower-cost amenities, in which summer tourism is of increasing importance. After Torrenueva the coastline is rugged and dramatic and Calahonda, in a cove, has the prettiest setting. The white and dozing village of Gualchos looks down on this part of the coast. Tucked within it, the small La Posada has a gourmet restaurant and offers quietly elegant accommodation.

MOTOR TOUR

The route takes in the Costa Tropical and a spectacular mountain road. If a very early start is made, the tour into Las Alpujarras, outlined on page 87, can be combined with this one.

From Granada take the N323, signposted Motril, for some 40km and go left on to the C333 to reach the spa town of Lanjarón. About 8km ahead you can branch off left to make the tour of Las Alpujarras or continue on to Orjiva, which overlooks the Guadalfeo Valley. A scenic road of some 32km runs to Motril via the village of Vélez de Benaudalla, where you should make sure to take the old Motril road – more winding and slower but more scenic. From Motril go west on the N340 coastal highway.

Salobreña

Winding streets lead up to the restored castle and its gardens, from which there are grandstand views of the coast and its intensively worked plain.

Twelve kilometres to the west along the N340, the tropical valley of the Río Verde comes into view with the clustered old town of Almuñécar on a hill surrounded by new development.

Almuñécar

It easily rates as one of Spain's most attractive seaside towns and is a very popular summer resort

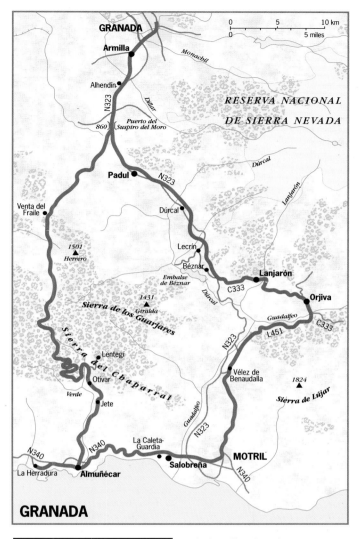

ROQUETAS DE MAR

MAP REF: 109 D1

On the western side of the Golfo de Almería, the village has three parts: a nondescript centre; an attractive fishing port; and a sprawling resort development.

Blocks of hotels and apartments, none reaching the highest classification or prices, line a long and wide beach, with the advantage, unlike many resorts, of not being separated from the seafront by a road – an important consideration for families with younger children. In the brash centre is a concentration of shops, bars and restaurants, many of which are foreign owned, especially by British and Germans. Parts of the resort have private villas, and the more recent development on the south side, at Playa Serena, is generally of a higher standard of design and quality. Here, too, there is a golf course. Saltpans lie beyond, and backing them are the shimmering acres of plastic-covered smallholdings.

Nearby Almerimar was started from scratch by British property developers to be an upmarket holiday and retirement zone based around a sports port and golf course. Economic difficulties made for stuttering progress. Japanese interests have moved in and building activity has increased. The area is attractively laid out with wide avenues and pleasing landscaping, and there is evidence of wealth in some fine villas.

Aguadulce, squeezed between mountain and sea along the N340 coastal highway, was a village where for a long time people from Almería city had enjoyed simple seaside pleasures. Its development quickened when film-making in Almería province was in its heyday. Now developments catering for seasonal tourism, mainly by Spanish people, have overwhelmed the village. Generally, the resort has no pretensions about being sophisticated, although newer developments are moving upmarket and the pretty new sports port on the eastern edge has added glitter to the image.

Gualchos, off the main tourist trail

SIERRA DE LOS FILABRES
MAP REF: 109 D1

Few visitors pass through this area of dramatic landscapes peppered with hamlets, in which time seems to have stood still. A day's tour of discovery, which will leave a lasting impression, can start by taking the C3325 road from Venta Los Yesos, between Tabernas and Sorbas on the N340, twisting northwards to Cantoria in the green valley of the Almanzora. A short distance west on the C323 is Olula del Río and south of it is Macael, a centre for marble quarrying. From here the AL840 twists back to the C3325.

Traditional kiln in Sorbas. Pottery workshops can be visited

SOLYNIEVE
MAP REF: 109 D1

'Sun and Snow' is an apt name for Europe's most southerly winter sports resort, based on the village of Pradollano in the Sierra Nevada, only 35km from Granada. There are more sunshine hours here each day than on any of the Continent's other snowy slopes, which gives more time for enjoying the sports. The resort also shows the advantage of a cost structure lower than those of most French, Swiss or Austrian resorts. Because of the southerly latitude, the season's start and finish is less predictable than in Alpine or Pyrenean resorts and late January through to March is the peak period.

A Parador del Turismo is among the resort's good selection of accommodation, eating places and nightspots. A lift and cable car give access to Veleta, Andalucía's second-highest peak, from where the Mediterranean and Africa may be seen. Different well-serviced, and generally unwooded ski-runs are ideal for novices and experienced skiers alike. Cross-country skiing, ice skating and indoor sports are among other attractions, as is hiking, and for the more intrepid there are *refugios* (huts) for overnight shelter.

Spain's National Sports Council is subsidising the construction of a

Mini Hollywood, Tabernas, a left-over from Almería's film industry

village-like High Performance Athletic Training Centre, which is intended to be the most complete of its kind in Europe. A large injection of new investment is being made to prepare the resort as the venue for the 1995 World Skiing Championships, an event Spain has not previously hosted.

SNOWS OF THE SIERRAS
The snow of the Sierra Nevada was sold by public auction in 1870 on the condition it be used in some productive way. In 1914 ownership passed to José Carrera, who became Granada's leading merchant of ice made from snow brought down from the mountains by donkeys. Modern methods of refrigeration and Don José's retirement in 1968 put an end to the business. *Escrituras* (title deeds) fully substantiate the claim to ownership of the snow, but not the land, by Doña Francisca, Don José's daughter, and her six daughters. Eager lawyers are keen to test this unique case in the courts with the claim that Cetursa, the company running Solynieve, should pay for its use of the family's snow.

Níjar

Nestling in the foothills of the Sierra Alhamilla and surrounded by citrus groves, the town appears as an oasis in the parched *campo*. Two towers, of its church and a Moorish sentry-post, stand out above the white splash of the town's buildings. Since Phoenician times, potteries have been in production here. Multi-coloured ceramics and handwoven blankets, *jarapas*, are now its craft specialities.

It is some 32km back to Almería along the N332.

VELEZ BLANCO Y RUBIO
MAP REF: 109 E2

Visitors entering Andalucía from Murcia along the N342 (Autovía '92) should detour into Los Vélez, two attractive towns only 8km apart. Vélez Rubio's pride is having the province's largest parish church. Its construction was subsidised by the local nobility, whose coats-of-arms appear on the main front, and it was completed in 1753 with two tall towers and a graceful cupola.

The high ground of Vélez Blanco is topped by the outline of a 16th-century castle, which was the noble family's home. Italian craftsmen worked on this Renaissance construction and fine examples of their work, like a marble patio and crafted woodwork, are now exhibited in New York's Metropolitan Museum of Art. Valuable finds from a number of prehistoric caves in this area have also been dispersed to several museums around the world.

The mountain village of Vélez Blanco dwarfed by its mighty castle

TABERNAS
MAP REF: 109 D1

Ruins of a Moorish *alcázar* (fortress) sit atop the small town, which eagerly hopes for a revival of the province's film industry. Its potteries are the draw for visitors. Near by is the Platforma Solar de Almería energy research centre, which may be visited by prior arrangement. Southwest of the town is the Parque Natural del Desierto de Tabernas.

MOTOR TOUR

The route passes through lunar landscapes reminiscent of Arizona, taking in old Wild West film sets and three towns where traditional ceramics are made.

From Almería take the N340 highway to Murcia, which for a while follows the Andarax valley where citrus fruits and palms grow. Between Rioja and Tabernas is 'Wild West' territory. Look out for film-set replicas of scenes from the American West - sometimes complete with cowboys acting out saloon fights or feats of horsemanship, for the benefit of tourists. After Tabernas, continue on the N340.

Sorbas
Advantage of this defensive position has been taken since prehistoric times. In the brown, arid landscape, the town perches dramatically above a gorge of the Río de Aguas ('River of Water', but usually waterless). The best view of its *casas colgadas* (hanging houses) is seen from the highway. The main attractions within the dusty town are its traditional ceramic workshops.

Return along the N340 for 9km and turn south on to the minor AL102 road, which twists through a rugged and desolate landscape for 25km.

•GLOSSARY•

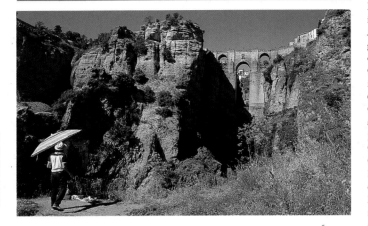

Andalucíans speak Castilian, the 'standard' Spanish, but with a variation known as the *seseo* in which *c* before *e* and *i*, and *z*, are pronounced as a hard *s* sound and not as the usual *th* sound. They often clip the endings of words and talk rapidly. A word is generally pronounced as it looks and exceptions are few. Correct grammar is obviously desirable, but correct sound formation and stressing are the key factors in starting to communicate verbally. A few basic rules follow.

Vowels: a - tar; e - let; i - marine; o - Tom; u - rule.

Consonants are pronounced like those in English, but there are some important exceptions:

b and v – similar and pronounced as a soft b;

c – like in keep before *a, o, u* or a consonant, but like thin before *e* or *i* (often as an *s* in Andalucía);

g – like get but before *i* or *e* it is like *j* below;

h – is always silent;

j – like loch but silent at end of word;

ll – like million;

n – like onion;

q – like keep (always followed by silent *u*);

r – strong and rolled and rr more so;

y – like yes;

z – like thin.

Stress: Words ending in *n, s* or a vowel have the stress on the second-to-last syllable. Other words have the stress on the last syllable. An acute accent on the syllable to be stressed is used for exceptions to the above rule. Accents are also used to differentiate between words of similar spelling but different meaning.

USEFUL WORDS AND PHRASES

Hello Hola

I am sorry but I don't speak Spanish (or only a little) Lo siento pero no hablo español (o solamente un poco)

Do you speak Danish/Dutch/English/French/German/Italian? ¿Habla danés/holandés/inglés/francés/alemán/italiano?

Is there someone who speaks ...? ¿Hay alguien que hable ...?

Yes/No si/no

Excuse me, I don't understand Perdón, no comprendo

Please speak slowly Por favor, hable despacio

Thank you (very much) (muchas) gracias

You're welcome/Think nothing of it de nada

Good morning buenos dias

Good afternoon buenas tardes

Good evening buenas noches

I am.../my name is... Soy.../me llamo...

What is your name? ¿Como se llama usted?

How are you? ¿Como esta?

I am... Estoy...

Very well muy bien

I (don't) know (something) (no) sé

I (don't) know (a person) (no) conozco

All right vale/de acuerdo

Good luck buena suerte

Goodbye adiós

See you again hasta luego

Where is...? ¿Donde está...?

Is it far/near? ¿Está lejos/cerca?

Very muy

Good/bad bien/mal

Left/right/ahead/at the end izquierda/derecha/delante/al final

Avenue/boulevard/road/street/passage/square avenida/paseo/carretera/calle/pasaje/plaza

Countryside/mountain(s)/hill/river/stream campo/montaña (sierra)/colina/río/arroyo

Castle/church/monastery/palace/school Castillo/iglesia/monasterio/palacio/escuela

Open abierto

Closed cerrado

Hour/day/week/month/year hora/día/semana/mes/año

Monday to Sunday lunes, martes, miercoles, jueves, viernes, sabado, domingo

Yesterday/today/tomorrow ayer/hoy/mañana

Last night/tonight anoche/esta noche

The weekend el fin de semana

Last week/next week semana pasada/semana próxima

Early/late temprano/tarde

I would like... me gustaría...

I'm looking for... Busco...

I want... Quiero...

I need... Necesito...

Do you have...? ¿Tiene...?

There is (not) (No) hay

How much (cost)? ¿Cuánto es/vale/cuesta?

Expensive/cheap caro/barato

Short/long/ corto/longo

Enough/too much bastante/demasiado

More/less más/menos

Good/better bueno/mejor

Big/bigger grande/más grande

Small/smaller pequeño/más pequeño

Quick/slow rápido/lente

Nothing more, thank you Nada más, gracias

NUMBERS

Zero to 10: zero, uno (a), dos, tres, cuatro, cinco, seis, siete, ocho, nueve, diez

11 to 20 once, doce, trece, catorce, quince, dieciseis, diecisiete, dieciocho, diecinueve, veinte

21 veintiuno

30 treinta

32 treinta y dos

40 cuarenta

50 cincuenta

60 sesenta

70 setenta

80 ochenta

90 noventa

100 cien

200 doscientos

500 quinientos

1,000 mil

Map symbols

━━━●━━━	Motorway and junction
▩▩▩●▩▩▩	Toll motorway
= = = = =	Motorway under construction
━━━━━	Single carriageway motorway
━━━━━	Primary route
━━━━━	Main road
━━━━━	Secondary road
───────	Other road
⊱::::::::::::⊰	Mountain road tunnel
━━━⏜━━━	Mountain·pass
+·+·+·+·+·+·+	Railway connection
━━━━━	Road Snowbound during winter
━━N18━━	Road number
⤙━22━⤚	Distance in kms.
▲	Mountain/Volcano
○	Town
Vasso ～	River and lake
– – –Ⓥ BASTIA	Vehicle ferry

Accommodation

Andalucía's accommodation was greatly increased and enhanced in preparation for EXPO'92. Officially registered accommodation is available in *hoteles* and *hotel apartamentos*, 1–5 star (5-star *Gran Lujo* is the top); *apartamentos turísticos*, 1–3 key; *hostales*, 1–3 star; *pensiones*, *fondas* (inns) and *casas de huéspedes* (guest houses); *campings*, 1–3 class.

Prices are officially registered annually and should be on display together with the applicable rate of value-added tax (IVA). Spanish tourist offices in other countries and local tourist offices will provide information about officially registered accommodation, but they will not make bookings.

The state-sponsored chain of Paradores de Turismo provides an exceptionally good ratio of price to quality, and Paradores are strategically placed through the region to facilitate their use by touring visitors. Most are in delightful or spectacular settings and have gardens and swimming pools. All have spacious, well-fitted bedrooms and bathrooms and public rooms are equally comfortable and welcoming. Local dishes are featured in their restaurants, where excellent value is also provided.

The Paradores at Arcos de la Frontera, Carmona, Granada, Jaén and Ubeda are in superb conversions of fine and historic buildings loaded with atmosphere. Others are at Antequera, Ayamonte, Bailén, Cádiz, Cazorla, Córdoba, Málaga, Mazagón,

Spacious gardens surround the well-positioned parador in Nerja

Mojácar, Nerja, Solynieve and Torremolinos. There is a Central Reservations Service: Paradores de Turismo, Calle Velázquez 18, 28001 Madrid (tel: (91) 435 9700; fax (91) 435 9869; telex 41461 RRPP).

Private enterprise has also tastefully converted palaces, convents and country houses into luxury hotels. More modest places have been turned into homely retreats in town or countryside locations, and many of these, not officially classified, are run by foreigners who rely on returning clients and their recommendations.

Andalucía has a crop of big hotels of the highest international standard in a variety of situations, like the Alfonso XIII in downtown Sevilla, Puente Romano by the sea in Marbella, and Bobadilla in the countryside of Granada province (see page 98).

The biggest choice of hotel and apartment accommodation of all grades is on the Costa del Sol west of Málaga. Here, and in other resort areas, there is also a wide choice of villas to rent. In some areas rural tourism is being encouraged by making *cortijos* available for rental and the opening of *villas turísticas* (holiday villages).

Modest, comfortable hotels at mineral spas in delightful locations or pampering places for convalescence and beauty care are other choices (see Health and Medical Care, page 113). Apartment complexes at Costa Natura (Málaga province) and Playas de Vera (Almería province) cater to naturists. Spick and span low-cost accommodation is offered by house-proud owners of *pensiones, fondas* and *casas de huéspedes* in villages, towns and cities. Many well-run sites serve campers and caravanners.

Arriving

Entry formalities

A valid passport is required for entry into Spain. Nationals of EC countries, the USA, and some other countries, do not need a visa for stays of up to 90 days. It is always wise to check the current situation with the Spanish Tourist Office or Spanish Consulate in your country. You are required by law to carry an official document of identification at all times. A good idea is to make photocopies of passports, driving licences and insurance certificates and to carry these rather than the originals. Visitors from most countries do not require any medical documents but, if in any doubt, check at one of the above places. Customs regulations are in line with those of other European Community countries. Details can be obtained from the above places, airlines and travel agents.

Conversion Table

From	To	Multiply by
Inches	Centimetres	2.54
Centimetres	Inches	0.3937
Feet	Metres	0.3048
Metres	Feet	3.2810
Yards	Metres	0.9144
Metres	Yards	1.0940
Miles	Kilometres	1.6090
Kilometres	Miles	0.6214
Acres	Hectares	0.4047
Hectares	Acres	2.4710
Gallons	Litres	4.5460
Litres	Gallons	0.2200
Ounces	Grams	28.35
Grams	Ounces	0.0353
Pounds	Grams	453.6
Grams	Pounds	0.0022
Pounds	Kilograms	0.4536
Kilograms	Pounds	2.205
Tons	Tonnes	1.0160
Tonnes	Tons	0.9842

By air

Iberia, Spain's national airline, and the airlines of other countries operate scheduled flights from many European airports to the international airports of Sevilla and Málaga. Jerez de la Frontera also has some scheduled connections. Charter companies operate to these airports as well as to Almería and Granada. Direct intercontinental connections are made to Sevilla and Málaga.

Other intercontinental connections are made via Madrid. Connections with Spanish cities are by Iberia or Aviaco, its affiliate. A shuttle air service operates between Madrid and Sevilla. Gibraltar airport is another entry point for the region.

By bus

Long-distance coach services connect other European countries with Andalucía's coastal resort areas and with a number of cities. Enquire from the Spanish Tourist Office in your country. A network of efficient and low-cost coach services links main centres in the region with other parts of Spain. Within the region, too, there is a comprehensive network of inter-provincial and local services in comfortable coaches. Details are available from local tourist offices and bus stations.

By car

An extensive road-building programme geared to EXPO'92, has greatly improved access to the region and passage across it. A driver can now go from Copenhagen, Frankfurt, Paris or Rome to Sevilla or the Costa del Sol without having to stop for a single traffic light. The NIV/E25 *autovia* (dual-carriage highway) from the north enters through the Despeñaperros Pass and is the main road access to the region. As the Autovia Andalucía it connects with Córdoba and Sevilla, from where there is a toll *autopista* (motorway) to Cádiz. Principal access from the east, connecting with the Mediterranean motorway network, is from Murcia along the N342/E26, which, as the Autovia '92, connects with Granada and Sevilla and then goes on to Huelva. Near Antequera, a new *autovia* links with Málaga and the Costa del Sol. On the western side of the region, main access is from Extremadura along the N630/E102 to Sevilla and from Portugal by a new bridge across the Guadiana River near Ayamonte.

By rail

RENFE is Spain's national rail company and its Talgo trains are the fastest and most comfortable along normal tracks. Spain's first high-speed track links Sevilla with Madrid via Córdoba, and the sleek AVE trains make the journey in under three hours. Many rail services within the region have also been upgraded.

By sea

Cruise liners regularly call at Málaga and less frequently at Cádiz and Almería. Regular passenger services of the Trasmediterránea company connect Málaga and Cádiz with Genoa, the Balearic Islands and Canary Islands. Ferry services operate from Almería and Málaga to Melilla; connecting with Ceuta and Tangiers are hydrofoils and/or ships from Benalmádena, Algeciras and Tarifa. Ferries also run between Gibraltar and Tangier.

Consulates

Many countries have consulates in both Sevilla and Málaga. Current addresses and telephone numbers can be obtained from the local police, tourist offices or telephone directories.

Crime

Carefree people in high holiday mood can be easy targets for opportunist criminals, many of whom take to crime to finance a drug dependence. Drunk foreigners are the easiest targets. The snatching of handbags and cameras, picking of pockets, running off with unattended luggage or bags and breaking into cars are the principal crimes against visitors. Muggings to steal jewellery and cash do also happen, more so in lonely streets, parks and seedier parts. Thieves (*semaforos*) sometimes even smash the windows of cars stopped at traffic lights, grab what they can and dash off on a moped or motorcycle.

Although the precautions that visitors can take are obvious, here are a few commonsense reminders. Deposit valuables (travellers' cheques, cash, passports, and so on) in a safety deposit box wherever you are staying. Take care with the security of apartment or villa accommodation. Wear handbags and cameras across your chest and wallets in your front trouser pockets. Do not be ostentatious with jewellery or cash. Keep an eye on your parcels and luggage. Keep car doors locked at all times, even when driving. Do not leave valuables in a car (even a bag holding nothing of value, but left in sight, may be a temptation to break-in). Avoid lonely, seedy and dark areas. Use taxis rather than public transport late at night. Be and look aware.

Disabled Travellers

In general, Andalucíans are
noticeably non-discriminating and
caring towards people with a
physical or mental disability.
Newer buildings are likely to have
amenities such as ramps, wider
doorways, and toilets. Local
authorities throughout the region
have also begun making such
provisions, but generally these are
still limited. Special needs should
be stated and full enquiries made
before making final reservations.

Driving

Breakdown
Special arrangements may be
provided by an insurance policy
bought from your motoring
organisation. In the case of hire
vehicles, contact the hire
company. Breakdown vehicles are
called *grúas* and a repair
workshop is a *taller*. The Real
Automóvil Club de España has
reciprocal arrangements with
motoring organisations elsewhere
and will usually offer advice to any
motorist in need. It has offices in
the provincial capitals and
strategically sited depots at
roadside locations. Emergency
telephones are available along
autovías and occasionally on other
roads.

Car hire
The big-name international firms
operate from offices at airports, in
the cities and in larger resorts, and
you can make bookings with them
in your home country. Holiday
operators have car-hire schemes
and airlines offer fly-drive deals.
Hiring from a smaller local firm
usually shows significant cost
advantage. Be sure to compare
fully-inclusive prices (with
insurance and taxes) and to check
that the insurance cover is
adequate and that there are no
hidden costs.

Documents
Valid driving licences issued by
European Community countries
are acceptable. Visitors from other
countries should have an
international driving licence,
which should be obtainable from
the motoring organisations in their
country.

Fuel
The different types are Normal (92
octane); Super (96 octane); Gas-oil
(Diesel); and Sin Plomo (lead-free),
which is increasingly available.

Parking
Finding legal parking within cities

**Bus is the cheapest way of getting
around a city like Sevilla**

and some towns can be very
difficult, and during high season
the problem extends to most
resorts. Car parks are the best
places to leave your car and they
are not expensive. But they are
few. Streetside spaces are
indicated by blue road and kerb
markings and tickets are bought
from machines on the pavement.

Road signs and rules
Generally they are in line with
those of other European countries,
with eccentricities that are
comprehensible only after
exposure to them. Spain's Ministry
of Transport publishes a small
leaflet of advice for drivers. Try to
get one at frontier posts or tourist
offices. If you are driving to Spain,
take advice and get information
from a motoring organisation in
your country and buy appropriate
insurance.

Eating

Breakfast *(desayuno)*, taken at
home or in a bar, is light, usually
coffee *(café)* or a chocolate drink
(chocolate or *cacoa)* with toast
(tostada) or pastries *(pasteles)*.
This is often repeated during the
morning. Lunch *(almuerzo)*,
traditionally the main meal of the
day and starting after 2pm, is
usually preceded by an *aperitivo*.
Around 6pm, a *merienda*
(afternoon snack) is taken – more
coffee and pastries. After work, it
is time for drinks and *tapas*. The
evening meal at home is light and
taken after 10pm. Around this

time restaurants are getting busy
with people wanting dinner
(cena).

Many restaurants are closed on
Sunday evenings and on Mondays
or another day in the week. In
inland cities, many are closed
during August for their annual
holiday. Restaurants are graded
with one to five forks, but this
reflects the standard of the
facilities, not necessarily that of
the cooking. In resort areas and
the cities, a wide choice of
international cooking is available.
There are also fast-food cafeterias,
chicken grills and other take-
aways, international franchise
operators, and 'milk bars'
(granjas). Traditional-style eating
and drinking places include
mesones in urban areas, *ventas* in
the countryside, and *merenderos,
chirinquitos* and *chamboas* at the
beach. In the western part of the
region *cocederos* or *freidurías de
pescado* are basic places at which
to enjoy freshly fried fish.

Ecological Hints

Seasonal and residential tourism
provides important economic
benefits for Andalucía and its
further growth is crucial to the
region's future prosperity, but
development has, and will
continue to have, an adverse
ecological effect in a region of
great natural diversity and beauty.
A few things that visitors can do to

help are: be sparing in the use of
water and electricity; collect and
dispose of rubbish in designated
places; be careful with cigarette
ends and making fires; and obey
signs, especially if you are in a
nature park.

Electricity

220/230 volts AC and 110/120 in
some bathrooms, and older
buildings. Plugs have two round
pins.

Health and Medical Care

Residents of European Community
countries are entitled to
reciprocal treatment from the
Spanish health service, if they
obtain form E110, E11 or E112
from their national health service.
However, the best advice for all
foreign visitors to Spain is to buy a
travel insurance policy from a
reputable company that provides
comprehensive cover in case of
accident and illness. It is wise to
enquire from the insurance
company exactly what procedure
should be followed in case of
misfortune.

It is also wise to carry a
photocopy of prescriptions for any
medication that you are taking.
Health problems are most likely to
arise from over-indulgence in
drink and food by people in
holiday mood; in summer, they
may be due to too much sun and
eating mayonnaise or 'sad' salads

and 'tired' *tapas*; or they may be a
reaction to unfamiliar tap water
(so stick to the bottled sort).

Pharmacies *(farmacias)*
As well as selling prescription
medicines, pharmacies will
provide free advice about minor
injuries or ailments and suggest a
non-prescription treatment from
their stocks. Or they may advise
a consultation with a doctor
(médico) and propose an
appropriate practitioner. They are
easily identified by a big green or
red cross sign and follow normal
shopping hours, but during other
times they will display a sign
indicating the nearest *farmacia de
guardia* that will be open. Local
papers also list them.

First Aid Centres *(casas de
socorro)*
These may be operated by the
Cruz Roja (Red Cross) or by the
SAS (Andalucían Health Service)
and are found in urban centres,
along country roads and at beach
locations.

Hospitals *(hospitales)*
Andalucía's *SAS* has modern, full-
scale hospitals, comparable with
Europe's best public hospitals, and
more are being built. They have
emergency *(urgencia)* depart-
ments. There are also private
hospitals.

Convalescence
Andalucía's climate and areas of
great natural beauty and peace-
fulness can do much for restoring
some health conditions in people
coming from colder, damper and
more stressful places. Eleven
mineral spas *(balnearios)* are
spread through the region and
provide treatment courses under
medical supervision. It is mostly
older Spanish people who have
patronised the low-key, sometimes
dated hotels, but the trend may be
changing as more people look for
natural treatments and realise that
these places are well-priced and
also well-sited to combine
relaxation and treatments with
sightseeing. Six modern clinics,
five on the Costa del Sol
Occidental and one in Almería,
offer pampered luxury and a
variety of traditional and modern
treatments, including diets and
exercise routines, in personalised
programmes that follow thorough
medical examinations.

**A potter with his traditional kiln
in Sorbas (page 105)**

Atlantic breakers make Cádiz popular with surfers...

Holidays

Besides the variable dates of Easter, when both the Thursday and Friday are holidays, and Whitsun, the principal holidays are:

Año Nuevo 1 January
Día de los Reyes 6 January
Día de Andalucía 28 February
San José 19 March
Día del Trabajo 1 May
San Juan 24 June
Santiago 25 July
Asunción 15 August
Día de la Hispanidad 12 October
Todos los Santos 1 November
Immaculada Concepción 8 December
Navidad 25 December

In addition, cities, towns and villages, as well as *barrios* within them, have their own list of feast days, when most businesses close. When a holiday falls on a Thursday or Tuesday, it is usual to make a *puente (bridge)* and also regard the Friday or Monday as a holiday.

Laundry and Dry Cleaning

Usually considerably cheaper than the services offered by hotels is a local *lavandería* and *tintorería* (often the same place). They mostly charge by weight and need 24 hours. Increasingly, there are also self-service places.

Lost Property

Oficinas de Objetos Perdidos are usually located at *ayuntamientos* (town halls), and/or with the *Policía Local*, and are open Monday to Friday 9.30am–1.30pm. Proof of identity is required for collections. Consulates should be advised about any loss of personal documents and, if necessary, credit card companies should be contacted.

Maps

Tourist offices provide free town plans and maps. Walkers and cyclists may need large-scale maps, available from the Instituto Geográfico Nacional. However, many of these are out of date.

Media and Entertainment Information

Newspapers

Many newspapers *(periodicos)* from other European countries are available by the afternoon. International editions are on sale in the morning. The 'liberal' *El País*, Spain's national daily with the widest respect internationally, publishes an Andalucían edition; so do other national dailies, like the 'conservative' *ABC* and the 'middleground' *Diario 16*. *El Correo de Andalucía* founded in 1899, is especially strong on coverage of the region. The daily *Sur*, published in Málaga, has a free edition in English each Friday.

Magazines

Spain publishes a plethora of magazines *(revistas)*. *Cambio 16* and *Tiempo* are two of the most respected weekly news and features magazines in the *Time/Newsweek* format. For coverage of personalities, *Hola* and *Semana* are the leaders. Among a number of monthly magazines aimed at foreign residents and visitors, and which have articles on Spanish affairs and places, are *Lookout* (English), *Aktuelle* (German) and *Solkysten* (Scandinavian).

Television

Two channels, *TVE-1* and *TVE-2*, are national and state-run; *Canal Sur* is sponsored by the Andalucían government; *Tele-5*, *Antena-3TV* and *Canal Plus* (subscription) are private stations. Some municipalities have their own local stations. Satellites beam in many European stations. BBC and Gibraltar TV programmes are available to parts of Málaga and Cádiz provinces.

Radio

Radio España, SER (Europe's biggest private network and linked with *El País*) as well as a host of other stations vie for space on the airwaves. In resort areas, local stations broadcast in foreign languages or have foreign-language slots.

What's on information

Relevant pages of daily newspapers, local or national with Andalucían editions, give coverage of current events. *Lookout* magazine has a good Agenda section detailing major events of the forthcoming month to help with forward planning. Small local publications provide information about more parochial events. Some cities have a monthly *Guía del Ocio* (leisure guide). The free monthly *Costa del Sol – What's On*, published by the Patronato Provincial de Turismo, covers events in Málaga province. Billboards, posters and leaflets are other sources of information

Money Matters

Banks

Spain has many banks with lots of branches and in recent years there have been major mergers. Foreign banks have also spread through the country. Savings banks, mostly also offering exchange facilities, are called *cajas*. Banks are open Monday to Friday 8.30am–2pm, Saturday (except June to September) 8.30am–1pm. In the summer, some banks may be open on the first and last Saturday of the month. Main branches in cities and large towns stay open until 4.30pm Monday to Friday.

Money exchange facilities are

... while others prefer a more sedentary occupation

available, outside these hours, at airports and points of entry to Spain. Cashpoints issuing money around the clock with use of a cash or credit card and PIN are plentiful.

Credit cards

The major credit, charge and direct debit cards are widely accepted. Make a note of your credit card numbers, and emergency telephone numbers to contact in case of loss, and keep it with your passport.

Currency

The peseta is available in the following denominations: notes – 10,000, 5,000, 2,000, 1,000; coins – 500, 200, 100, 50, 25, 10, 5 and 1.

Tax

IVA, a value-added tax, is currently applied at 6 per cent on most goods and services and at 13 or 33 per cent on luxury items and some services. People resident outside Spain can gain exemption from tax on large individual purchases, but may incur a higher tax on importation into their home country. Shops will provide information and necessary forms.

Nightlife

Like other Spaniards, Andalucíans are night owls, coming out late and hooting loudly until the dawn, especially during the warm months. Streets and places that are quiet at 11pm, when people are

dining, can be buzzing with activity two hours later, when open-air *terrazas* and music bars are throbbing and discos are starting to hum.

Sevilla, followed by Málaga and Granada, has the widest range of cultural and entertainment events on offer, and all types of places in which to while away the dark hours. Nightlife in resort towns comes alive over the Easter weekend and builds up to full power in July and August. Many nightspots are foreign owned, predominantly British, and some feature live performers from their countries or may have sing-alongs and talent contests. Tourist complexes have entertainment programmes aimed at foreigners.

Tablaos (flamenco perform-ances) can be seen in most cities and resorts. Big-name international stars are increasingly including Sevilla, Málaga, Granada or Marbella on their European tour itineraries.

Watersports equipment for hire

Opening Times

The majority of shops are open Monday to Saturday from 9.30am or 10am–1.30pm or 2pm, and then from 4.30pm or 5pm– 7.30pm, 8pm or 9pm. Department stores do not close for lunch, and during peak shopping periods may be open on Sundays. Some shops close on Saturday afternoons and inland most do so in the summer, while in coastal areas they may stay open even longer on Saturdays, as well as being open on Sunday mornings.

Business offices work Monday to Friday between 9am–2pm and 4pm–8pm. In the summer, many businesses work *horas intensivas*, 8am–3pm. Official organisations are generally open to the public from Monday to Friday, 8am or 9am–1pm or 2pm.

There are plenty of campsites

Pharmacies

See Health and Medical Care.

Places of Worship

The great majority of churches are Catholic, with services in Spanish. In a few churches Catholic masses are also said in other languages at specified times. Other denominations and faiths in Andalucía have communities and services in cities and resort areas, especially on the Costa del Sol. Information on places and times of worship is obtainable from foreign-language publications (see Media), tourist offices and consulates.

Police and Emergencies

Officers of three police organisations have different, sometimes confusingly overlapping roles. Andalucía is also creating its own police corps, which initially will be charged with protecting the government buildings, politicians and functionaries. It does not matter to which police an incident is reported in the first instance.

The municipal police (Policia Local) are mainly responsible for traffic matters and the protection of property in urban areas. They have blue uniforms and white checked bands on their vehicles and caps.

Spain's national police (Policia National) also in blue, are responsible for law and order in the major urban areas and for the country's internal security. It is at their *comisaría* that serious crimes or losses should be reported and a statement (denuncia) should be made.

Officers in the olive-green uniforms of the Civil Guard (Guardia Civil) are mostly seen at border posts, in country areas and along the coastline. A branch of the organisation is responsible for highway patrols.

Emergency telephone numbers
Policia Nacional 091; Policia Local 092. These 24-hour numbers will not necessarily connect you with the nearest station, but will get your message relayed. Clearly state the nature of the emergency (urgencia), for example: accident (accidente); robbery (robo); serious illness (enfermedad grave); heart attack (ataque cardiaco). Also state your name, location and the services required, for example: ambulance (ambulancia); fire brigade (bomberos); doctor (médico).

The tower of the parish church overlooks Estepona's old quarter

Post Offices

The post office (correos) is usually clearly signposted in towns. Normal hours are Monday to Friday 9am–2pm, Saturday 9am–1pm, but those in cities stay open later Monday to Friday. Parcels are handled in an adjoining *paquetería*, which is usually open Monday to Friday 9am–1pm. Mail can be sent to you at Lista de Correos (poste restante), followed by postcode, town name and province. Take personal identification when collecting. Post-boxes are yellow and some have different sections for different destinations. Stamps (sellos) can also be bought at tobacconists (estancos).

Public Transport

Air
Travel agents are the best source of information for the traveller. IBERIA has offices in Sevilla, Málaga, Granada, Córdoba, Jerez de la Frontera and Torremolinos.

Bus
All sizeable communities have bus networks operated by local authorities. In resort areas, routes link urban areas with the centre and with nearby towns. A network of scheduled inter-urban routes criss-crosses the region and fares are comparatively low.

Taxis
Taxis are licensed by municipal authorities and are easily identifiable. They show a green light and *libre* sign when available for hire and can be flagged down in the street. In larger urban areas they have meters; others have fixed rates for various destinations or distances and the fare should be determined in advance. There are supplements for baggage or for trips at night, and for those departing from railway stations and the airport.

Trains
Changes and improvements are being made in the region's rail network. Current information can be obtained from travel agents and from RENFE offices.

Senior Citizens

Public authorities and private organisations run various centres and programmes for senior citizens, but these are generally not accessible to foreigners. Specialist operators offer holidays tailored for senior citizens from their countries. Some include tours of the region combined with relaxation in a resort. In the winter months, the tourist industry provides low-cost, long-stay holidays for senior citizens on the Costa del Sol.

Sports

The opportunities to enjoy various participant sports in ideal conditions are increasingly the main attraction for many visitors to

Andalucía. Sports publications, clubs and federations in other countries can be sources of information and, within the region, tourist offices have brochures giving details of local facilities. Some specialist holiday operators offer sports-based packages.

Golf
Predictions are that by 1995 Andalucía could have around 90 courses. The 'Costa del Golf', west from Málaga city and into Cádiz province, has Europe's densest concentration of courses and most of them are of championship standard. Robert Trent Jones, Severiano Ballesteros, Tony Jacklin and Gary Player are among the designers. Heavy booking by members at peak times can make it difficult for visiting players to get a game except during the hottest part of the day. Solutions are booking well in advance, taking a golfing package holiday or staying at a hotel that has preferential arrangements with courses. An explanation for rising green fees is that water is a scarce and costly commodity and one day's feeding of a course is equivalent to the full daily usage of some 80,000 people.

Horse riding
The *Andaluz* love of horses means that there are many stables and riding schools throughout the region where horses can be hired by experienced riders. Most also cater for first-timers and some provide tuition. Centres at Coín in Málaga province and Capileira in Granada province organise horseback excursions of a few days or a week.

Tennis
Courts are plentiful in the coastal resorts, and inland, too, it is not difficult to get a game. Most courts have Tennis Quick surfaces, while others are clay. At some hotels, tennis clubs or integrated sports centres there is tuition at all levels. Wimbledon champions Manuel Santana and Lew Hoad have tennis centres at Marbella and Mijas respectively.

Watersports
All along the coast, and on some lakes, there are seasonal facilities, including tuition, for waterskiing, parasailing and boardsailing. Tarifa is one of the favourite places among the world's top board-sailers. Training in diving is given in Almuñécar; Cabo de Gata has perfect waters for snorkelling.

Sailing and boating
Modern marinas with all facilities and attractive quayside recreational areas are conveniently spaced along the coastline. Boats of all descriptions are available for hire or charter from most of them.

Winter sports
Solynieve is Europe's most southerly winter sports resort and among its most modern (see page 104).

Other sports and activities
Squash courts are among the amenities of many tennis clubs and sports centres. Mountaineers head mostly for the heights of Granada's Sierra Nevada and Jaén's Cazorla mountains; pot-holers find more in the depths of Málaga and Cádiz provinces. Paragliders try it wherever they can, but Málaga's Valle de Abdalajís and Granada's Las Alpujarras are becoming the favourite places. Fishermen also try their luck wherever they can: sea fishing is best off the coasts of Cádiz and Huelva; inland, there are lively streams for sport fishing in all the provinces, and many reservoirs are also well stocked.

Student and Youth Travel
Young travellers should consult with specialist travel agencies, tour operators and youth organisations in their home countries. Within Andalucía, enquiries about events or amenities of special interest for young people, as well as about discount schemes and student hostels, can be obtained from tourist offices and from offices of the *Sección de Juventud* of the municipality. Student activity is liveliest in Sevilla and Granada. These and other places, like Málaga and Almuñécar, have good language-learning schools. There is no shortage of inexpensive accommodation and simple places for cheap meals. Buses are a low-cost way of getting around. Hitch-hiking is not recommended.

A herd of goats seeks the shade near Trevélez

Telefax, Telex, Telegrams

Many hotels provide all of these services, but supplements can at least double the cost. Business bureaux offer telefax and (some) telex services. The telegram office is at the *correos* (post office). Telegrams by telephone – 24-hour service (tel: 422 2000 for services within Spain; 422 6860 for services abroad).

Telephones

The dialling code for seven-digit numbers in Sevilla and Málaga (cities and provinces) is 95. All numbers in Sevilla start with 4 and all those in Málaga start with 2. Other provinces have six-digit numbers and their codes are as follows: Almería 951; Cádiz 956; Córdoba 957; Granada 958; Huelva 955; Jaén 953. The code is used when dialling from other provinces, but not when dialling from within the same province.

To call from outside Spain, dial the international service access code applicable in your country, then 34 for Spain, 5 for Sevilla, or 58 for Granada, and the seven- or six-digit number.

Public phone booths are plentiful. They take 100, 25 and 5 peseta coins and some accept credit cards. Instructions for use are displayed in a number of languages, as are provincial and international dialling codes. Many bars also have telephones for use by customers.

To make direct international calls, put at least 200 pesetas in the groove at the top (or in the slot of some telephones), dial 07 and wait for a changed tone, then dial the country code, the town code (without the initial 0) and the number. Country codes are: Australia 61; Canada 1; New Zealand 64; UK 44; US 1.

You can get assistance, make reversed charge calls and pay after your call at *locutorios* run by Teléfonica, the national telephone company. Cheap rate applies from 10pm to 8am Monday to Friday and from 8pm Saturday to 8am Monday.

Time

Like most of Europe, Spain is two hours ahead of GMT (Greenwich Mean Time) in the summer and one hour ahead in the winter.

There are three types of police

Tipping

Although most hotel and restaurant bills will include a service charge, you may still want to give a tip of between 5 and 10 per cent in restaurants and for special services in hotels. At bars leave more or less 5 per cent from whatever change you get. The same applies to taxis. Other people who usually get tips are car-park attendants, shoe-shines and tour guides.

Toilets

Public lavatories are few and far between. There are toilet facilities at department stores, some museums and places of interest. Bars and restaurants have facilities for their customers.

Tourist Offices

Turespaña of Spain's Ministry of Tourism operates offices in Argentina, Australia, Austria, Belgium, Brazil, Canada, Denmark, Finland, France, Germany, Italy, Japan, Mexico, The Netherlands, Norway, Portugal, Sweden, Switzerland, the UK and the US.

Within the region there are three tiers involved in tourism's administration, promotion and the provision of information: *ayuntamientos* (municipalities) and *diputaciones* (provincial councils), both of which may be linked with local business in *Patronatos de Turismo*, and the Direccíon General de Turismo of the Andalucían government. Offices of the latter in the provincial capitals are as follows:

Calle Hermanos Machado s/n (tel: 23 0858) Almería;

Calderón de la Barca 1 (tel: 21 1313) Cádiz;

Torrijos 10 (tel: 47 1235) Córdoba;

Libreros 2 (tel: 22 5990) Granada;

Avenida Alemania 12 (tel: 25 7403) Huelva;

Arquitecto Berges 1 (tel: 22 2737) Jaén;

Pasaje de Chinitas (tel: 221 3445) Málaga;

Avenida de la Constitución 21 (tel: 221404) Sevilla.

·INDEX·

ACKNOWLEDGEMENTS

The Automobile Association wishes to thank the following
photographers and libraries for their assistance in the preparation of this
book.

DOUGLAS ROBERTSON was commissioned to take all the photographs
for this book except those listed below.

AA PHOTO LIBRARY
Jerry Edmanson 1, 3, 6b, 7a, 7b, 12a, 14a, 14b, 17, 20b, 24, 25a, 30a,
30b, 32a, 36a, 39a, 40b, 43, 44a, 47, 50, 51, 52a, 54b, 64a, 64b, 66a,
66b, 67, 70a, 72a, 72b, 73, 74, 81, 83, 85, 88b, 92a, 94, 96a, 96b, 98,
106, 118a, 118b
Andrew Molyneux 27, 32b, 33b, 34a, 34b, 36b, 37, 38, 39b, 100a, 100b,
110a, 111, 112
Jens Poulsen 11 26a, 42b, 46b, 53, 54a, 55a, 55b, 56a, 56b, 57b, 58a,
58b, 59, 60a, 60b, 61, 62b, 63a, 63b, 89, 110b, 115a, 115b, 116

MARY EVANS PICTURE LIBRARY 19 Trafalgar – 'Belleisle' crippled, 22b
Turks torture Christians, 23 Philip II

ZEFA PICTURE LIBRARY Cover Hill-top town, Málaga

All Tanked Up ...

**The Canadians
in Headley
during World War II**

*compiled from the memories
of Villagers and Veterans*

by John Owen Smith

For those to whom
'Peace in our Time'
came too late.

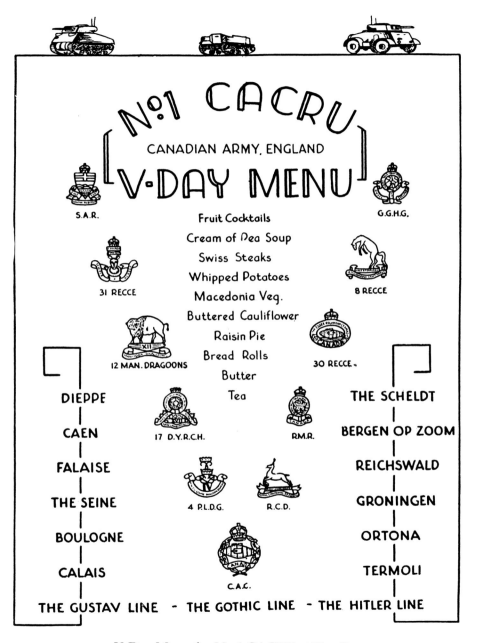

V-Day Menu for No.1 CACRU at Headley
(see page 24)

Author's Note

During a summer visit to a particularly peaceful location in our area with other members of the Headley Society, talk turned to recollections of other less restful times. Thoughts of the 50th anniversary of D-Day, coming up in June 1994, brought back memories to those who were in the village then, of tanks negotiating narrow lanes and Canadian troops packing the pubs. Surely someone should write a history of it all, while people were still around to tell the tale, they said. And so the project started.

We had a certain amount of information to hand locally: lists of regiments which had stayed in the village, back copies of local newspapers, parish magazines and, of course, the memories of those who were here. But to get the Canadian point of view, I decided to advertise in their Veterans' magazines, both in Britain and in Canada, for anyone who remembered Headley. I'd thought this might draw a blank, but I needn't have worried - every week seemed to bring new letters and fascinating stories from across the Atlantic and, conveniently, addresses of several Canadian ex-servicemen now living in England.

In particular I wanted to discover facts about Erie Camp, the military detention centre situated where Heatherlands now stands, and was delighted when one of the letters from Canada turned out to be from an ex-inmate, who was able to give me an informative and amusing, if in parts unpublishable, view of life behind the wire.

Visiting museums, reading regimental histories and talking to those who had served in armoured divisions gave me background material to add to the personal stories of men who had passed through the village on their way to Normandy or Italy, and one lucky find in a local house-clearance sale brought me notes from a wartime course on 'how to service armoured vehicles'.

Stories of wartime are bitter-sweet affairs - a mixture of pride and poignancy extends through both personal and public events. The story I'm telling belongs not to me, but to the people of Headley and Canada who entrusted me with their memories, and I thank them for so willingly volunteering their information. I have tried where possible to let their voices speak, and keep my own comments and additions to a minimum; after all, I wasn't there at the time and they were. I sincerely hope both they and many others will enjoy reading the book.

John Owen Smith
Headley, 1994

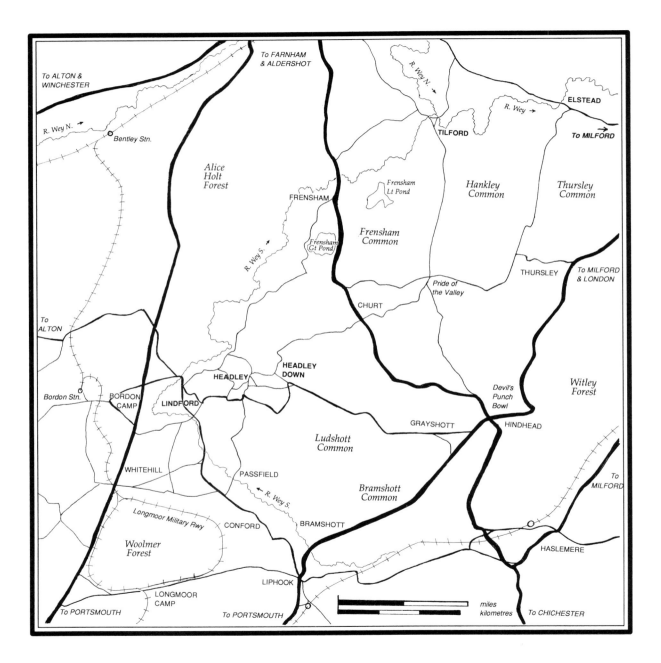

To ALTON & WINCHESTER

To FARNHAM & ALDERSHOT

R. Wey N.

R. Wey N.

Bentley Stn.

Alice Holt Forest

FRENSHAM

R. Wey S.

Frensham Lt Pond

Frensham Gt Pond

Frensham Common

Hankley Common

Thursley Common

ELSTEAD

R. Wey

TILFORD

To MILFORD

To ALTON

THURSLEY

To MILFORD & LONDON

Pride of the Valley

CHURT

Bordon Stn.

BORDON CAMP

LINDFORD

HEADLEY

HEADLEY DOWN

Devil's Punch Bowl

Witley Forest

GRAYSHOTT

HINDHEAD

Ludshott Common

WHITEHILL

PASSFIELD

To MILFORD

Longmoor Military Rwy

CONFORD

R. Wey S.

BRAMSHOTT

Bramshott Common

Woolmer Forest

LONGMOOR CAMP

LIPHOOK

HASLEMERE

To PORTSMOUTH

To PORTSMOUTH

miles
kilometres

To CHICHESTER

General Map of the Area

Including Bentley to Bordon branch railway line and Longmoor Military Railway, both now closed.

Note that Frensham Great and Little Ponds were drained during the war, to prevent enemy aircraft using them as navigational aids.

All Tanked Up ...

Introduction

The village of Headley sits just across the River Wey from Bordon Camp. This was constructed at the turn of the century on land first purchased by the army in 1863 for use as a training area and, until the end of the 1920s, formed an integral part of Headley parish. Through the years, therefore, the village has become familiar with the presence of the military close at hand. Older residents tell of hearing the bugle calls from the Camp, and today we can hear quite distinctly the firing coming from the Woolmer ranges.

During the First World War, villagers saw troops, led by their military bands, marching through from Bordon to Ludshott Common in order to practice digging trenches. They remember a meat depot and bakery being established on the Village Green, bread being baked in open ovens for the soldiers of several local camps, and the Institute adjoining the back of the Congregational Chapel (both since demolished) being used to give soldiers a cup of tea on Sunday afternoons.

Sadly, all too few years were to pass before the village and common were again used for similar purposes.

The Village Prepares

Britain declared war on Germany on 3rd September 1939 and, as Mrs Katie Warner puts it, "immediately there were plans made to billet soldiers everywhere in the village." She lived in the School House at the time, and recalls that initially tents were erected on the Village Green, and a field cookhouse "like a huge saucepan for producing stew" arrived to provide hot food for the soldiers there. Winter was soon upon them - that first year there was a lot of snow - and when eventually it began to thaw, the soldiers were "ploughing around ankle deep in mud."

In fact that winter was the coldest on record since 1894, although this could not be publicised at the time, as the weather was a military secret during the war.

A number of houses, such as *Belmont* in the High Street, were already owned by the Army, but others in the area were quickly requisitioned. Herbert Price with 'D' Company of the 1/6th South Staffordshire Regiment was billeted in *The Mount*, through the archway at the top of Barley Mow Hill, from October 1939 until March 1940. In letters written to Pauline Grove, who lives there now, he says: "That winter was very cold, and I remember the trees were all turned more or less into glass. The track from *The Mount* was very rough, and we used to 'Get fell in' and march, or rather slide, down the track to the Green where the marquees were set up to serve as dining quarters. Very primitive, but looking back it was fun. Frozen tea, spuds, veg, you name it and we had it."

The tents remained on the Green for "maybe the best part of a year", according to Katie Warner, while other more permanent accommodation was found or built. Nissen Huts were constructed in the Rectory Field, on the Village Green and elsewhere in the village, and eventually a proper brick canteen was built on the Green during 1941. At the top of Rectory Field there were also two dining halls, which were of brick, "but they never had roofs put on - they had huge canvas marquees put over them instead." *Apparently there was a similar pair erected on Crestafield along with a NAAFI according to David Whittle, one used as a dining room and the other, he thinks, as a QM stores.*

"We didn't have a lot of pay in 1939", says Herbert Price, "but what we had we were happy to spend on Friday and Saturday evenings in the *Wheatsheaf*. Mostly though, during the week, we used to frequent the tea room in the village for a cuppa, and sometimes a cake. My memories of Headley are very pleasant. I can see that room now, round tables, flowers in the middle, home from home. *The words 'Headley Restaurant' were, according to Sue Allden, painted on the side wall of Radford's Shop, now Long Cross House, but removed as a security measure when the war began.*

"We were inspected by HM the King and Queen at Bordon prior to going to France with the BEF. I wonder how many recall that, in 1940? It was a fair march from Headley."

There were other British regiments stationed in the village at this early stage in the war. Betty Roquette's cousin by marriage, Lord George Scott who was Colonel in charge of Hussars, was billeted in *Beech Hill House*. Ironically her brother, Jim Richards, was also here later as part of the Canadian Provost Company guarding Erie Camp just up the hill, but the two men never knew each other.

Betty Parker remembers the South Staffordshires, Jim Clark the 9th Lancers and the 10th Hussars, and Joyce Stevens also recalls the latter, mostly conscripts she thinks, who were here for some time. Arthur Dean remembers they were parked in Headley, "for a long time in the early part of the war - mainly up from the *Wheatsheaf* alongside the road - and they had the old Crusader tanks."

But eventually the British troops left, and Headley's special relationship with the Canadians was to begin.

The Canadians Arrive

Canada declared war on 10th September 1939, and the first 'flight' of Canadian troops for Britain sailed in a convoy from Halifax, Nova Scotia to arrive safely in the Clyde on 17th December of that year. The 7,400 servicemen on board included men from Infantry regiments, the Army Service Corps and the 'Mounties'. The latter formed the No. 1 Provost Company, some of whom were to serve, like Jim Richards, in

Headley as 'provos', supervising the Canadian military detention centre. Many further 'flights' followed over the next 4 to 5 years, bringing a large variety of Canadian regiments to these shores. During the whole of this time only one ship carrying Canadian troops was torpedoed.

It seems that no Canadian troops were stationed in Headley itself until 1941, but several of their service units were located in Bordon from the early days of the war and, since Headley was regarded as a good place in which to 'get away', Canadian soldiers soon became a familiar sight in the village. Not all of the resulting encounters were as cordial as might be hoped. Tom Grisdale, who ran a poultry farm in Liphook Road at the time, recalls: "One night I looked out of the window and saw a light down the field. I took my gun and a torch, and found two French Canadians who'd just hunted this sack full of chickens. Fortunately they hadn't killed them, so I rammed the gun in their backs and they dropped the sack and put their hands up. They said if I let them go they wouldn't come again, so I did - otherwise I thought I'd probably have the whole regiment."

John Ellis (who later was to transport American armour to Utah Beach in LCTs) also remembers the Canadians' partiality for supplementing their rations with local fresh meat. He says: "Before 1943, we had a pig farm adjoining the stores and buildings at Headley Mill, including a breeding section. One night, someone got into the pigsties and took a whole litter of suckling pigs. In the morning, the sow was standing there alone, and we found a full bottle of beer, which had been used to stun the pigs, and a forage cap complete with the badge of the Canadian Provost Corps!" On another occasion, one moonlit night near Christmas time, his sister saw some Canadian soldiers strip off and plunge into the ice cold water of the mill pond to try and catch the geese there - but this time they failed.

The Canadians also had their own reservations about some of our British ways. One ex-soldier recalled that British instructors tried to teach him, unsuccessfully, how to bowl a grenade. Another remembers the very elderly Brigadier who, "at the completion of our training at a battle school in Wales explained the purpose of the final exercise: 'You Canadian chaps will be the Swazi tribesmen in the hills and we British will dislodge you.' Churchill was saying Nazis while the Brigadier was saying Swazis, and Lord it was a confusing war for us at the muddy boots level."

A detachment of 6th Field Company Royal Canadian Engineers 3rd Division arrived in Headley on 16th July 1941, with instructions to build a military prison camp. Tom Grisdale recalls that it was built using timber brought all the way over from Canada. It was to be on "what seemed to be a piece of wasteland", according to Fergus Steele, who helped construct it. They lived in tents nearby and "completed the job about the middle of October." This "wasteland" was part of the Land of Nod, owned by Major Whitaker, and some villagers still remember it as being "the prettiest spot in Headley - wonderful view from there - pure unspoilt common land, heath, pines and heather." It became Erie Camp, now Heatherlands Estate.

Whether by coincidence or design, the new Headley Down automatic telephone exchange opened at about the same time as Erie Camp was completed. It stood halfway down Glayshers Hill, just across the road from the camp, in a building dated 1939. We have records showing that the phone number given to the 'Canadian Detention Barracks' was Headley Down 2174.

During September 1941, while the Detention Barracks were still being built, the Calgary Regiment moved into Headley having lived under canvas on Salisbury Plain for a couple of months since arriving in the country. It was one of three regiments in the 1st Canadian Army Tank Brigade, which was now being concentrated "in the Farnham area" to perform training "on the moors" with the 3rd Canadian Infantry Division.

The Calgarys arrived with old 'Waltzing Matilda' tanks, but these were soon replaced by new Churchills. Jim Clark remembers watching them waterproofing the Churchills on Openfields - "putting black bituminous stuff, round the doors on the side", and Arthur Dean, whose sister married Jim Hanczin of the Calgarys, recalls: "we used to go up to Rogers Field, by the *Holly Bush,* and see them putting waterproofing all round the turrets - they put thick tape over the joints and anything that opened or moved - then they got the exhausts right up in the air, so they could go through the water."

"We knew something was *on*", Jim Clark said - and suddenly they all left and never came back. He links this in his mind with the raid on Dieppe, in which the Calgary Regiment was involved, but regimental records show that they left Headley in December 1941 to take up a role guarding the South Coast of England, eight months before the Dieppe operation occurred.

The largest body of troops to sail from Canada during the war embarked at Halifax in November 1941, and included the 5th Canadian Armoured Division. The convoy of 12 liners arrived on this side of the Atlantic on 22nd/23rd November. On landing in Britain, the regiments were first sent by rail to Aldershot, and Pete Friesen of the Fort Garry Horse remembers marching from Aldershot station through the town at midnight to full musical accompaniment from their trumpeters, of whom he was one, and being booed by the residents for waking them.

They stayed there in old, cold barracks which were not at all popular. As Pat Lewis of the Sherbrooke Fusiliers, who came along the same route a year later, said: "Nobody liked Aldershot - you got one bucket of coke and a few bits of wood and you had a grate, and that's all you had to heat a massive room - and there were 15 people in that room. As soon as you had a penny in your pocket you ran out of there as fast as you could go - sometimes you didn't know where you were going to - you just got on a bus and went somewhere, anywhere." Pete Friesen added that the piles of coke in Aldershot barracks used to be sprayed white so that the authorities could see if anyone had been stealing it overnight.

A Popular Station

After a few weeks, the regiments were moved to other locations more suitable for tank training. One of these was Headley, and the official history of the Lord Strathcona's Horse recollects that "the march from Aldershot to Headley was one of the most pleasant ever made, through small lanes." It includes a photograph taken of the men marching along what could be Bacon Lane, although the location is untitled, and continues: "On arrival, the troops were delighted to find that the

new billets were requisitioned civilian houses which, although not mansions, were vastly more pleasant than the damp, dark barracks of Aldershot." They were also to live in Squadron groups (of about 80 to 90 men) for the first time. "The final item which filled our cup to overflowing was the fact that a short 15 minute walk in any of three directions brought us to one of 3 delightful country pubs. One of these, *The Wheatsheaf*, was perhaps a little too handy, as the members of 'A' Squadron will remember."

This was April 1942, a time of many Canadian arrivals in the area. Men from other armoured regiments also marched or drove along the lanes from Aldershot during the month, including the Fort Garry Horse, who were to become the best known regiment in the village, as they and their mascot 'Whitey' were stationed here not once, but twice during the run up to D-Day. Their official record states that Headley "proved to be one of our most popular stations; we soon got to know the natives, who we found very agreeable - it was really our first meet up with the English folk." Each regiment had a compliment of 660 'all ranks', and at least two regiments at a time were stationed here, so accommodation for more than 1,300 men must have been required in and around the village.

There were normally three regiments attached to an armoured Division or Brigade, and these tended to move station together. In the case of the 5th Canadian Armoured Division, two regiments (Fort Garry Horse and Lord Strathcona's Horse) were placed in the Headley area, while the third (1st Hussars) was placed in the Elstead area. This continued to be the pattern for future postings here.

The 5th Division, which at this time included the British Columbia Dragoons who are also reported to have come here, stayed for about 4 months, until the beginning of August 1942, then left for Hove. Shortly afterwards, three regiments of the 4th Division arrived in the area: the Elgin Regiment, the South Alberta Regiment, and the British Columbia Regiment, who also stayed with us for about 4 months.

The first two of these were replaced in January 1943 by other regiments of the 4th Division, at a time when the Canadian

Armoured Divisions were being re-organised. The Governor General's Foot Guards and the Canadian Grenadier Guards stayed for about a month before they moved on. Marcel Fortier of the Foot Guards notes: "The citizens received us with customary English reserve, but this atmosphere soon gave way to one of warm hospitality. Headley became one of the homes that was eventually left with deep regret."

Almost immediately, in February 1943, the newly formed 3rd Canadian Army Tank Brigade arrived, but consisting largely of familiar faces: the Fort Garrys were back in Headley, and the 1st Hussars were back in Elstead; only the Sherbrooke Fusiliers were new, and Pat Lewis found: "We weren't accepted by the others. They wanted the pubs and the girls and they'd already made the contacts, so we had to go elsewhere for our entertainment." They stayed for 3 months until the end of May 1943 but, with all the 'schemes' that were going on at the time, they were probably living in the area for only half that period.

The 3rd Brigade left Headley at about the time the last armoured regiments were coming over from Canada. Two of these were stationed here: Al Trotter of the 16/22 Saskatchewan Horse recalls: "We arrived in Headley late one summer evening in '43, and were billeted in Nissen huts near an Anglican Church very close to the village" - presumably these were the ones in Rectory Field; and William Curtis of the Essex Regiment remembers: "We were stationed in and around Headley in the fall of 1943 until the spring of 1944." Both these regiments, and the others which came over with them, were disbanded, and their men sent to augment existing regiments.

But earlier, when the 5th Division had arrived here in the spring of 1942, where was the armour? The Straths had only a "few old Lees and a couple of Rams which had just arrived in the third week of March", and the Garrys had "very few tanks" then, according to Harvey Williamson. The full complement for a regiment at the time was supposed to be in the region of 50-60 tanks, and these were eventually delivered in batches over the next few years as the regiments moved around Britain from location to location. In April 1942, however, the tank regiments had arrived, but effectively they had no tanks.

Billets and Parking Lots

Although the army already owned a number of properties in Headley, others were requisitioned in order to accommodate the hundreds of troops coming into the village. Grace Barnes (née Snow), who lived then as now down Glayshers Hill, remembers: "My husband had been called up in 1940, so I was here on my own, and they wanted to billet troops on me - I wasn't having that, so I went down the road to my parents' home and lived there." Her house was let to two different families during the war, and suffered cracks in the ceilings due to the constant tank traffic up and down the hill.

Generally the Canadians were moved into empty houses rather than sharing with the local householders. Some of these were up Barley Mow Hill, and others mentioned were *Belmont, Hatch House Farm, Kenton House, Windridge, The Mount, Beech Hill House, Walden* (now *Heathfield*) and *Pound Cottage*. Jim Clark's father worked for the army during the war as a carpenter, though he was a wheelwright by trade, and he used to go round these houses doing repairs. Sometimes the damage was substantial; Sue Allden recalls that *Sunnybank* (by Arford Farm) was almost torn to bits by Canadians billeted there.

Church Gate Stores in the High Street was used as a squadron orderly building, and Canadian troops there added to the wealth of graffiti already in the attic from domestic servants of previous generations *(see photo)*. In addition, Nissen huts were erected all over the place: in the Rectory Field beside the hedge from the school up to the *Holly Bush*, on the Village Green, on Openfields, in gardens along Barley Mow Hill, in woods behind *The Mount*, in Crestafield (now the Windmill estate), in fields now occupied by Hilland estate, on Cricket Lea in Lindford, and on the edge of Ludshott Common next to Seymour Road. Erie Camp, of course, was a special case - the 66 wood and brick buildings there were for the exclusive use of the prisoners and their guards.

Pat Lewis recalls the NAAFI on Ludshott Common and the two ladies who ran it with great affection: "We didn't have much money and our regiment felt, to some extent, like outcasts - we were the new guys brought into the Division. That was the reason we used the NAAFI so much, and these ladies were marvellous, absolutely marvellous - the army food was pretty good, but we never liked it, and they would supply us with sandwiches and souffles and things."

Harvey Theobald, in 'A' Squadron of the Garrys, also tells of the joy of supplementary provisions: "To add variety to the monotonous army rations, we were indeed grateful for the greens, in season, provided by the fforde's farm (*Coolgreany*); the green spring onions from Rogers store - devoured by the troops like candy bars; and milk products from the dairy (*The White House*) run by Percy and May Wilcox.

Grace Barnes remembers there was a cookhouse behind *The Mount*. She had two Labrador dogs which she kept in a big run in her garden, and when they caught the scent of cooking they tore holes in the netting to get out - however, she always knew where to go and find them. The sign "Regimental Butcher" is still to be seen painted inside the door to the garage at *Headley Mount Cottage*, as are the blue lines painted on the wall outside to separate the bins for "swill only" and "ashes only".

For young Canadian men seeing life in rural England for the first time, Headley seemed to take on a magical quality. Pat Lewis recalls: "We were amazed at how tidy the people were, how they looked after their environment in those days. You had the guy with the wheel-barrow, the shovel and the brush, and he kept the gullies along the road clear, and he swept up the leaves. You looked out of the window in the morning in Headley and saw flowers all over the place, and what impressed us most was the tranquillity - you'd do guard duty, and from 2 to 4 o'clock in the morning you'd hear all kinds of bird songs as the false dawn came in." Harvey Theobald noted that the sound of the cuckoo was first treated by them as a novelty, but very soon wore out its welcome.

Al Trotter recalls a different sort of attraction: "One evening an NCO and I went for a walk along one of those nice footpaths. The flowers were blooming all over the place. The trees just about covered the path in areas. It was beautiful. Anyway, we came across this tennis court. Two real pretty girls were pushing a lawn mower and they were having a hard time as the grass was pretty high. This NCO volunteered him and me to cut the grass for them. I wasn't keen on the idea, but nevertheless went along with it. We cut grass and trimmed flowers for about an hour, then, lo and behold, a couple of young officers came upon the scene with their tennis gear on. They thanked us, but I had the feeling we were being had. All the rest of the evening I gave this Corporal a hard time, and asked him what we were trying to prove, as we didn't even know how to play the game." *Now then, you Headley locals - own up, who was it?*

When the tank regiments received their tanks, these were often parked near to the troops. Mrs Warner remembers: "You would sometimes find a tank in the corner of someone's garden - they just put down a slab of concrete under overhanging trees, and drove a tank in there." There were tanks parked up Barley Mow Hill and Headley Hill Road, down Beech Hill Road where the scout hut is, along the Grayshott Road opposite Ludshott Common, at Crestafield where the Windmill estate is now, along Liphook Road where Hilland estate is, down in Lindford by the cross roads, in Openfields where the school is now, and behind *Rowley House* in what was known as 'Rogers Field' *(see map opposite and Appendix I)*.

Jim Clark, who was a schoolboy at the time, lived then as now in Church Lane and remembers the tanks just at the top of his road in Openfields. "They used to take us on the tanks - it was one big adventure - they sat us in the seats. We had Churchills here and then Shermans, and some small tanks we called 'Littlies'. He also recalls being in school one afternoon when the Canadians decided to have a grenade-throwing practice in the Rectory Field: "Old Amos sent us home from school early that day, saying there's no point in trying to teach us with all that noise going on."

"Quite an exciting time for us", he continues. "We used to wander round the tanks up there - they had everything all laid out - I remember seeing a load of revolvers and Sten guns beside the tanks. They were very irresponsible in a way - they used to leave ammunition all over the place, and you could go along and just pick it up - take the bullets, knock the heads off, take the cordite out and make rockets of them."

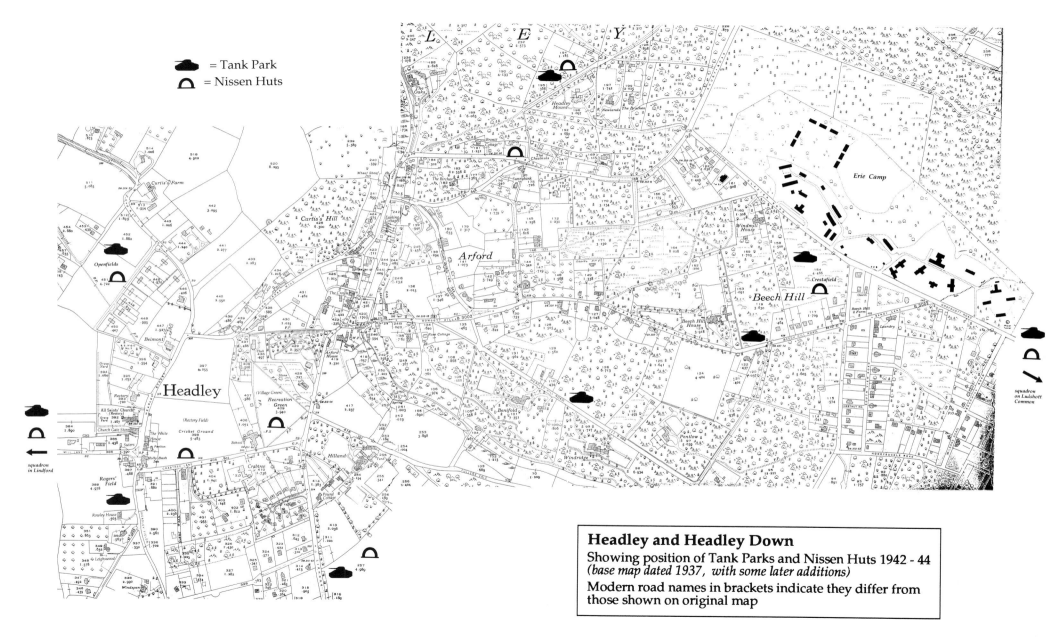

= Tank Park
= Nissen Huts

Headley and Headley Down

Showing position of Tank Parks and Nissen Huts 1942 - 44
(base map dated 1937, with some later additions)

Modern road names in brackets indicate they differ from
those shown on original map

Encounters with the Locals

The local population were in two minds about their visitors from abroad. Joyce Dickie (née Snow, Grace Barnes' younger sister) worked at the telephone exchange in Bordon and recalls the first Canadian soldiers she met there: "They were all bad ones that they'd taken from prison - I got into contact with them quite a bit and they were really horrible." She used to say this to her mother, but was told: "You shouldn't talk like that, they've come over to help us." Her mother ran dances and social evenings on behalf of the Red Cross in the Village Hall, which the War Office had commandeered. People promised to give a penny a week towards the cost, and Joyce went round the village to collect the pennies every Monday. There were plenty of young Canadian soldiers at these dances, and Joyce met one there who she later married. "So I changed my mind about them eventually", she said.

Many villagers would invite servicemen in for a cup of tea on a more or less regular basis, and others organised small parties for them. "We used to have little parties up on Headley Down and invite the soldiers", Joyce Dickie remembers. "We couldn't get very many in because it was only a little hall (along Fairview Road, now a dwelling). We each used to ask one soldier, and we'd supply cider and crisps - we had some jolly good times up there." Jim Richards told his sister, Betty Roquette, how he would go across from the huts at Crestafield to get fruit and fish & chips from Mrs Eddey, who had open house for the Canadians on Sundays. Mr Eddey also used to run dances.

Some of the Canadians remember the time when Jack and Marjorie Harrison invited them round to their house *(in Reynolds, Standford Lane)* for a corn roast. John Whitton, an officer in 'B' Squadron of the Garrys, recalls: "It was a very North American event. Marjorie was an American by birth, English by education, and had grown the corn at Headley from seed sent to her by her father in Connecticut. It was delicious."

The soldiers held social events of their own. Joyce Dickie recalls: "They used to have parties in Bordon, and come round in a big truck to pick up all the girls. There was so much food, and we were rationed. They had lots of cigarettes with flip-tops, and sweets." On a more formal level, some of the village ladies were invited round by the Canadians for supper evenings. Joyce Stevens remembers going with the rector's daughter and others to *The Mount*, off Barley Mow Hill, where they were given what they assumed to be a typical Canadian meal - heaps of food, and all on one plate. John Whitton recalls the time the 'A' Squadron officers gave a garden party and invited all their neighbours round. "There was tea, sandwiches, punch and other refreshments. One or two of the elderly guests didn't fully realize what the other refreshment really was - their systems weren't accustomed to it and they were helped home with much laughter."

Village men serving in the British forces returned on leave to find Canadians "all over the place" and were not altogether happy about the situation, but the local girls were of a different disposition. As Pat Lewis put it: "They'd been brought up on American movies, and they associated us with the Americans and the great prairies of Canada, and thought it would be marvellous to live out there." Local girls remember being told: 'Marry me - I own a gopher farm back home'. "If I'd been a young Headley village boy I'd have been very uptight about things", said Pat; but he adds, "we fought more among ourselves than we did with the villagers." Tom Webb of the Garrys writes: "I do know that the people of the village were most gracious and friendly to us, and even forgiving, for we were not exactly angels."

Betty Parker (née Aldred), who lived then as now in *Eashing Cottages*, remembers going down the alley beside *Belmont* with a friend and putting sticks out for doughnuts - the Miss Laverteys used to scold them for it, she says. She was aged about 14 or 15 at the time. "We used to have good fun with their boxes of chocolates and cookies - we'd say 'any gum chum', and they'd give us a big packet of gum. We used to go up by *The Chestnuts* (now *Hill Cottage*, on Barley Mow Hill), and they'd say 'mend my socks and you'll get some chewing gum', and we girls used to mend their blooming socks - darn them just for a piece of chewing gum. They were always chewing gum - always."

They also had a reputation for drinking a fair amount. The pubs were very different to Canadian bars - and "they got so wild because they drank here as they never could in Canada - and they had more money than our men", as one local remembers it. The three pubs in Headley seemed to be packed out most of the time. "It wasn't just the troops based in Headley", said Pat Lewis, "we had the Canadian Army women in Bordon plus the laundry (on Broxhead Common) which most of them worked in - for some reason or other they all seemed to be in the pubs at Headley, at least while we were there, so you had to hold onto your glass - if you put it down, it disappeared and you couldn't get another drink.

"Sometimes you couldn't get into the bar - there was a stairway in the first pub as you go down the hill (the *Wheatsheaf*) that went up to the snug - well that staircase, it used to be full - no room inside." He was stationed in the huts on Ludshott Common by Seymour Road, and says he used to do most of his drinking in the *Fox and Pelican* at Grayshott, where it was quieter. Troops from his regiment were also taken by trucks to Haslemere and "dropped by the two hotels" there. More than once he had to walk back when he missed the return lift.

Betty Parker, too, recalls that the pubs were packed. She lived between the *Crown* and the *Wheatsheaf*, and remembers them charging 2/6d deposit on a glass, so her father used to take a jam jar along. Arthur Dean recalls that Mr Smallbone, the landlord of the *Crown*, would get two or three local lads to go round and pick up the glasses, so when the soldiers wanted another drink they had to go and pay their half crown again.

The troops would sit in a row opposite the *Wheatsheaf*, where the phone box is now, and Betty remembers the publican there following them up the road asking for their glasses back, and seeing them drop them on the road in front of him. John Whitton recalls: "I've forgotten the owner's name, but his teen-aged daughter was called Jeannie, I believe, and while really too young to be drawing beer for us, she was very good natured and popular with us all."

Harvey Williamson says: "'Old Charlie' played the piano in the *Crown* - not very well, not much more than 'You Are My Sunshine', but he'd keep playing so long as you put a pint on his piano." Sometimes they'd send out the jeep to find out the opening times of the various pubs - it seemed that one would open as another closed. He admitted that when they went out, the emphasis was on the drinking. Tom Webb, of the same regiment, remembers good times at the three pubs, and "an unforgettable pint of Old at the *Wheatsheaf* after a drinkless trip from Glasgow. I still taste it", he says.

Pat Lewis commented that with many Canadians it was the way they drank it which gave them problems with English beer - mixing it up with spirits or drinking whisky chasers. They were also "knocked around a bit" by the old ale which came out in winter time, but Al Trotter says he found his first Mild & Bitter quite potent enough, "much to my sorrow the next morning."

Even those who couldn't get to meet the locals still have their memories of them. Len Carter of the 1st Canadian Parachute Battalion who, after taking a prolonged and unauthorised leave in London, found himself behind the wire of Erie Camp, remembers: "From those days I came away with an impression which has stayed with me all this time. Gazing one day at freedom beyond the wire, I saw this elderly grey haired lady, a stately looking person on a high-seated bicycle pedalling slowly, almost majestically, along the road with a cigarette hanging from the side of her mouth. I believe that if an army convoy had come along it would have pulled over to accord her right of passage, and I thought at the time it was she, not Britannia, who typified the Brits." *Many readers in Headley will have their own ideas as to who this lady might have been.*

Services and Entertainments

The Parish Church at Headley became a garrison church for the Canadian troops in the area, and was later presented by the Canadians with a beautiful silk flag with a maple leaf on it, in grateful memory. Mrs Warner played the organ here for many years, and remembers that the soldiers' service was held an hour or so before the regular village service - and when the villagers arrived, there were complaints from certain Headley residents about the smell of 'wet khaki' lingering in the church.

Non-conformists used to go to the Congregational Chapel off Long Cross Hill, and Betty Parker recalls that a lot of Canadians went there - "I think they liked that kind of service", she said. Pat Lewis, as a Catholic, went to St Joseph's church at Grayshott in whose churchyard so many of his Catholic compatriots from the First World War lie buried. Others may

---

'Whitey', the Fort Garry mascot

Villagers such as Katie Warner have fond memories of the Garrys mascot, 'Whitey' the Collie dog (see photo): "He used to lead the regiment to church. They'd bring him in, and he would lie down in the aisle right by the front pew, and would stay there the whole time. If you couldn't see him you wouldn't know he was there - and when the service was over he would get up and lead them out again."

'Whitey' had been smuggled into England in a box under anaesthetic, and was a great favourite with troops and villagers alike. Rod Waples, secretary of the Fort Garry Horse Association, says: "'Whitey' was a Fort Garry Horse member - his Regimental No. was H 26001/2 - and he came to us one cold night in the winter of 1939. He appeared on the doorstep, was invited in to warm up, and stayed."

John Whitton remembers: "Whitey lived with 'B' Squadron, and at morning parade time, when the Sgt. Major would shout his orders to "fall in", Whitey would literally herd the men into their various troop formations, all the while barking and rounding up the slow movers. He knew to be quiet when the Sgt. Major was about to give forth with subsequent 'orders', but would then give more barking, just to punctuate the occasion." E C Brumwell, also of 'B' Squadron, recalls: "He would attach himself to a Trooper as his master for a couple of weeks, then move on to another troop."

Sadly, 'Whitey' was accidentally run over and killed by a truck shortly before D-Day, and buried with proper military ceremony at a spot code-named 'Shangri-La' near Fawley in May 1944.

---

have attended Mass in Mr Alex Johnston's garage at *Leighswood* along Headley Fields, which he offered for use when petrol rationing made travel to Grayshott increasingly difficult.

The army had requisitioned the Village Hall, and various entertainments were put on here for the troops. (The floor had to be replaced after the war due to the damage caused by the soldiers' boots.) Betty Parker and Jim Clark both remember the cinema shows there, and how the local children would creep into the front in the dark - "they weren't supposed to be there of course." Dances were on Friday or Saturday, with the villagers providing cakes, refreshments and raffle prizes. These were generally happy events, and although the local *Herald* newspaper of the period reported three separate 'incidents' in which Canadian soldiers were brought to court for molesting local girls, this can hardly be considered exceptional over a four year period.

Soldiers stationed away from the centre of the village often went elsewhere for their entertainment. Those on Ludshott Common tended to go to Grayshott and Haslemere - Pat Lewis, who was in Nissen huts by Seymour Road with the Sherbrooke Fusiliers, says that he never heard of a dance going on in Headley. The only village function he remembers attending in his 3 months here was at Grayshott, where they had a regimental sports day at the playing field just before they left the area, and the ladies put on tea for them.

Those based in Lindford had cinema shows in *Hatch House Farm*, and walked to dances at Liphook Village Hall, according to Pete Friesen of the Garrys 'HQ' Squadron, which was quartered in Nissen huts at Lindford during both visits here - they knew the *Holly Bush*, but otherwise rarely visited the centre of Headley. His elder brother Jack ('Shorty') and younger brother Dave *(see photo)* were with him here. They were all in the Garrys' regimental band, which was the HQ Squadron scout car troop, the Sergeant in charge being the band leader. The residents of Lindford should have heard some fine reveilles!

Soldiers and civilians alike from Headley used to go to the two cinemas in Bordon during the war: the *Palace* in Deadwater and the *Empire* behind the Post Office (now the sorting office) off Camp Road. Sue Allden remembers catching the bus from the village to the *Empire* and seeing many films there - she remembers it was always full of soldiers, and had that distinctive smell of khaki uniforms about it. Close to the *Empire* was the 'Church of England' club, which also proved popular with servicemen in the area.

Treats and Recreations

As well as participating in village entertainments, the troops organised their own recreations. The official records of both the Garrys and the Straths mention a full programme of sports competitions, including baseball, boxing, hockey and cross-country running, held between Canadian regiments. 'Slim' Bradford, now living in Hindhead, though not based in Headley at the time, remembers visiting the village to take part in a boxing match. He recalls too the 24-hour gambling schools which "took place in all locations."

The Canadians gave treats to the locals, especially at Christmas time. Katie Warner says: "When the Canadian soldiers realised that sweets and chocolate and everything were so very scarce here, they sent over big boxes of them which were taken to the school and distributed among the children. I'm sure there must be hundreds of children around here who received some of those sweets." They organised Christmas parties at the Village Hall, and gave the Holme School children a party *at Hatch House Farm* in Lindford. "They picked us up in a lorry", Jim Clark recalls, "and at Wellfield Corner we hit another lorry coming the other way - no-one was hurt, but I remember the bang." He also remembers the wooden yacht he was given - "a super little boat with sails and everything."

They arranged parties at Erie Camp for the local Headley Down children, at which they gave out presents made by the prisoners - and some of these are cherished to this day. Grace Barnes still has the lovely doll's cot which her daughter received there. "They were very good at making different things you know", she says, "and the food was alright. It was behind the barbed wire, coils of it - you had to go up into the camp and into one of their recreation rooms, I suppose it was." Mary Fawcett (née Whittle) remembers her disappointment when the gifts were given out in alphabetical order - there were no prams left when they got to her, and she received a small rocking-horse instead.

Some of the 'treats' were somewhat more illicit. Betty Parker remembers her father complaining that they had no sugar one day, only to find a military lorry arriving later with a big bag for him. Others remember a 'black market' going on round the village for cans of petrol and other rationed material.

The Canadians also did their bit to 'dig for victory'. The official record of the Straths tells how "spare time was devoted to the planting of gardens", and mentions that "Squadron-Sergeant-Major Sam Heinrich, thanks largely to a hothouse which he usurped, was able to supply 'A' Squadron with fresh radishes a full week ahead of all the others."

Len Carter too, behind the wire in Erie Camp, was planting Brussels sprouts "and other edible albeit disgusting things" between the buildings there, having "finally managed to escape the 'infernal rectangle' or parade square" because he remembered a little maths from school. The RSM had demanded if there was anyone who could figure out the square area of a triangle - he was the only one to volunteer, and was detailed to help Staff Sgt Williams who was in charge of "planting every available foot in the compound with vegetables." This NCO had to submit a statement to the Commandant showing the total area under cultivation, and hence his need for Len's mathematical skills! Len drew up a coloured plan of the entire compound area under cultivation - which largely consisted of a lot of yellow areas indicating Brussels Sprouts, "one of the dirtiest gastronomical tricks the Belgians ever played on us."

And finally, we should not forget that there were some particular skills which the Canadians brought with them, as John Ellis discovered one day. He remembers: "The last horse to be used for the delivery of animal feedstuffs at Headley Mill was named *Boxer*. Some pasture land adjoining the mill had been requisitioned to produce cereals under the War Emergency Act, and *Boxer* was needed to haul a trailer to help with the harvesting. We tried to catch him one summer's evening, but without success - he dashed around the field and we found it impossible to get him. A crowd of Canadian soldiers came and leant over the gate to see what was going on, and eventually one of them came into the field and asked if we had a long rope. We produced one - and *Boxer* was lassoed within seconds."

A Few Problems

Given the large number of troops, both British and Canadian, who passed through the village during the war, it is gratifying to find how fond are people's memories of that time, and how few the problems which they now recall. Reactions against the first Canadians stationed at Bordon, mentioned earlier, might have stemmed from the fact that some of the initial 'waves' contained ex-convicts. "If you had six months to go in prison, you could apply for early release to join the army", said Pat Lewis. "To some extent, the army were looking for this sort of person - who was prepared to take chances and to fight. A lot of us went straight from school into the army, so we were high on dreams, but these guys were in jail and used to hard living - it takes a crook to catch a crook, sort of thing - so the army was glad to have them."

"Before you could get into the tank regiments, however, you had to sit an education and an intelligence test." The Sherbrookes started off as a mounted machine-gun regiment, "but then", Pat says, "they decided to make us a tank regiment, and the test they gave us took away nearly half of our people." This didn't necessarily weed out all the rougher elements though, and indeed those who were more 'street-wise' helped the rest of the men in the regiment look after themselves.

The local press, being censored, was very restricted as to the hard facts it could publish, but any case that came to a civil court seemed to be fair game. Thus we read that Canadian soldiers were involved in a number of vehicle accidents: such as the Bombardier driving his Colonel's car at night along the Grayshott straight in October 1940 who "did feloniously kill and slay" a trooper of the 10th Hussars walking along the road outside *Stonehaven*; and the Canadian despatch rider who was killed when his motor bike ran into a 3-ton anti-aircraft lorry crossing the road at Headley Mill in July 1942.

Other reported incidents involved accidental deaths among Canadian servicemen in Headley, such as the soldier who shot his friend while fooling around with a loaded pistol outside *Church Gate Stores* in August 1942. Joyce Stevens, who lives next door in *Suters*, remembers hearing it happen. She also remembers a couple of soldiers arguing over a girl outside the little wooden shops (now the parade of shops) next to the *Holly Bush*. "It ended up with a gang fight and one of them was kicked to death", she said. This was probably the incident recorded in the *Herald* as occurring on 15th March 1943, in which a Canadian soldier was found guilty of manslaughter and given 13 days imprisonment. The judge said it was "one of those cases where death resulted unexpectedly from a blow struck in a fight."

The Strathcona's first fatality occurred on 17th June 1942 when, according to a *Herald* article which was surprisingly uncensored for the time: "Lieutenant Richard Anderson Squires, 2nd Armoured Regiment, Canadian Forces, lost his life as the result of falling from a tank at Ludshott Common. The deceased officer, who was in his 32nd year, was the son of the late Sir Richard Anderson Squires, twice prime minister of Newfoundland." The Straths' official record adds: "He was our only Newfoundlander, and very popular." He was buried in Brookwood Cemetery.

Towards the end of the war, when the Princess Louise's Fusiliers had returned from Italy and were stationed for a short time at the Headley end of Ludshott Common, the body of a 24 year-old Private was found, "in full battle dress but without his cap", in a frozen static water tank underneath an inch of ice. He had arrived at the camp on 30th October 1944, and should have proceeded to Canada with a PoW escort group on 23rd November. Posted as 'absent without leave' on 9th November, his body was not discovered until the beginning of January 1945. The *Herald* describes the water tank as "brick, 20ft diameter, 12 ft deep and holding 12,600 galls. It was mainly below ground level. Its edges were surrounded by grass which sloped up from the main drive in and a footpath - a rise of about 1 ft in 1 ft. The tank was right opposite the NAAFI canteen. The top was in no way protected - wire netting and poles had been removed in September." An open verdict was recorded by the Winchester District Coroner.

Some Memories

For every event which was reported there must have been dozens which remain only in the memories of those involved. Joyce Stevens, right opposite the *Holly Bush*, recalls hearing "an awful kerfuffle at turning out time when Sally Stevens, the landlady, was saying goodnight to everybody as she always did. I remember she was wearing a white blouse, and she'd got blood all down the front of it because one of the soldiers had broken off a bottle or something and cut someone."

Sally is fondly remembered by the troops; as Major Macdougall writes in his *Short History* of the South Alberta Regiment: "We must not forget to mention that 300 lb bundle of good humour, whose only regret was that, while she had played with Canadians in the last war, in this war she could only mother them." He also recalls Christmas here in 1942, when "all ranks enjoyed themselves to the full, and I mean to the full." He continues that: "Apart from a few slight run-ins with our friends the Elgins, who were at Headley Down, the day passed peacefully enough."

Elsie Johnson (née Pearce) was living with her parents in their shop (now closed) in Fullers Vale at the bottom of Beech Hill. She says: "I can remember one incident on a Saturday night. Mabel and I had come home from work - we often didn't get back till nine - and mum and dad were scrubbing out the shop. We had a plain white wooden floor and stairs, and every Saturday night without fail they were scrubbed. Newspapers were put down, and the lights were on downstairs, though you couldn't see much of them through the shutters, and some Canadians walking back down to the village tried to get in. They thought it was a pub. Father shouted to them that we were shut and we didn't sell liquor, but they climbed the bank on the left hand side, and walked in through the kitchen door. I can see dad now, coming up the stairs with a scrubbing brush in his hand - and with brute force we all pushed these lads out. We didn't know any of them, but they were determined it was a pub and that they were coming in for a drink."

John Ellis at Headley Mill found a different way to deal with such things: "One night after midnight, a party of noisy Canadians, obviously the worse for drink, took a short cut past the mill to get back to Bordon Camp. When they got to the house they stopped just under our window, and created the most frightful din. The house was not then modernised, and each bedroom had a wash hand-stand complete with wash bowl and water jug. I got out of bed, in spite of Dorothy's protestations, eased up the sash window, took the 3 gallon jug of cold water and poured it over them. There was deathly silence. We didn't hear another thing - we didn't even hear them move away."

Betty Parker remembers talking to a Canadian motorcyclist and his pillion passenger outside *Eashing Cottages* in Arford - the passenger decided to get off, but the other drove away. Almost straight away he ran into a lorry at the corner, and was killed. "Those Harley Davidson machines always looked powerful to us", Jim Clark says, "and so did the 'Indians', which were the other motorbikes they used." He too remembers a fatal motorbike accident nearby: "One of them hit a tank by Arford House - went straight into it as he was coming down the hill." *Not a nice place to meet oncoming traffic even now.*

Mary Fawcett, living down Beech Hill at the time, recalls a Canadian on a Harley Davidson crashing through the hedge at the Honeysuckle Lane bend, hitting an electric pole and taking out the whole of the public electricity supply in the area. She also remembers a tank coming along Fullers Vale failing to take the bend at the bottom of Beech Hill and hitting the post box which was then in the gatepost at the bottom of *Kenton House* drive. *The post box was then moved to its present safer place.*

Joyce Dickie, on her way home from Bordon telephone exchange where she sometimes had to work until midnight, was walking up Barley Mow Hill when she heard a girl screaming her head off from a piece of common land opposite *Barley Mow House*. "I thought, 'Oh my golly, now what do I do? I can't just walk by and not do anything when somebody's screaming for help'. And yet I had in my mind what was going on, but I didn't know what to do. Anyway, I put on as gruff a voice as I could, and I said, 'What's going on over there?' And this girl came out, and the soldier with her. Well, she was terrified, and I think she'd taken on a bit more than she'd realised.

She begged me to take her home, and I thought, what if I meet the fellow when I come back up again? I did go home with her, but that chap plagued me for weeks afterwards - wanted me to go out with him, but eventually he got fed up."

Altogether, Barley Mow Hill seemed to be quite a centre of activity at this time. "The 'provos' were always busy up this road", says Grace Barnes speaking of Glayshers Hill, "because we had an 'interesting' house just round the corner where the telephone exchange is now." Glayshers Hill led from the Provo's quarters in Erie Camp down to Barley Mow Hill. "We didn't dare get out and about in the road much - you kept yourself pretty quiet", she said.

However the Provost Corps themselves, according to *Battle-dress Patrol*, the official war memoirs of the Royal Canadian Mounted Police, felt that: "Despite long years of training and waiting and the consequent boredom, I think it fair to say that our troops were well behaved. Provost units had much less trouble with them than might be thought. We like to think our approach helped; provost men were taught and encouraged to help soldiers who were in trouble - sick, broke or overdue off leave. At times more stern action was necessary when dealing with public disorder and drunkenness, but these causes were surprisingly rare."

Air Raids

While spared the intensity of the air attacks which were hitting Portsmouth and other strategic locations, the residents of Headley nevertheless became all too familiar with the sound of sirens. Joyce Dickie recalls an occasion when it went just as she was due back at work in Bordon. "When the siren went you were supposed to stay put, but on this occasion it was such a long time before we got the all-clear, I said to myself: 'I can't wait here any longer - there's no sign of anything, so I'll go'. Well, I'd just got to Lindford when the planes came over. I was stopped there and had to get down in the pit with the men at the garage. Then it seemed to be alright, so they let me get on my bike and off I went - and I was almost at the cross roads, where the Military Police had an office, when they came over

again. The police stopped me - they wouldn't let me go any farther and made me go in with them. I ended up under the billiard table with these men all round me. A bomb fell right on the cross-roads - the people had been evacuated, but an old lady was worried because her little bird was in there and had gone back to get it, and she was killed - the little bird in his cage was alright."

Tom Grisdale, who was in the Home Guard at the time, remembers the same event: "I was out at five o'clock in the evening, on my field down Liphook Road, and we saw the bombs leave the plane. Me and Derek jumped on our bikes and went down. They dropped all by the Fire Station cross roads - and I think the only person that was killed was the turncock's wife - she came out and went down the shelter, then remembered she'd left the canary, ran back to get it, and she just got caught in the middle of it."

He also remembers Canadian soldiers sharing his dug-out in Mill Lane, opposite Churchfields, during air-raids: "We used to get down there at about 6 o'clock in the evening, and regularly this used to be when, as it got dark, the siren would go - and they'd all come out from Bordon and spend the night with us." Betty Parker remembers Canadians from Bordon sheltering in Headley too: "They slept in the woods by *Brontë Cottage* up Barley Mow Hill - you'd see them come up every night with their packs on their backs and their blankets - they'd sleep there, and you'd see them going back in the morning."

Katie Warner recalls: "There were air-raid shelters in the school gardens which had been built there for the school children - I used to go in with them and the teachers - as an extra helper with the little ones, the 5 and 6 year-olds - when there was a warning."

Jim Clark says: "For us, ten and eleven year-olds, an air-raid was just one big adventure - we didn't realise the fact that the Germans were across the channel - we didn't think about that. I remember a German plane coming across here, and they opened at it with the Bren guns on tripods."

On 10th February 1943, according to Marcel Fortier of the Foot

Guards, "the nearby town of Bordon was heavily strafed, near misses landing in HQ Squadron area and in No. 1 Squadron Tank Park (probably in Lindford), while hits were made on the walls of the Sergeants' Mess"; and both the 1st Hussars and the Sherbrookes recall that on 8th March 1943 a German raider dropped bombs in the Haslemere area. In a footnote to the latter incident, we are told that one of the pilots shot down had studied English in Haslemere before the war - and the local population did not appreciate his return visit.

Another more mysterious visitor from the sky was reported by Jim Clark. One night he and two other village lads saw quite clearly a lone parachutist dropping across the full moon, to land, he would reckon, on Ludshott Common. He reported this to the authorities, and was visited the next day by plain clothes security men in the traditional trench coats, but never heard any more of it.

However, it was not all one-way traffic up in the air. John Whitton says: "We seemed to be on a direct path between an airfield and targets on the continent, as light bombers frequently flew low overhead in formation. They looked very serious." Al Trotter of the Saskatchewan Horse remembers that in the summer of 1943: "Every evening the RAF bombers would pass over Headley on the way to Germany and occupied countries and return the next morning. The count was not always the same next morning." Jim Clark recalls seeing the Americans, when they started the daylight bombing: "They used to meet almost over here - they came from two directions just as we were walking to school, and they used to fire these red flares - I don't know what that was for, but I remember the sky being full of Fortresses." Tom Webb of the Garrys saw what was rumoured to be an early experimental jet that went overhead pouring black smoke, and aeroplanes 'sans propellers' from Farnborough were also sighted here by Harvey Theobald.

Tanks Around the Block

"The British tank regiments came first", said Tom Grisdale. "They were all up on Ludshott Common - it was just a sea of mud." Jim Clark remembers these being light tank regiments,

with 'Matildas' he thinks. But it is the Canadians who the villagers remember most vividly.

"The first lot of Canadians came without tanks - we thought that was bad enough, but then we had Canadians plus tanks", said Joyce Stevens, echoing the feelings of many residents at the time. The squadrons which were parked in the village and in Lindford had to drive through the village to take part in exercises on Ludshott, Frensham and Thursley Commons. Katie Warner remembers: "It was nothing to go up and find a line of tanks all down the High Street, some of them with their tracks off being repaired."

Pat Lewis recalls driving tanks from Headley to Aldershot when they had to do repairs, and going through the lanes to Farnham. "They specialised in tanks at Aldershot, while Bordon was more for the other vehicles", he said. Katie Warner recalls: "They widened our roads for us considerably - especially Mill Lane - it's difficult to imagine it now, but it used to have quite high banks each side going down the hill. But when two tanks met on the hill, nobody was going to stop and go back - and so they each carved into the bank." She remembers the resulting mud at the top of Mill Lane, by the chestnut tree. It was so bad that when her six year-old son slipped and fell there on their way to church, she had to take him straight home to clean him up, and missed the service.

"If you look around the area now you'll find concrete in the oddest spots", she continues, "maybe in somebody's garden - and there's a bit along the Liphook Road just outside *Littlecote*, where they used to turn to go into the field, in what is now Hilland Estate. Where they were turning on this same spot all the time, they scooped out the road blocking the ditch - so they had to put in this big slab of concrete which allowed them to turn more easily."

Concrete slabs put down to assist tank movements can still be seen in many other parts of the village: for example, at the sharp corner of Churt Road at Hearn Vale, by the scout hut up Beech Hill Road, at various places along Headley Hill Road (*see photo*), and at the entrance to Headley Fields. According to David Whittle, parts of Carlton Road (as far as the dip) and

Seymour Road were made up for tanks to go along and there was a Tank Repair Shed in the middle of Ludshott Common. "Just inside the fence of the school grounds at Openfields, there's concrete still under the grass", Jim Clark says. "They tried to break it up afterwards, but it must be nearly three foot thick - they couldn't touch it, so they just put earth over it - and of course if you get a hot summer now, that grass all dies off first."

"There was a tank shed by where the scout hut is now", Mary Fawcett recalls, "with several tanks parked near it, and there was always a guard standing there, day and night." There were also tank parks laid down opposite Ludshott Common along the Grayshott straight, according to Pat Lewis. At each of these, up to three tanks would run in onto concrete slabs arranged in a 'trifurcated' pattern, hidden under the trees which were there at the time. From these parks the tanks had only to cross Grayshott Road to get to the training area on the Common. This at least saved them from having to drive through the village.

Many residents remember the incident when a tank ran into the side of a house in Arford. The house (see photo), since demolished during post-war development, stood at the narrowest part of Arford Road just down from the junction with Long Cross Hill. It had been built with a rounded corner, and according to Katie Warner, "they had a go at that rounded corner more than once." Betty Parker, who lived close by, said that the husband of the lady living there was away in the Navy at the time. "She was Irish, and flew out of doors demanding a guard until it was repaired. He stayed on duty outside there with a rifle at night for several weeks." Sue Allden, who supplied the photograph of the house, recalls the lady telling the tank driver he "couldn't drive a wheelbarrow."

Joyce Stevens (née Suter) remembers that the tanks "kicked up at the back when they started off", and more than once demolished different parts of their garden wall in the High Street. She still has one of the forms from the Canadian Claims Commission, proposing to pay £10 for "damage to stone wall by unidentified C.M.V." on 19th November 1943 (see copy p.29). *In fact the bill from Johnson & Sons of Liphook for repairing the wall came to £12, so the Suters were £2 out of pocket on this occasion.*

Harvey Theobald recalls that their C.O. had ordered that any crew damaging walls, etc, would be responsible for repairing same within 48 hours. "The walls near the entrance to 'A' Squadron tank park and the narrow bridge at Lindford came in for a lot of special attention. Most of our tank crews soon became very proficient as stone masons!"

Sue Allden says the wall by the road shown in her photograph of Arford was "continually being knocked down by tanks", and confirms the report in a contemporary Parish Magazine which mentions the 1914-18 War Memorial being hit and damaged by an army vehicle. *The Memorial was subsequently moved back from the road after the war to its present position, in order to protect it from traffic.* Pat Lewis remembers how he once hooked a woman off her bicycle - though not in Headley: "I had a recovery tank, with plenty of room, but I misjudged the width, and at the side of the tank there were booms which hit her. She and the bike went over, but thank God there was road works going on, and she landed in a pile of sand there." No wonder veterans tell the tale that the last vehicle in a tank convoy was always the regimental paymaster, who paid out for damage caused along the way.

Vehicle Identification

Each tank carried a squadron sign and tank number painted on the turret for identification. "I remember the squadron signs", says Jim Clark. "There were squares, circles, diamonds and triangles on the turret - and the squares were parked up here in Openfields. I can remember in the evenings, we were by the *Holly Bush* when all the tanks were coming back up from Bordon, and we looked to see which ones came down our road and which went elsewhere - and when we saw the ones with the squares on we said, 'They're our lot', and sure enough they turned down our way." According to convention in both the British and the Canadian army, the diamonds signified HQ Squadron, and the triangles, squares and circles belonged to A, B and C Squadrons respectively.

Other official identification marks included the *Formation* and

Some Familiar Sights in Headley - 1994

The Holly Bush

Entrance to The Mount

The Crown

The Wheatsheaf

Concrete laid for tank movements in Headley Hill Road

Hut on Erie Camp after the war (see arrow on map p.31).
Mrs Callaghan (later Mrs Wells) with her daughter Kathleen.

Pearce's shop (now closed) in Fullers Vale today (see p.19).
The kerb was raised to keep out flood water from Ludshott Common.

Arford. The house in foreground (now demolished) was hit by the tank (p.16).
Eashing Cottages (background) were among those flooded (p. 19).

Canadian Armour and Armoured Regiments

Old Renault tank bought from USA for training in Canada.
Pete Friesen of the Fort Garrys in Camp Borden, Ontario.

Fort Garry Horse in Aldershot, winter 1941.
There are 84 men and 3 tanks on parade.

Fort Garry Horse with Grant type tanks near Aldershot, early 1942.
There appears to be one tank per squadron here.

South Albertas with Ram tanks in England, 1943.
Tac sign of 45 indicates a Recce Regiment.

Canadian Snap-shots

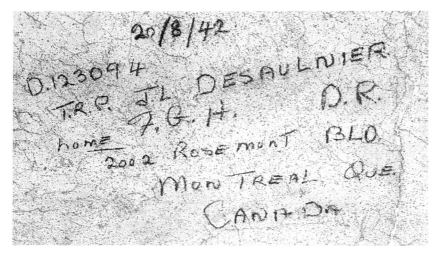

Part of the Graffiti in the attic of Church Gate Stores.
It is thought that Trooper D.123094 James L. Desaulnier was
a Despatch Rider (D.R.) with the Fort Garry Horse (F.G.H.).
The date 20th August 1942 was one day after the ill-fated Dieppe raid.

Headley Church in 1942, taken by John Whitton of the Fort Garry Horse.
A motorbike and side-car stands outside the Stores, and he says: "I believe
the figure leaning against the fence is the then Captain Alex Christian."

William Curtis
Essex Tank Regiment (30 Recce)
taken in 1944

The Friesen brothers (Jack, Pete and Dave), who were all in the Fort
Garry Horse regimental band. This picture was taken in Canada.

'Whitey', mascot of the Fort Garry Horse.
(see page 10 for his story)

Cameraman Visits Mechanized Fort Garry Horse Over There

A cheerful Garryman from Toronto is W. E. Mitchell,

Now "somewhere in England" is the famous Canadian regiment, the Fort Garry Horse, originally a cavalry unit now an armored regiment. Tall and short of the outfit are Trooper D. G. Tweedie (left) of Sault Ste. Marie and Trooper M. P. Manion, from Swift Current, Sask.

From Selkirk, Man., is G. Gunter, member of a Fort Garry Horse tank crew.

It's kit inspection time for the Fort Garrys with Sergt.-Major R. M. Davies, of Winnipeg, checking the kit of Trooper P. Friesen, also from Winnipeg. The Fort Garrys carry a proud record from the last war into the present battle.

Ram tank of Fort Garrys being loaded onto a transporter.
This would have been a familiar sight in Headley.

'Swimming' Sherman of 1st Cdn Hussars, now displayed in Normandy.
The 'skirt' on the hull supported a canvas screen to achieve buoyancy.

Ram variant now on display at Aldershot Military Museum
(see page 28)

Churchill variant (AVRE) now on display in Normandy.
These cleared a path for Canadian Shermans to land on the beaches.

Dieppe

We and British invade France.

(American Journal)

„If then this is not in any sense the opening of a „second front", what may it be taken to mean?.. (Times)

451/DE/VIII/42

Tactical signs on the front and rear of each vehicle. The Formation sign for the Canadians was a maple leaf superimposed on a rectangle of the relevant Division's colour - green for the 4th, and maroon for the 5th Armoured Division, and so on. The Tactical (or 'Tac') sign was a number denoting the 'seniority' of the regiment within the Brigade. Conventionally for tanks, this was normally '51', '52' or '53'. Thus, for example, the Foot Guards, as senior regiment in the 4th Brigade *(see Appendix III)*, had a Tac Sign of '51', while the Garrys, second in the 2nd Brigade, would display '52'. Reconnaissance ('Recce') regiments, such as the South Albertas became after they left Headley, displayed '45'. *Other numbering systems existed - for example it can be seen that the 'Tac' sign of the Calgarys at Dieppe was '175'.*

Tanks were also given names according to a convention which varied from unit to unit. Sometimes they were chosen to start with a letter relevant to the Regiment's name: for example all tanks of the Foot Guards carried names beginning with the letter 'F' (Marcel Fortier's tank was 'Fitzroy'); whereas in the Straths and certain other regiments, the names began with the letter of the squadron: A, B or C.

But identification marks shown in photographs, even where the censor has let it through, are not always to be trusted. Pat Lewis recalls: "Wherever we were stationed, we were involved in 'away activities', loaded on tank landing craft, doing fake runs here and there - up to Wales, up to Scotland and then back. We didn't realise at first, but the 'Scam' was on as well - we were taken down the road and they'd tell us to change the lettering on the tank, or something. We'd think, 'What stupid thing's this? We've just done that'. But it was all trying to screw up the German intelligence."

Whereas the Calgarys arrived with British 'Matilda' and then 'Churchill' tanks, all subsequent Canadian regiments here used the American M3 'Grant', M4 'Sherman' or Canadian 'Ram' types. The *Grants* were relatively old-fashioned, and noted for having their main gun 'sponson-mounted' in the body of the tank rather than in the turret *(see photo)*. This gave them a very limited angle of fire unless you turned the whole tank, and they were eventually replaced by Shermans which did not suffer from this problem. The *Sherman* became the main battle-horse of the Canadians during the Normandy campaign, and was usually powered by dependable twin Diesel engines. *See Grant and Sherman specifications in Appendix IV.*

However, the *Ram* was probably the tank seen most in Headley *(see photos)*. It was a Canadian manufactured version of the Sherman, of all-welded construction, powered by an aeroplane engine running on 100% octane petrol, and is said to have taken its name from the ram on the family crest of General Worthington, the 'father' of Canadian armoured forces. These tanks were relatively fast, but only did 1 mile per gallon with a maximum range of some 100 miles, and also required a great deal of maintenance on their engines. Their protective armour was not very heavy - the Garrys discovered on visiting the Linney Ranges in Wales that a shot from their 2 pounder main armament would go right through them. They were used for training and eventually replaced by 'real' Shermans for operational armoured work, but the changeover was not complete until April 1944 - just 2 months before D-Day.

Exercises and Inspections

While the tank regiments were here, they took part in any number of exercises. As Pat Lewis put it: "Headley was the ideal place to get yourself orientated with your tanks to the English countryside. Later, we were involved in what they called 'schemes' as we were moved around the country prior to D-Day. The British army, often the Home Guard, fought you in mock battles and they gave us a hard time throwing mattresses over the tanks so the driver couldn't see, and so forth. We had to get through towns and countryside as we would see it in France - trying to use tanks in roads where there's hedges all over the place and you can't see what you're doing. But basically we came to Headley to learn how to handle the tanks."

Harvey Theobald recalls that they used 'A' Squadron tank park as a primary area to train new drivers. "Once they became proficient within its confines, our main training could be concentrated on Ludshott and Frensham Commons - which became very busy at times considering that these somewhat small areas had to be shared by three regiments."

Marcel Fortier of the Foot Guards remembers: "Convoy and harbouring schemes occupied much of the time. During the first of these hasty harbour changes it was soon discovered to be not the proper training area, but the private property of the Right Honourable David Lloyd George!"

Individual regiments were inspected during their time here by a number of dignitaries and various Generals, but in April 1942 the 5th Canadian Armoured Division as a whole was inspected by the King and Queen on Frensham Common. Pete Friesen of the Garrys has a picture from a Canadian newspaper showing him with his kit laid out for inspection just prior to the visit (see photo). He remembers thinking that the King looked very ill and white - 'not real'. The official record of the Straths tells how they were wearing their new Maroon patches for the occasion, with 'L.S.H.' inscribed on them, but the King suggested the letters might be confused with other regiments, and recommended they should be changed to 'Ld.S.H.' - which was duly done.

Tanks based in the Headley area used Frensham, Thursley, Hankley and Ludshott Commons for training, as did those based in the Elstead/Tilford/Milford area. The 1st Hussars noted that at one time: "The brigade was awaiting repairs to be completed on Ludshott Common before beginning to fire Browning practices at moving targets." They also did tank firing on the 30 yd Conford ranges.

But tanks were in short supply. In the *History of the 1st Hussars*, it states that around June 1942 "the number of our [Ram] tanks never exceeded 18, and the necessary 100 hour inspection of the radial engines meant that several tanks were always off the road for maintenance." It continues by saying that: "The problems were accentuated by the fact that the tanks arrived in England without wrenches and tools, so needing a continual improvisation of the required articles."

Nearly a year later than this, things had not improved much. In early 1943, Pat Lewis remembers sharing the few Ram tanks the Sherbrookes had between their four squadrons: "When we didn't have the tanks, we would use pieces of timber with a centre piece and a rope, and you hung that over your neck, and the group commander was behind with a piece of rope in his hand, and we used to run round Ludshott Common acting as a tank to learn the commands."

One time when he did have a tank to drive, "it was a clapped out Grant, and it broke down in a gully on Ludshott Common. The spares took 3 days to arrive, and we had to stay with the tank until then." By the end of May 1943, the supply of Rams had improved somewhat, and the Sherbrookes were able to transport 'all 49 tanks' when they moved out of the area to go to Worthing.

Al Trotter of the 16/22 Saskatchewan Horse recalls that they started to receive tanks from Bordon when they arrived in the summer of 1943, only to find the regiment was to be broken up. He transferred to the British Columbia Regiment (28th Armoured) and did his armoured training with them around Brighton and Tunbridge Wells.

Floods and Fires

Despite complaints from the regiments of insufficient vehicles, enough tanks were in evidence for the commons to suffer serious loss of vegetation through their movements during the war. Comments from villagers and servicemen sum it up: "Ludshott Common was absolutely barren except for the bigger trees - it was as bare as could be" - "... just a sea of mud where the tanks were - it was so muddy they had duck boards for the troops to walk on where the tanks had cut it up - not a bit of green or anything" - "... it was the tanks and the lorries and what not, going backwards and forwards, that killed the heather and everything" - "... it was just like a rice field - churned up the entire common - no vegetation left on the common at all" - "Ludshott Common was desecrated by the time we'd gone." Jane Durham recalls the common was polluted with oil. At the end, in April 1945, the Ludshott Common Committee reported: "The restoration of the common to anything resembling its pre-war state will be an uphill task which the committee view with great anxiety."

Those of us lucky enough to live near that Common now, nearly 50 years on, know that thanks to the dedicated work of the National Trust, it is once again a glorious habitat for heathland flora and fauna. But during the war years, with nothing growing there to absorb the water, heavy rains ran straight off, down Pond Road and into Arford causing major flooding. Pat Lewis noticed the results of it: "By the time we arrived in Headley (February 1943), the road near the *Wheatsheaf* was a sea of sand washed down there with all the rain."

The water came across the bottom of Beech Hill and down Fullers Vale by Pearce's shop. Elsie Johnson recalls: "We had such terrible floods in October 1942, a particularly wet period - it just came down the full width of Pond Road like a river - it went past our shop and washed the garden of Rose Cottage away - the high kerb was built after that *(see photo)* - the water was up to the second stair in the shop. That was the first time - after that it flooded more often." Tom Grisdale remembers going down Beech Hill one morning after it had flooded overnight, and right opposite Elsie Johnson's shop the water was still deep, and there were "all these tents that had been washed down off the common flopping about in the road." Sue Allden recalls buses were diverted down Barley Mow Hill when Fullers Vale flooded badly, and Mary Fawcett remembers cycling along Fullers Vale each morning to catch the No.6 bus at Bordon for Petersfield, where she went to school: "It was nothing to come home and find it flooded along Fullers Vale."

"It really was bad", said Katie Warner, "I went to the fish shop (also a chip shop, run by the Jelphs) in Arford one morning, and the fishmonger's wife said, 'Have you seen the flooding? You should go down and have a look'. So I walked down as far as Eashing Cottages and the front door of the lowest house was wide open and the water was up to the second step of the stairs - flooded to that depth. Not funny for the people. Every house there was flooded - plus others lower down."

There were times, however, when a spot of water might have been welcome. The 1st Hussars, stationed in the Elstead area, were called out on the night of 9th May 1942 for fire fighting duties on 'Grayshott Common'; and in the *History of the Sherbrooke Regiment* it notes that: "On the afternoon of the 19th May [1943] the unit practised tank-infantry co-operation on Ludshott Common, training which did not occur as planned, because the infantry were chiefly occupied in extinguishing fires started by their mortars."

On a lighter note, Tom Webb of the Garrys writes: "While having an after-duty game of volleyball, our squadron was informed there was a grass fire somewhere and that the Duty Sgt was on his way. Everyone vanished so quickly that the ball was still in the air when he arrived. Being good soldiers, no-one ever volunteered!"

Erie Camp

There were four Canadian camps locally each named after one of the Canadian Great Lakes: Huron and Ontario Camps were on Bramshott Common near to the Portsmouth Road, Superior Camp was at the Grayshott end of Ludshott Common (the concrete road and footings are still very much in evidence there), and Erie Camp was at Headley Down, in the area now occupied by Heatherlands estate.

Of these four, Erie Camp was the 'odd man out', being used exclusively as a military detention centre for Canadian servicemen. "Here we gathered both the casual, happy-go-lucky offenders, and the really bad actors of the army", as the official record of the Provost Corps puts it.

The villagers have many stories to tell of the 'provos' and the prisoners. Betty Parker says: "Whenever anyone escaped, the siren would go and the Provos would be down through the woods with their sticks and red armbands looking for them. This seemed to happen quite often." Grace Barnes, who lived quite close to the Camp remembers: "They often used to get out over the wire - they threw their blankets over the top - and they'd go down into the woods. You used to find bundles of prison clothes down there, and I've always been wondering - someone outside must have been helping them, because what did they wear?" Mary Fawcett remembers seeing prisoners on the run as she picked potatoes in the Land of Nod with David, now her husband. "They would tear off their trouser legs and throw away their jackets", she said, in order to get rid of the red rings marking them as convicts.

Tom Grisdale says: "I remember when I was on leave, a prisoner had escaped and he got on the bus at Beech Hill Garage. The 'Red Caps' jumped on to arrest him, but the conductor wouldn't let them - he said 'you can't touch him on here - you can have him when he gets off'. So they followed the bus with a jeep and when he got off at the terminus in Haslemere they took him." He adds: "I didn't realise that they couldn't touch him on a public bus." He also recalls: "Some days you'd be on the bus going up towards Grayshott, and the Military Police would be out there seeing prisoners onto the bus when they'd finished their detention."

Servicemen in the area were told to keep away from Erie Camp, "and we did", according to Pat Lewis. However, since it was on the route between Ludshott Common and the village, they could hardly fail to notice it. "We passed the gate and saw the MPs and the guys who came out with them when they took them on a run - forced route marches and things like that." Pete Friesen remembers seeing prisoners from the Detention Centre having to run at the double as soon as they came out of the gates. "The truth is", said Pat Lewis, "we didn't want to go in there not so much for being penned up, but you lost your money - that was the biggest worry - not only did you lose your money while you were in there, but it was also taken off your pension at the end of the war."

One serviceman who did see the inside of Erie Camp for three months in late 1944 was Len Carter, mentioned earlier. On discharge from No.10 Canadian General Hospital at Bramshott, having just won £40 in a game of dice, he decided to turn east and visit London instead of turning west to rejoin his regiment at Bulford. On returning 37 days later he was court-martialled and sent to 1st Canadian Detention Barracks, as Erie Camp was officially called. Some memories of his time in there are included as Appendix V.

According to Len it had two compounds for prisoners, A and B (see p.31), where A was for second offenders and incorrigibles, and B for the first offenders. Compound A, towards the northern end of the camp, consisted of concrete cell blocks.

Villagers remember the problems these caused after the war when the council tried to remove them. "They had an awful job - tried knocking them down and everything - even used explosives, but in the end they were covered up, not removed."

Compound B consisted of wooden and brick buildings (see photo), as did the staff barracks at the south-eastern end of the camp. According to locals, the camp had "huge big gates and rolls of barbed wire" at the main entrance (where Larch Road goes in now) and an observation tower with a searchlight on it. There were offices just inside for admission of prisoners and kit storage. Villagers also remember a water tower, which remained for some time after the war standing opposite Wilson's Road - having survived being burnt in a riot - and some recall a second being down at the Glayshers Hill end.

There was a parade ground at about the point where Maple Way now meets Larch Road, and a large natural depression nearby (where the playing field is now) which Len Carter says had been used as an assault course, though not in his time. Paula Wadhams remembers she called it the 'bomb crater' - it had trees growing in it, and they used to get their Christmas trees from there. After the war it was used by the Council as a Refuse Tip and filled to its present level.

Discipline in the camp was strict and living conditions spartan. As the records of the Provost Corps put it: "One field punishment camp commanding officer said it was his plan to make it so tough that his customers from the front line units would rather go back and stay there than return to his care." He was not talking about Erie Camp, but Len Carter's recollections make it clear that much the same principle applied there. Len says he has never remembered any of the Provost staff there with enmity - "they had a job to do" - but riots took place in the camp at other times when he was not there, during which it seems a few old scores were settled. According to Dot Myers, the prisoners once made the Colonel in charge march up and down with heavy packs on his back.

Jim Clark says: "I can remember going up there when they'd rioted and the whole camp was surrounded by Canadian troops, about four or five deep, like a big wall round it. My

20

father worked for the army as an unofficial locksmith, sort of self-taught, and quite a lot of them had smashed the locks of the cells so they couldn't get out or in - he had to go there and repair them. Quite a big thing, the riot - quite a serious thing."

There was also a "massive break-out" around VE Day. Katie Warner says a lorry was used to charge the gates - "I don't know how they got hold of the lorry, but I do know that some of those prisoners came down to the Village Green and spent the night in the two air-raid shelters in the school garden. We had a big bonfire on the Green that night and some of these prisoners were mingling with us there and admitting that they'd just come out - I think at the time people didn't believe them, but apparently it was so, and of course it wasn't long before the military police were around collecting them up. I think their stay outside was rather short-lived."

Anthony Vella of the Royal Canadian Electrical & Mechanical Engineers had been sent to 'Headley Detention Barracks' in 1944 to be a part of a rehabilitation programme for prisoners charged with 'Self-inflicted wounds' (SIW), who were "serving 2 yrs detention and facing a subsequent dishonourable discharge." He says: "The programme was designed to teach a trade (I was in charge of the welding school) during their incarceration, and if successful, and if they volunteered to return to their unit and the front, then the dishonourable discharge was withdrawn." Relating to the events described above: "I am happy to say that this re-hab programme was very successful and that during the riots in this camp, when almost everyone was running amok and vandalizing property and manhandling officers and staff, our 'students' did not take part."

The Regiments in Action

When the Canadian regiments rolled out of Headley, they passed out of sight of the villagers, but not out of mind. With the strict censorship during the war it was difficult if not impossible to know how individual units were faring, and while this book is not intended to cover events which occurred outside Headley in any great detail, it will interest a number of people to know where the troops eventually went:

The Tragedy of Dieppe

On 19th August 1942, a force consisting mainly of the 2nd Canadian Infantry Division mounted a sea-borne raid on Dieppe. In this they were supported by the Calgary Regiment, using the Churchill tanks which had been issued to them in Headley the previous year. The purpose and timing of the raid remains controversial, and many pages of analysis and comment have since been published on it.

Essentially it seems to have been designed as a test of the Allies' readiness to take a French port and the German's readiness to defend it. There was no intention to follow up with a full-scale invasion at the time; the orders were to take and destroy key objectives in the area, and then execute an orderly withdrawal. In the event, it was a disaster. Every tank that landed was lost, and over 65% of the 5,000 Canadians involved were either captured or killed.

Barbara Boxall's Canadian cousin, Ralph Spencer, who was billeted in Headley during the war, landed in Dieppe and was one of the lucky ones to return. Survivors were given 48 hours leave afterwards to recover. In a taped message sent to Barbara in 1979, he told her: "I managed to get invited to Buckingham Palace for a decoration, which amazed me, and I'm still trying to figure out what happened." Apparently it was for shooting a German sniper who was causing problems there.

He went back to France on D-Day, at H-Hour on Juno Beach, with the Regina Rifle Regiment, and was almost immediately wounded in the legs by machine gun fire. After "quite a few operations" and a long period of convalescence in England, he returned to the continent in time for the war to end while he was in Germany.

About four weeks after the raid, the Germans dropped propaganda leaflets over Headley. Sue Allden and Jim Clark both kept copies (*see photo*) which they picked up then. These show photographs of the wrecked Churchill tanks, and of dead, wounded and captured soldiers - some recognisable as men who had been in the village not so long before.

In passing, it has become almost a legend in Headley that the tanks 'suddenly left' the village to go on the Dieppe raid; but, as mentioned, *the Calgary Regiment had moved away from the area some eight months previously and, according to their 'short history', were not stationed here again. However the Fort Garry Horse and Lord Strathcona's Horse regiments <u>did</u> leave the village suddenly at that time, though for a different purpose, and the village would indeed have seemed deserted then.*

The Canadians suffered a higher casualty rate at Dieppe than they did in Normandy . Most of their tanks were destroyed before they could get off the beaches, and from this experience it is said many lessons were learned, including the need to develop 'floating' tanks for D-Day.

Lord Mountbatten, then Chief of Combined Operations, said after the war: "The Battle of Normandy was won on the beaches of Dieppe. For every one man killed in Dieppe, at least ten more had their lives spared on the beaches of Normandy." Nonetheless, the Dieppe raid remains one of the most tragic and contentious events of the Second World War.

As a postscript, on 1st September 1944, during the rush to the Seine and Belgium following the defeat of the German Seventh Army in the 'Falaise Pocket', the 2nd Canadian Infantry Division captured Dieppe without a fight. This division consisted of the same brigades and the same regiments that had suffered on the raid two years previously, with one notable exception - the Calgary Regiment was then fighting in Italy.

To 'Juno Beach' and Beyond

In December 1942, a decision was made to reorganize the Canadian armoured regiments in preparation for specific roles in Normandy and elsewhere. The immediate effect of this, as far as the village was concerned, was to bring the Garrys back for their second visit to Headley (and the 1st Hussars back to Elstead). They were now destined to play an infantry support role in the D-Day landings on 'Juno' beach, forming the 3rd Canadian Tank Brigade (subsequently re-named 2nd Canadian Armoured Brigade) along with the Sherbrooke Fusiliers.

Meanwhile, units of the 4th Canadian Armoured Division had already passed through. Four regiments of this Division, the Governor General's Foot Guards, the Canadian Grenadier Guards, the British Columbia Regiment, and the South Alberta Regiment were destined to land in Normandy about a month after D-Day, to join up with and reinforce the 2nd Canadian Armoured Brigade forming the 2nd Canadian Corps and eventually the 1st Canadian Army. From then on they battled virtually side by side through France, Belgium and Holland to Germany. The Elgin Regiment was responsible for delivery of armoured vehicles to the combat zone.

It should be mentioned here that John Boxall, a long time resident of Headley after the war, also landed at Juno Beach on D-Day. He was in the RASC and part of a DUKW unit, bringing in troops and supplies in these amphibious vehicles. His widow Barbara tells us they had a live duck as their mascot which they took to Normandy with them. Just after the Canadians had landed, she says, the duck disappeared in mysterious circumstances, and nearly started World War III among the Allies. *So come on you Canadian guys - you can safely admit it now - who did for the RASC's duck?*

The 'Northern Ireland' Campaign

The Straths, previously colleagues and friendly rivals of the Garrys, and with them in Headley earlier in 1942, got what they considered at the time to be the better treatment - retained in the 5th Canadian Armoured Division as the *5th Canadian Armoured Brigade* along with the British Columbia Dragoons. On 12th November 1943 they boarded the "Scythia" at Avonmouth, thinking they were going to Northern Ireland - and arrived in Algiers at the start of the Italian campaign!

The Calgary Regiment, severely depleted after Dieppe, was 'reinforced, reorganized and retrained'. Their *Short History* records that they were given Rams in place of Churchills in November 1942 (presumably these were replaced by Shermans later) and in June 1943 the regiment embarked from Greenock for Sicily. There they distinguished themselves, fighting their way up through Italy as part of the *1st Canadian Armoured Brigade*. At the end of the Italian campaign they moved to NW Europe until the end of the war.

After the War

It is perhaps some measure of the popularity of the Canadian troops in Britain that, at the end of hostilities, there were over 40,000 brides and 20,000 children waiting to be shipped to Canada to meet up with their Canadian husbands and fathers. Pete Friesen of the Garrys stayed on to help with the Canadian Wives' Bureau in London where they took 800 girls at a time into the Portman Hotel (there were also two other hotels) for one night before sending them by boat train to Southampton.

Pete himself married Enid, an English girl; his younger brother Dave married Betty, a Scottish girl; and his elder brother Jack ('Shorty') married Joan, a Welsh girl.

In Headley the redundant army huts were quickly occupied, legally or illegally, by those who would otherwise have been homeless. Tom Grisdale recalls: "I came back after the war, and we lived with mother-in-law for a while up Liphook Road till we eventually got this Nissen hut in Rectory Field. They were moving in all these displaced Poles and Ukrainians - you came home out of the army and you couldn't get anything.

"There were about 10 or 12 huts down by the side of the field opposite Tonards - we were No. 2. It was the remnants of an army camp, and squatters moved in after the army moved out. Then the Council took them over and put in a kitchen sink and a range, and made it into 3 rooms, but they could only brick it up three-quarters of the way because it was that shape, and if you got a frost, when it used to thaw out it was ghastly. All you had was a window at each end made of that reinforced glass so you couldn't see out. They gave you a bath which you hung on the wall and put down in front of the range."

Then in the early 50s: "We were about the second family to move into Erie Camp, No. 7. They bricked up these huts which were one big room - not up to the ceiling, half way - and at one end they divided in the middle so you got two bedrooms and one big room. There was still the old tin roof, and with the condensation we had to put umbrellas over the bed and the cot. The floors were concrete - and where they'd been breaking up wood for burning it was like dust, so we put roofing felt down.

"The Council put in a little range in the middle of this room, and you had one cold water tap, that's all. The toilet was a little wooden place outside with an earth bucket which the Council used to come round at midnight to empty, slopping it all up against the door. It wasn't bad - you had a bathroom with hot water and all that. We were happy there."

Tom also remembers: "When you dug in your garden, you dug up knives, forks, spoons - they buried everything, and the story is they even buried army motorbikes." They may or may not have buried motorbikes in Erie Camp; from recent stories in the local press, they do seem to have buried jeeps on Thursley Common, and Don Heather, as a lad, remembers seeing them burying a whole tank in a crater on Ludshott Common.

Over the years the huts disappeared from the village or were reused, in some cases more than once. One, for example, was moved to a site opposite Alex Johnston's house in Headley Fields and used as the village's Catholic Church until 1965, when a more permanent building was erected there. It was then moved again, this time to Beech Hill Road, and used as the Scout Hut until it finally burnt down spectacularly in 1985.

The huts at Erie Camp were replaced by council houses in the 60s and 70s, and this estate, now called Heatherlands, was eventually completed in 1978. The only reminder of its link with the Canadians is the name given to one of the roads there - 'Maple Way'.

Still We Remember

We cannot close this book without mentioning just a few examples of the happy memories which the name Headley evokes in many parts of Canada.

A young man from Headley Down went to work in Newfoundland in the fifties and met many Canadians there. They asked him from where he came. "Oh just a very tiny village called Headley Down." "Really? We know it well! We were in Erie Camp and on Ludshott Common during the war!"

When Barry and Wendy Ford moved into Erie Estate they had one of the first telephones, needing it to run their business, and he suggested she should surprise her aunt in Canada by giving her a call. "In those days you had to go through the operator", said Wendy. "The man in Canada asked me which exchange I was calling from, and was amazed when I told him Headley Down, saying he'd been at Erie Camp during the war - then when I said I was actually ringing from Erie Camp, he could hardly believe his ears. 'Of all the calls I could have answered!', he exclaimed - and we spent a long time chatting about Headley before I was put through to my aunt." She adds:" It's a pity, but I forgot to ask him his name."

More recently, Katie Warner was visiting her sons in Canada: "I got off the plane in Toronto one afternoon and a man just outside the door said, 'cab, madam?' - I said, 'no thank you', but he said, 'where do you come from?' I said, 'England, Hampshire' - 'What part?' - and I started to explain, and he said, 'Do you know Superior Camp? Do you know Erie?' and he went all round the camps, around Longmoor, Bordon, the lot, Huron - all of them - he said, 'I was there for about 4 years during the war' - and when I mentioned this part of Headley he said, 'I know it'. And another man I met actually knew the Congregational Institute - 'I know the house you lived in' - we were living in *The Old Manse* at one time."

Mary Fawcett started writing to a Canadian pen friend during the war, and they still correspond 51 years later. Lieut. Jack Casey of the Sherbrooke Fusiliers gave her the address of his sister-in-law Joan, who was two years older than Mary, being 13 while Mary was 11 years old. Jack, a "very handsome man" according to Mary, had opened his own restaurant in London, Ontario, before joining up in 1941 and coming to England with his regiment late in 1942. He was billeted in *Kenton House* during his time in Headley, and is mentioned in Lt. Col. Jackson's book on the *Sherbrooke Regiment* for his 'coolness and disregard for personal safety' having saved the lives of a party of troopers at a grenade-throwing practice in Wales when one of them dropped his grenade with the pin pulled out.

Jack Casey landed on Juno Beach during the D-Day invasion, and received a severe head injury there. He was brought back to Brookwood Hospital, but sadly died of his wounds. However, Mary kept up her correspondence with Joan - they met for the first time on Mary's 21st birthday, and have continued to see each other many times since then.

No.1 CACRU V-Day Menu

While Jack Casey was in *Kenton House* he used to walk up to *Windridge* in Headley Hill Road for meals - from which we presume it was an officers' mess. At the end of the war, a 'V-Day' meal was held there for the No.1 CACRU (Canadian Armoured Corps Reinforcement Unit). We don't know whether all these regiments were in Headley during the war - but if so, then at least 21 Canadian armoured units came rather than just the 13 mentioned opposite. Those whose badges are shown (left to right) on the menu, above that of the Corps, are:

S.A.R.	South Alberta Regiment [29]
31 Recce	15th Alberta Light Horse [31]
12 Man. Dragoons	12th Manitoba Dragoons [18]
17 D.Y.R.C.H.	17th Duke of York's Royal Cdn Hussars [7]
4 P.L.D.G.	4th Princess Louise's Dragoon Guards [4]
R.C.D.	Royal Canadian Dragoons [1]
R.M.R.	Royal Montreal Regiment [32]
30 Recce	Essex Tank Regiment [30]
8 Recce	14th Canadian Hussars [8]
G.G.H.G.	Governor General's Horse Guards [3]

The Menu is next to the Author's Note at the front of this book.

Note - Canadian Armoured Regiment Numbers shown thus: [32]

Appendix I. List of Canadian Regiments in the Headley Area

	Arr:	Dep:	
Royal Provost Corps & RCMP *[Erie Camp]*			
Royal Canadian Army Service Corps			
Royal Canadian Engineers (6 Fld Co, 3 Div)	Jul 41	Oct 41?	
1st Cdn Army Tank Bde + 3rd Cdn Inf Div			
Calgary Regiment (14th C.A.R.) *at L/H*	Sep 41	Dec 41	to Seaford
Regina Rifles + possibly other infantry regiments with Calgary Regiment?			
5th Cdn Arm'd Div			
Lord Strathcona's Horse (2nd C.A.R.) *at HD*	Apr 42	Aug 42	to Hove
1st Hussars (6th C.A.R.) *at Elstead*	Apr 42	Aug 42	to Hove
Fort Garry Horse (10th C.A.R.) *at L/H*	Apr 42	Aug 42	to Hove
British Columbia Dragoons (9th C.A.R.)	???		
4th Cdn Arm'd Div			
Elgin Regiment (25th Recce Reg) *at HD*	here with S. Albertas		
South Alberta Regiment (29th Recce Reg) *at L/H*	Sep 42	Jan 43	to Aldershot
British Columbia Regt (28th C.A.R.) *at Elstead*	Sep 42	Feb 43	to Hove
Gov. Genl. Foot Guards (21st C.A.R.) *at L/H*	Jan 43	Feb 43	to Hove
Cdn Grenadier Guards (22nd C.A.R.) *at HD*		Feb 43	to Hove?
3rd Cdn Army Tank Bde (later re-named 2nd Cdn Arm'd Bde)			
1st Hussars (6th C.A.R.) *at Elstead*	Feb 43	Jun 43	to Worthing
Fort Garry Horse (10th C.A.R.) *at L/H*	Feb 43	Jun 43	to Worthing
Sherbrooke Fusiliers (27th C.A.R.) *at HD*	Feb 43	Jun 43	to Worthing
16/22 Sask Horse (20th Recce Reg) *at L/H*	Sum 43	Broken up: Nov 43	
Essex Tank Regt (30th Recce Reg) *at HD*	Aut 43	Broken up: Spr 44	
Elgin Regiment (25th Recce Reg) *at Elstead*	Noted on 26 Nov 1943		

Notes:

C.A.R. = Canadian Armoured Regiment.

Recce = Armoured regiment equipped for reconnaissance.

> *There were 31 Canadian Armoured and Recce regiments formed, of which 28 came to the UK. Nearly half of these visited the Headley area.*

L/H = Lindford/Headley

HD = Headley Down

Elstead = Elstead/Milford/Tilford.   This location included here for completeness, since regiments of the same armoured Brigade or Division were stationed both here and at Headley, occasionally taking part in joint exercises.

Billet locations in the Headley area

Taking as an example the three regiments stationed simultaneously in our area in February 1943, the 3rd Canadian Army Tank Brigade (later re-named 2nd Canadian Armoured Brigade) is believed to have been billeted as follows:

1st Canadian Hussars - *Elstead/Milford/Tilford*

Regimental HQ & HQ Sqn	Elstead
A Squadron	Milford
B & C Squadrons	Tilford

Fort Garry Horse - *Lindford/Headley*

Regimental HQ & HQ Sqn	Lindford (Officers' mess *Hilland*)
A Squadron	Rectory Field
	(tanks Rogers Field; Officers' mess *Walden*)
B Squadron	Openfields (Officers' mess *Belmont*)
C Squadron	Barley Mow Hill & Hilland field
	(Officers' mess *Pound Cottage*)

Sherbrooke Fusiliers - *Headley Down*

Regimental HQ & HQ Sqn	The Mount
A Squadron	Ludshott Common
B Squadron	Beech Hill Rd/Headley Hill Rd
C Squadron	Crestafield
Intercommunication troop	Hearn

It is unclear whether other regiments distributed their squadrons in the same pattern.

D-Day at Juno Beach

The 2nd Canadian Armoured Brigade landed on D-Day at Juno Beach in support of the 3rd Canadian Infantry Division. Each of the three armoured regiments was assigned an infantry brigade, as shown in the diagram below:

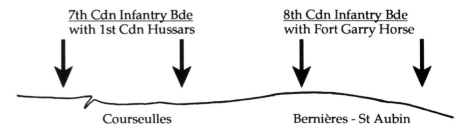

Naval Force 'J'

9th Cdn Infantry Bde
with Sherbrooke Fusiliers

7th Cdn Infantry Bde
with 1st Cdn Hussars

8th Cdn Infantry Bde
with Fort Garry Horse

Courseulles   Bernières - St Aubin

Appendix II. Calendar of events

1939
Sep 3	War declared by Britain on Germany
Sep 10	War declared by Canada on Germany
Sep 19	BEF lands in France.
Oct	South Staffordshire Regt arrives in Headley
Dec 7	'First flight' of Canadian troops embark - 7,400 men on 5 ships

1940
Mar	South Staffordshire Regt leaves Headley for BEF
May 10	Germans invade Belgium
May 20	Dunkirk evacuation of BEF

1941
Jul 16	Canadian Engineers arrive in Headley to start building Erie Camp
Sept	Calgary Tank Regiment arrives in Headley
mid Oct	Engineers finish Erie Camp
Oct 19	Trooper Nip Keys of Oshawa, Ont. signed his name in the *Church Gate Stores* attic
Oct 25	Automatic telephone exchange opened in Headley Down
Dec	Calgary Tank Regiment leaves Headley for Seaford

1942
Apr 1	1st Cdn Hussars arrive in Elstead area Fort Garry Horse & Ld Strathcona's Horse arrive in Headley area
Apr 24	Review of 5th Cdn Arm'd Div by King & Queen - Frensham Common
Jun 6	Garrys visited in Headley by Maj. Gen. Montague
Jun 15	James Desaulnier "came from Canada" - signature in *Church Gate Stores*
Jun 17	Lieut. Squires of the Straths killed falling from a tank in training on Ludshott Common
Aug 5/6	Fort Garry Horse & Ld Strathcona's Horse leave Headley, and 1st Cdn Hussars leave Elstead area for Hove
Aug 8	Trooper Mitchell accidentally shot Trooper Brooks outside *Church Gate Stores* ('B' Squadron orderly room)
Aug 19	**Dieppe raid:** Calgary Regiment involved
Aug 20	T.R.P. J.L. Desaulnier F.G.H. D.R. signed his name again in the *Church Gate Stores* attic *(see photo)*
Sep 2/3	British Columbia Regiment arrives in Elstead area South Alberta Regt (& Elgin Regt?) arrive in Headley
Dec 17	Abnormal rains cause floods in Headley - report in *Herald*

Dec	Split up of Cdn Arm'd Divs: Straths, BC Dragoons and 8th Princess Louise NB Hussars stay with 5th Cdn Arm'd Div (destined for Italy); Garrys, 1st Hussars and Sherbrookes form new 2nd Arm'd (initially 3rd Army Tank) Brigade (destined for Normandy). "In the future the Canadian Armoured Divisions were to have only one brigade of tanks instead of two, following the precedent set by the enemy and afterwards by the British and Americans."

1943
Jan 13	Governor General's Foot Guards arrive in Headley
Jan 15	South Alberta Regt (& Elgin Regt?) leave Headley for Aldershot
Jan 28	Mayor Lewis of Ottawa visits Foot Guards in Headley
Feb 19	Foot Guards and Cdn Grenadier Guards leave Headley, and British Columbia Regiment leaves Elstead area for Hove
Feb 22	Sherbrooke Fusiliers & Garrys arrive in Headley 1st Cdn Hussars arrive in Elstead area
Mar 15	Tpr Michaelis killed Tpr Gibbs in a brawl near the *Holly Bush*
May 10	Garrys inspected in Bordon by Gen. Montague
Jun 1	Sherbrookes & Garrys leave Headley, and 1st Cdn Hussars leave Elstead area for Worthing
Jun 17	Calgary Regiment embarks for Sicily
Summ	16/22 Saskatchewan Horse arrive in Headley; later broken up
Fall	Essex Tank Regiment (30th Recce) comes to Headley - assembling trucks in Bordon
Nov 12	Straths embark for Algiers

1944
	RCEME run rehab course at Erie Camp
Spring	Essex Tank Regiment leaves Headley; later broken up
May	'Whitey', mascot of the Garrys, buried near Fawley
Jun 6	**D-Day:** Garrys, Sherbrookes and 1st Hussars land on Juno Beach
July	4th Cdn Arm'd Div lands there about a month later
Oct 30	Princess Louise's Fusiliers arrive at Ludshott Common from Italy

1945
Jan 14	Frozen body of Pte Lasky of Princess Louise's Fusiliers found in water tank on Ludshott Common
May 8	Riot in Erie Camp on VE day V-Day Menu for No.1 CACRU

Appendix III. Order of Battle for Canadian Regiments in 1945

1st Infantry Division *RED shoulder patches*
4th Princess Louise's Dragoon Guards (Recce) *[4]*
Saskatoon Light Infantry (M/c Gun Bn)

1st Infantry Brigade
Royal Canadian Regiment
48th Highlanders of Canada
Hastings & Prince Edward Regiment

2nd Infantry Brigade
Princess Patricia's Canadian Light Infantry
Seaforth Highlanders of Canada
Loyal Edmonton Regiment

3rd Infantry Brigade
Royal 22nd Regiment
Carleton & York Regiment
West Nova Scotia Regiment

2nd Infantry Division *ROYAL BLUE shoulder patches*
14th Canadian Hussars (Recce) *[8]*
Toronto Scottish (M/c Gun Bn)

4th Infantry Brigade
Royal Regiment of Canada
Essex Scottish Regiment
Royal Hamilton Light Infantry

5th Infantry Brigade
Black Watch of Canada
Regiment de Maisonneuve
Calgary Highlanders

6th Infantry Brigade
Fusiliers Mont Royal
Queens Own Cameron Highlanders of Canada
South Saskatchewan Regiment

3rd Infantry Division *FRENCH GREY shoulder patches*
17th Duke of York's Royal Canadian Hussars (Recce) *[7]*
Cameron Highlanders of Ottawa (M/c Gun Bn)

7th Infantry Brigade
Canadian Scottish Regiment
Regina Rifles
Royal Winnipeg Rifles

8th Infantry Brigade
Queens Own Rifles of Canada
Regiment de la Chaudière
North Shore Regiment

9th Infantry Brigade
Stormont Dundas & Glengarry Highlanders
North Nova Scotia Highlanders
Highland Light Infantry of Canada

4th Armoured Division *DARK GREEN shoulder patches*
South Alberta Regiment (Recce) *[29]*

4th Armoured Brigade
Governor General's Foot Guards *[21]*
Canadian Grenadier Guards *[22]*
British Columbia Regiment *[28]*
Lake Superior Regiment (Motor Battalion)

10th Infantry Brigade
Argyll & Sutherland Highlanders of Canada
Lincoln & Welland Regiment
Algonquin Regiment
New Brunswick Rangers (M/c Gun Bn)

5th Armoured Division *MAROON shoulder patches*
Governor General Horse Guards (Recce) *[3]*

5th Armoured Brigade
Lord Strathcona's Horse *[2]*
8th Princess Louise's N.B. Hussars *[5]*
British Columbia Dragoons *[9]*
6th Duke of Connaught's R. Cdn Hussars (HQ Sqn) *[15]*
Westminster Regiment (Motor Battalion)

11th Infantry Brigade
Irish Regiment of Canada
Perth Regiment
Cape Breton Highlanders
Princess Louise's Fusiliers (M/c Gun Bn)

Independent Brigades *BLACK shoulder patches*

1st Armoured Brigade
Ontario Regiment *[11]*
Three Rivers Regiment *[12]*
Calgary Regiment *[14]*

2nd Armoured Brigade
1st Canadian Hussars *[6]*
Fort Garry Horse *[10]*
Sherbrooke Fusiliers *[27]*

Troops *ORANGE shoulder patches*

1st Corps Troops
Royal Canadian Dragoons (Recce) *[1]*

2nd Corps Troops
12th Manitoba Dragoons (Recce) *[18]*
Prince Edward's Island Lt Horse (Corps HQ Defence) *[17]*

Army Troops
Elgin Regiment (Armoured Delivery) *[25]*
Royal Montreal Regiment (HQ Defence) *[32]*

Note - Armoured Regiments numbered thus: [32]

Appendix IV. Specifications of Tanks

The following details *(except for notes in italics)* are copied from sheets of paper issued and notes taken in early 1943 by S. G. Vane-Hunt of *Square House*, Headley, at the Electrical and Mechanical Engineering School.

Survey of A.F.Vs in the Service - American Tanks

Note: ALL American tanks have the Engine and Clutch at the rear and the Transmission at the Front, with a Propeller Shaft in between. Tracks are built of rubber and steel. The rubber is vulcanised to the steel pivot pins.

Medium Tank M3 - General Grant I

Crew of Six: Commander, Driver, WT Op, 37 mm Gunner, 75 mm Gunner, Loader.
Weight 26 ton (30 US tons), length 17', width 8'11", height 9'11", ground clearance 24", fording depth 42", ground pressure 17.5 lb/sqin.
Armour plate thicknesses: front lower section 2", front upper section 1.5", sides & rear 1", ceiling & floor 0.5", turret cast armour 2", around pistol ports 3."
Armament:- Co-axial 37mm gun and .30 Browning in a power operated turret (combined electrical & hydraulic operation) and a 75mm gun in forward sponson.
Powered by a 400 BHP radial air cooled petrol engine at 2400 RPM. Engine has 9 cylinders and fan and flywheel are incorporated in one casting. Weight of engine and accessories 1,390 lbs - engine change in 7 hours with 'four good men'.
*(See notes on **Starting Procedure** following)*
Fuel capacity 150 galls.
Normal type clutch. Synchromesh gearbox (five forward and one reverse speed) with direct drive to a controlled differential.
Steering by application of brake bands to either side of the differential, so reducing the speed of one output shaft and proportionally increasing the speed of the other.
Drive from differentials to sprockets is through a double helical toothed reduction.
Suspension:- Three pairs of bogie wheels, each pair controlled by a volute spring.
British designed turret with no commanders cupola on top (unlike General Lee).

Medium Tank M3 - General Grant II

Similar to General Grant I, except that it is powered by twin 185 BHP GM two-stroke compression ignition engines at 2100 RPM.
A cross-drive carries the drive from the two engine clutches to the propeller shaft.
Both the 37mm and 75mm guns are fitted with gyro-stabilizers.

Medium Tank M4 - General Sherman

Weight 27 ton. Crew of five.
Armament:- Co-axial 75mm gun and .30 Browning in a power operated turret (combined electric and hydraulic operation). The gun is fitted with a gyro-stabilizer.
There are three types of hull used on this tank:-
   1. Where all the hull is built up by riveting.
   2. Where the top half of the hull is built up of welded plates.
   3. Where the top half of the hull is a casting.
In the official history on the 'Garrys' it is noted that experienced crews added old track links to the front armour of their Shermans for added protection.

The type of power unit will depend on the type of hull:-
Types 1 and 2 will be powered by either:
   a). A twin 185 BHP GM two-stroke compression ignition engine at 2100 RPM, or
   b). A Ford 8 cylinder V8 450 BHP petrol engine, or
   c). A Chrysler 30 cylinder 500 BHP petrol engine using five engine blocks and crankshafts driving a single master pinion.
Type 3 will be powered by either:
   a). A 400 BHP radial air-cooled petrol engine at 2400 RPM, of same design as the engine fitted to the General Lee, or
   b). A nine cylinder Guiberson radial compression ignition engine of 400 BHP.
The transmission, steering, suspension and tracks are similar in design to the Generals Lee and Grant.

*Note that **Duplex Drive** (DD) amphibious versions of the Sherman were produced which could swim ashore under their own power. They achieved buoyancy from a rubberized canvas screen attached to the hull deck. Two propellers were fitted to the rear of the tank, driven by off-takes from the rotating tracks, giving a speed through the water of approximately one hundred yards per minute. Steering was provided by a tiller. The screen doubled the tank's height and had to be collapsed quickly once ashore for the gun to be used. DDs were used with mixed fortunes on D-Day; some sank on their way to shore, but those that arrived proved very effective. There is an example on display in the Tank Museum at Bovington Camp, Dorset.*

Medium Tank - Ram I

Canadian manufactured tank similar to the American Medium tank but equipped with a 2 Pdr.

Medium Tank - Ram II

Similar to the Ram I, but equipped with a 6 Pdr.

There is a version of a Ram tank standing outside the Aldershot Military Museum *(see photo)*. It bears the name "Elverdinge" - the following notice is displayed on it:

> ### Sexton (Self-propelled 25 pdr gun)
>
> The Canadian Ram Tank, built by the Montreal Locomotive Works between 1943-45, was found to be underarmed and underarmoured for combat in Western Europe. In this model the turret has been replaced by an open top welded armoured superstructure mounting a British 25 pounder field gun. It carried 105 shells, and weighed 24.5 tons. A total of 2,150 were produced. It had a top speed of 25 mph.

Ram tanks were retained for a number of operational roles: to be used as self-propelled guns *(as above)*; as flame throwers; or as 'kangaroo' troop carriers which, with turrets off, could transport infantry to the front at high speed.

General Grant - Starting Procedure

1. Make sure that the master switch and ignition switch are 'off' and that the gear lever is in neutral.

2. Check the level of the engine oil by the dipstick on the filter cap of the oil tank (do not overfill).

3. Inspect the engine compartment for loose and missing parts.

4. If engine has been stationery for five hours or more it must be turned by the starting handle over at least eight compressions (to check for a Hydrostatic Lock). If a lock is evident, remove spark plugs from lower cylinders to pump oil out.

5. Check the transmission and final driver for oil.

6. Check the voltmeter: it should read zero.

7. Close the master switch and the voltmeter should read 24 volts.

8. Turn on the required petrol tanks.

9. Turn on HYCON pressure cock and check for leaks.

10. Prime engine if necessary (not more than four pumps).

11. Check clearance of the clutch pedal and then depress it.

12. Close starter and booster switches together.

13. Let the engine turn for a short while then switch the magnetos on to 'Both'.

    NOTE:- Do not prime engine whilst it is turning or switched on.

14. Check oil pressure gauge: should read between 60-80 lbs per sq. in. (If the oil fails to show within 45 seconds, switch off the engine).

15. Check the flow of the gearbox oil by the tap situated at radiator.

16. Check for leaks throughout the engine and transmission.

17. Check the running of the engine on each of the magnetos.

18. Let the engine warm up before moving the tank. (The minimum oil temperature should be 80 degrees to 100 degrees).

19. Do not attempt to move off until engine has warmed up for at least 10 minutes.

NOTE:- If engine fails to start, check fuel cut-off valve for poor seating or sticking. Over priming and under priming will cause engine to be stubborn in starting.

Pat Lewis's comment: *"Can you imagine doing all this in action?"*

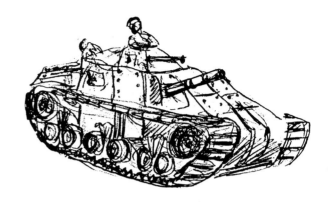

To be completed in Triplicate.
One copy left with Claimant.

CANADIAN CLAIMS COMMISSION (OVERSEAS)
Canadian Military Headquarters, London

PROPOSED SETTLEMENT AND RELEASE OF CLAIM
by

Claimant .... PERCY SUTER .... - .... gardener ....

Address .... 1, High Street, Headley, Bordon, Hants .... Claim made £ Unstated

Proposed settlement £.10.0.0 .... (... TEN .... pounds ... NIL .... shillings ... NIL .... pence)

Place, date and nature of occurrence from which alleged claim arose:-
Headley; 19 Nov 43; damage to stone wall by unidentified C.M.V.
....

Officer, soldier, etc. ....

I UNDERSTAND THAT THE CLAIM I HAVE MADE AS HAVING ARISEN OUT OF THE ABOVE OCCURRENCE AND ALSO THE ABOVE AMOUNT OF THE PROPOSED SETTLEMENT ARE SUBJECT TO THE CONSIDERATION AND APPROVAL OF THE CANADIAN CLAIMS COMMISSION (OVERSEAS).

I also understand that payment, if any, will be made on the basis of my representation hereby made that I have not received and am not entitled to demand any insurance compensation in connection with such claim.

The following Release will only be effective upon my receiving payment of the proposed settlement.

In consideration of the payment to me of the above amount of the proposed settlement, I hereby release the Crown in the right of Canada, all members of the Canadian Armed Forces, and all officials and employees of the Crown in the right of Canada from liability to me in respect of all claims which I now have or may hereafter have arising out of the above occurrence.

I have received a copy of the above terms.

Witness .... (Claimant) .... P Suter ....

Address .... (4d. stamp)

Occupation .... (Date) .... 24/1/44 ....

C.M.H.Q. 1000;7
40/P & S/43 (2745)

Proposed Settlement for damage to *Suters* wall

Appendix V. Len Carter's memories of his time in Erie Camp

While serving with the 1st Canadian Parachute Battalion in 1944, I spent three months as a soldier-under-sentence (SUS) in Erie Camp Military Detention Centre. Because my offence was not 'refusing to jump' I was permitted to retain my maroon beret, but being the only one with this distinctive headgear, it was not always a blessing. Whenever there was a *merde* detail the cry was, "That man with the red hat!"

The Commandant of the place was a little Scot who strutted about in his trews and Glengarry, and who had a penchant for ordering that all the windows in the hut be flung open on the coldest of days. He had won the VC during WWI so I suppose he had earned the right to freeze those military culprits in his charge.

Conversation between SUS was forbidden except for that short daily spell on the parade square when you were formed up in two ranks - 'Front rank - about turn. Ten minutes - talk.' You might find that your *Tete-a-tete* partner was a soldier from a French speaking regiment, who was still upset about that business on the Plains of Abraham, but any conversation was better than endless silence ...

There was a locked box of books in the center of the hut, and we were allowed to read for an hour in the evening. I applied to see the Commandant about purchasing a couple of books so as not to waste the time, but this VC-winning red-faced gentleman bellowed: "You are not here for an education, you are here for punishment."

We probably spent most of our time looking for cigarette butts, which we could furtively smoke by pretending we were stoking one of the two Quebec heaters in the hut, blowing the smoke into the open door, or we could turn up the shower very hot to create a lot of steam and stand at the back of the stall to hurriedly inhale a combination of smoke and steam.

There were two Provost bodies sitting at a table in the middle of the hut at all times - they all had to be addressed as 'Staff' even those who were only privates - and some of them had keen noses. Caught smoking and you existed on bread and water for a few unenjoyable days. "On the ding" was a cute Provost euphemism for 'on charge'.

I believe the 'fast food' concept originated at Headley. I've forgotten the exact number of minutes we were allowed to finish our meal, but if you weren't a fast eater you could often leave the Mess Hall very hungry. Mother may have told you to chew each mouthful at least ten times, but in your letter home you told mother she was out of touch with the real world. Just inside the door was the table where those sentenced to bread and water had their frugal repast.

They say you could tell a Headley graduate by his foot drill - he had that certain Headley stomp, as if there was something evil on the parade square that he was trying to stomp to death. I finally managed to escape the 'infernal rectangle' because I remembered a little maths from school - one morning the RSM demanded if there was anyone who could figure out the square area of a triangle. These requests in the army are pretty tricky and you have to be careful, but I was willing to try anything to get off the 'strutting ground' and I hesitantly raised my hand - the only one to do so. "Right that man with the red hat go with Staff Sgt Williams."

It seems that the S/Sgt was in charge of planting every available foot in the compound with vegetables, and had to submit a statement to the Commandant showing the total area under cultivation, (multiply the length by half the base of the triangle for the number of square feet). With that bit of magic I became the S/Sgt's trusted assistant, mathematician and graphic artist. By drawing up a coloured plan of the entire compound area under cultivation I became the darling of the cultivation gang which consisted of the S/Sgt and myself.

When my kids in later years wanted to leave school early I told them to hold on at least until they had learned how to work out the square area of a triangle, that one day that knowledge might come in handy.

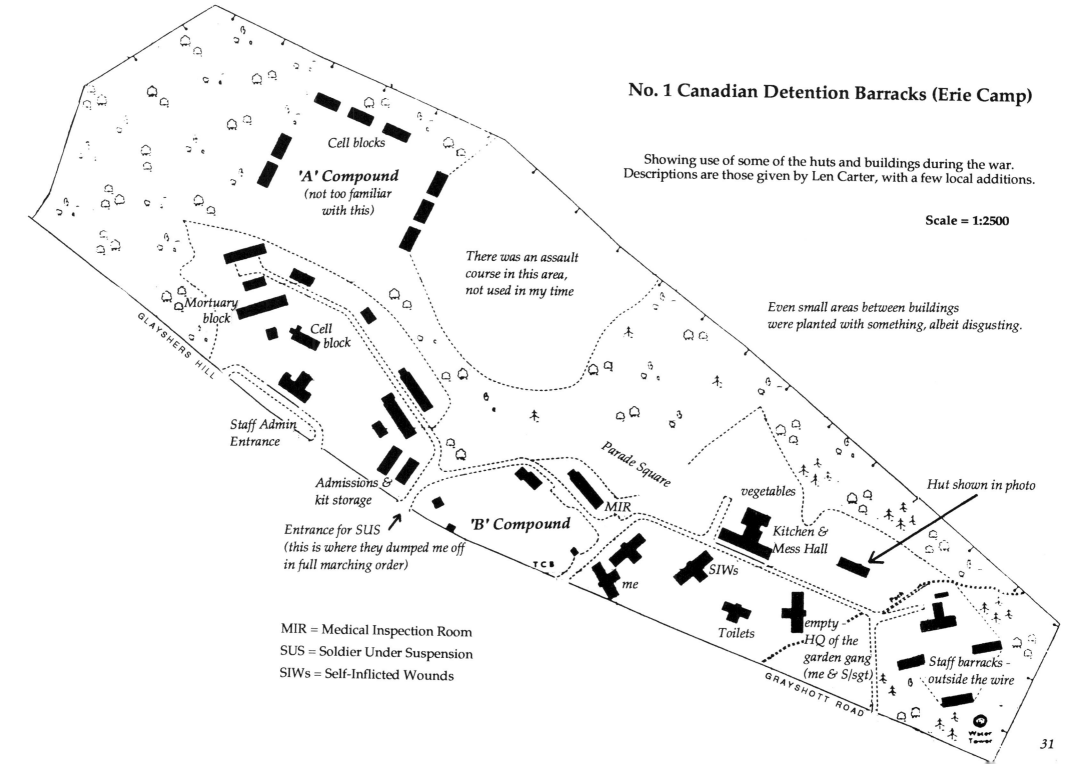

No. 1 Canadian Detention Barracks (Erie Camp)

Showing use of some of the huts and buildings during the war.
Descriptions are those given by Len Carter, with a few local additions.

Scale = 1:2500

Cell blocks

'A' Compound
(not too familiar with this)

There was an assault course in this area, not used in my time

Even small areas between buildings were planted with something, albeit disgusting.

GLAYSHERS HILL

Mortuary block

Cell block

Staff Admin Entrance

Admissions & kit storage

Entrance for SUS
(this is where they dumped me off in full marching order)

Parade Square

vegetables

Hut shown in photo

'B' Compound

MIR

Kitchen & Mess Hall

TCB

me

SIWs

Toilets

empty - HQ of the garden gang (me & S/sgt)

Staff barracks - outside the wire

GRAYSHOTT ROAD

Water Tower

MIR = Medical Inspection Room
SUS = Soldier Under Suspension
SIWs = Self-Inflicted Wounds

31

Appendix VI. List of Contributors & Acknowledgements

From the Village:

Sue Allden	Don Heather
Grace Barnes	Elsie Johnson
Barbara Boxall	Dot Myers
Jim Clark	Fred & Betty Parker
Arthur Dean	Betty Roquette
Joyce Dickie	Joyce Stevens
John Ellis	David Sulman
David & Mary Fawcett	Paula Wadhams
Wendy Ford	Katie Warner
Tom & Barbara Grisdale	David Whittle

- and the many others who have given their help, advice and information so willingly.

References:

Vanguard - the Fort Garry Horse in the Second World War, by Col. R E A Morton
Lord Strathcona's Horse in the Second World War, by Lt. Col. J M McAvity
The Sherbrooke Regiment, by Lt. Col. H M Jackson
A Short History of the 29 Can Arm'd Recce Regiment, by Maj. G L Macdougall
The Calgary Regiment - a short history
A History of the First Hussars Regiment 1856-1945
Battle-dress Patrol, the military contribution of the RCMP to the Canadian Provost Corps 1939-45, by Commissioner L H Nicholson
1st Battalion The Regina Rifle Regiment 1939-1944
The Story of the British Columbia Regiment 1939-1945
Light Dragoons, by Allen Mallinson
The Half Million, by C P Stacey & Barbara M Wilson
British and Commonwealth Armoured Formations 1919-46 by Duncan Crow
Dieppe 1942, by Ronald Atkin
The Churchill, by Bryan Perrett
Wartime copies of *The Herald*

From the Regiments:

Patrick Lewis	(Sherbrooke Fusiliers)
E C Brumwell	(Fort Garry Horse)
Pete Friesen	(Fort Garry Horse)
Erle Kitching	(Fort Garry Horse)
Harvey Theobald	(Fort Garry Horse)
Rod Waples	(Fort Garry Horse)
Tom Webb	(Fort Garry Horse)
Charles Wendover	(Fort Garry Horse)
John Whitton	(Fort Garry Horse & Calgary)
Harvey Williamson	(Fort Garry Horse)
William Curtis	(Essex Tank Regiment)
Marcel Fortier	(Governor General's Foot Guards)
Al Trotter	(16/22 Saskatchewan Horse)
Fergus Steele	(RCEME)
Anthony John Vella	(RCEME)
Len Carter	(1st Canadian Parachute Battalion)
'Slim' Bradford	(various)

Other Acknowledgements:

Glenn Wright, Staff Historian, RCMP Ottawa
Access to History Publications, Ottawa - for *Battle-dress Patrol*
Staff of *Legion* Magazine, Ottawa
Vic Waller - information about Canadian forces Order of Battle
Staff of Aldershot Military Museum
Staff of Imperial War Museum, London
Staff of The Tank Museum, Bovington Camp
Roger & Lyn Butcher - *Church Gate Stores*
Jane Durham - information about Ludshott Common
Pauline Grove - letters of Herbert Price
Vivien Hardy - information about British D-Day landings
Mr & Mrs Bill Hinson - *Headley Mount Cottage*
Carl Tantum - information about Headley Catholic Church

Photographs & Illustrations:
As acknowledged opposite
All recent photographs are by the author

Front cover drawing by Hester Whittle
Cartography by Dil Williamson

Illustrations & Maps

Contents

My apologies to those whose information arrived too late for inclusion in this edition. I hope it may be possible to use such material in a future reprint.

Almost inevitably there will be omissions and a number of errors in a compilation such as this. The author would be grateful to hear of these.

Please write to:

John Owen Smith
12 Hillside Close
Headley Down
BORDON
Hampshire GU35 8BL
England